W9-ACU-521

TESORO BOOKS

Ambassador's Journal: A Personal Account of the Kennedy Years
John Kenneth Galbraith

Here to Stay
John Hersey

The Road Back to Paris
A. J. Liebling

On Becoming American
Ted Morgan

ALSO BY

JOHN HERSEY

THE CHILD BUYER
(1960)

THE WAR LOVER
(1959)

A SINGLE PEBBLE
(1956)

THE MARMOT DRIVE
(1953)

THE WALL
(1950)

HIROSHIMA
(1946)

A BELL FOR ADANO
(1944)

INTO THE VALLEY
(1943)

HERE
TO STAY

HERE
TO STAY

JOHN HERSEY

PARAGON HOUSE PUBLISHERS
New York

First paperback edition, 1988

Published in the United States by

Paragon House Publishers
90 Fifth Avenue
New York, NY 10011

Copyright © 1988 by John Hersey

All rights reserved. No part of this book may be
reproduced, in any form, without written permission from
the publishers, unless by a reviewer who wishes
to quote brief passages.

OF THE material in this book, the following articles—some
in slightly different form—were first published in *The New
Yorker*: "Over the Mad River," "Survival," "Journey
Toward a Sense of Being Treated Well," and "Hiroshima."
The following—in somewhat different form—were first
published in *Life*: "Joe Is Home Now," "A Short Talk
with Erlanger," and "Prisoner 339, Klooga."

Library of Congress Cataloging-in-Publication Data
Hersey, John, 1914-
Here to stay / John Hersey. — 1st pbk. ed.
p.   cm. — (Tesoro books)
Reprint. Originally published: New York: Knopf, 1963.
ISBN   1-55778-100-1
1. Survival (after airplane accidents, shipwrecks, etc.)
I. Title.
G525.H43   1988
904—dc19   87-30446

FOR

ALFRED

PREFACE
TO THIS EDITION

THE GREAT THEMES are love and death; their synthesis is the will to live.

The middle years of the twentieth century witnessed some of the most revolting events in human history. The nine true stories of survival in this book all come from that short span of time, and they tell of the various ways in which a handful of people held on to their lives when millions of others were dying.

I could wish that a great secret could have been embedded in these tales, so that a reader could unriddle it between the lines—a clear answer of some kind to the most mysterious of all questions, the existential question: What is it that, by a narrow margin, keeps humankind going, in the face of its crimes, its follies, its greed, its passions, its sorrows, its panics, its hatreds, its hideous drives to pollute and waste and dominate and kill?

But the nine stories here cannot be anything more than exemplary. They do share the theme of the will to live—the drive to keep going, a deep wish not just for survival but that the saved life may prove to be better than what has been. This urge, thrilling whenever it manifests itself, has many modes. The first story told here is of an escape from drowning, the watery form of death that is said to be a reciprocal of birth, and the last is a story of quite another order of meaning, about the deliverance of a few human beings from an atomic attack, which might be likened, at least in its potential, to a reciprocal of the creation of the earth. Between, there are instances of survivals that were not at all noble, but rather mean, and even squalid; of strength given from without, by partners, friends, families; of utter dregs of desperation; of the force for life that we call zest; of a frightful selfishness that in certain competitive struggles is the margin of survival; of an altruism that sometimes also saves; and of interventions of luck, fate, chance, or a plan.

The years since mid-century have not encouraged the belief that mankind learns much from its bitterest experiences. The world since then has suffered wars, insurrections, terrorism, racist atrocities, fanatical bombings, the holding of hostages, avoidable famine, and that dangerous sort of hostility, distilled from irrational fear, which is euphemistically called deterrence of nuclear war. Our only hope is memory. We need to remember the Holocaust; we must remind ourselves of what Hitler stood for; we must not forget Hiroshima.

Enough years have passed so that direct memory is already fading out. Of the six people in the last account in this book, three had died when this edition went to press. As the witnesses disappear, we are obliged to fall back on recorded memory. For this reason I am glad that this book, for what small contribution it may make to remembrance, is having its own survival in a new edition.

CONTENTS

ix

CHANCE

Over the Mad River

CHANCE

ONE August night in 1955 a tropical hurricane, which had been given by the United States Weather Bureau the winsome name Diane, bore off her course and skittered up the state of Connecticut. Its winds spent, the storm unloaded on the New England hills millions of tons of water it had scooped up from the Atlantic Ocean during its voyage from the Caribbean Sea.

This is a tale of how one little old lady survived the floods that ensued; I got the account from her and others in her town a few days afterwards. It is a story, really, of the part chance can play in survival, and it tells what bizarre forms chance can take, for there could scarcely be a wilder incongruity than the one provided by its central figures—the tiny, sickly heroine, seventy-five years old, and the burly, disenchanted diabolus ex machina who came to save her life.

3

Over the Mad River

THAT EVENING, a delicate little old widow named Jessica Kelley spent three pleasant hours in her apartment, at the rear of the fourth floor of Anna Landi's tenement block, at 375 Main Street, in Winsted, Connecticut, chatting with her nearest neighbor, a middle-aged maiden lady of French-Canadian descent, Yvonne Brochu, who had the fourth-floor front. It was raining very hard, and several times the two women remarked on the pounding of the water on the roof.

"I love that noise," Mrs. Kelley said at one point. "It's so soothing to sleep to. But, gracious, it *is* teeming tonight, isn't it, Yvonne?"

Mrs. Kelley, who was seventy-five years old, had long since made it clear to Miss Brochu that she considered conversation one of the purest joys in her altogether joyful life. She once said to her that she had always loved to talk. Just before her marriage, in October, 1903, her fiancé, a salesman of bars, handles, and trimmings for funeral caskets, told her that the very first things he intended to buy after their wedding were a parrot and a brass bed. On their honeymoon in New York, Mr. Kelley did indeed purchase a fine brass bed; nothing more was said about the parrot, and some weeks later Mrs. Kelley asked her husband why he had not bought one. "Jessica, dear," he said, "I have you."

The talk with Yvonne Brochu that evening was pleasurable,

for Miss Brochu, a tiny person, barely five feet tall, who was a factory worker at Dano Electric, in Winsted, was sweet and patient and a loving listener. Mrs. Kelley had moved into the Landi block only two weeks before. She and Miss Brochu were old friends, however, having shared light-housekeeping privileges in a boarding house on Case Avenue several years earlier. For the last three and a half years, Mrs. Kelley had taken room and board in the east end of Winsted, near the Gilbert School, and on this particular rainy evening she told her friend Yvonne how trying things had been there. Mrs. Kelley had been a diabetic for three decades, and so, as it happened, had both her landlady and her late landlord in the east-end home. How prodigally those people had eaten! They had pretended to stay on a diabetic diet, but they had thought nothing of gulping down four or five bananas at a clip, a bag of cherries, a box of prunes—between meals, too. *He* had died from it; he did not live to tell of his gourmandizing. And *she* had been so close-fisted! Could Yvonne imagine? Mrs. Kelley had been obliged to keep her perfectly good bedside radio wrapped up in paper and string for three and a half years because *she* hadn't wanted even a tiny dribble of electricity used on her premises. Be saving of hot water! Don't waste a cracker crumb! Mrs. Kelley, the soul of charity, spoke of her former landlady not bitterly but in sadness, with a hesitant, sensitive smile from time to time, as if to ask her friend, "Aren't people a puzzle?"

At about ten-thirty, which was nearly her bedtime, Mrs. Kelley said, "It's so muggy and close, why don't you and I take baths before we turn in?"

So they did. Mrs. Kelley's apartment consisted of a bedroom and a kitchen, each about eight feet by ten and as clean as a pin, and a tiny bathroom. When Mrs. Kelley took her bath, she was very careful to keep her left foot dry, because while she was walking to St. James Episcopal Church on the previous Palm Sunday morning she had stepped off the curb in front of the

First National Store at Park Place, with the stoplight in her favor, and a lady hit-and-run driver had dropped, it seemed, out of the carless sky right in front of her and had run over her foot and knocked her down, and as a consequence she had spent four months in Litchfield County Hospital and had had to have her little toe amputated. The foot was still bound up in bandages; a visiting nurse, who helped her with her insulin shots, kept it dressed for her. The winter before, she had sprained that same foot when she slipped on an icy sidewalk on her way to the post office; because she had a will of iron, and because it was what she had set out to do, she had walked all the way to the post office and home again on her throbbing foot. That, too, had cost her some time on her back, though, thankfully, not in the hospital. It seemed that her left foot was her Jonah; nothing had ever happened to her right foot. "That's my kicker!" she once said to Yvonne Brochu, giving her sound right foot a sharp little swing.

After her bath, Mrs. Kelley dressed for bed and then sat on a small straight chair in front of her dressing table, fixing her gray hair for the night. She walked out into the hall and called good night to Yvonne, who had finished bathing in her apartment. Mrs. Kelley returned to her bedroom, pulled down her tufted bedspread with two bright peacocks on it, got into bed, read a page or two of her prayer book, and dropped off, under the soothing influence of the still drumming rain, into deep slumber.

While Mrs. Kelley slept, hundreds of millions of gallons of rain, part of the fantastic load of water that had been shipped by the hurricane designated as Diane during its voyage up the Atlantic Ocean, were being bailed out on certain hills of northern Connecticut and were washing down them toward Winsted.

Winsted's Main Street lies along the north bank of the Mad River. For several hundred yards downstream from what Winsted people call "the center"—the point where Elm Street crosses Main and then the river—nearly all the Main Street stores backing on the watercourse were surmounted by rickety wooden tenements, mostly three or four stories high, many of them connected to each other on the river side by continuous wooden porches. These porches were tied together vertically by stairs here and there, which were supposed to serve as fire escapes by way of the stores below. Anna Landi's tenement block, in which Mrs. Kelley slept so soundly that night, was the fourth building below the center bridge; it contained, on the street level, the county agent's office, the Metropolitan Cleaners & Dyers, and Irving's Smart Shop. Directly across the river from the Landi block, and facing on Willow Street, was the upper end of a substantial factory building, Capitol Products, where electric toasters and hot plates were made. The backs of the buildings on both sides of the river made a kind of canyon about forty feet wide, with the Mad River in its bed. The river there is normally five or six feet deep.

The Mad River rises in the town of Norfolk, about five miles west of Winsted's center; its watershed lies in rugged foothills of the Green Mountain range, most of which are precipitous on their eastern slopes and are blanketed by forests of birch, ash, basswood, black oak, hemlock, and laurel. Winsted itself lies in an irregular bowl formed by the steep slopes of Street Hill, Platt Hill, Ward's Hill, Second Cobble, and several lesser hills. Southwest of the city and high above it is Highland Lake, which has become a pleasant summer resort not only for inhabitants of Winsted but also for vacationers from far-flung areas of Connecticut. Highland Lake is two miles long and averages a third of a mile in width, and it runs north and south; at its northern end, which is about half a mile from Main Street, it empties into a ravine leading to the Mad River. In 1771, the surface of the lake was raised four feet by a wooden dam and bulkhead. Thirty-five years later, a spring freshet and thaw broke the dam, but the weakness had been spotted beforehand, and a working party of men and teams was standing by when the break occurred; they hauled a huge tree trunk into the breach and with spars, planks, straw, swingling tow, and gravel prevented a disaster. The next year, a new bulkhead raised the surface of the lake another foot. In 1860, a causeway was built across the northern end, protected by a strong retaining wall and two wide overflow spillways, which raised the surface of the lake five feet higher yet. All this damming was for water power. At one time, the waters of Highland Lake turned the wheels of eleven factories scattered down the ravine, which drops a hundred and fifty feet in its half-mile course before it joins the Mad River in Winsted's west end.

Over the years, while Winsted has grown from a cluster of villages to a city of eleven thousand inhabitants, the Mad River, swollen by overflowing water from Highland Lake, has several times risen abruptly and washed out here a bridge and there a house or two. During a spring freshet in 1936, and in the New England hurricane of 1938, the Mad River overflowed into Main Street, and after a flash flood on New Year's Eve of 1947–48, the Mayor of Winsted, P. Francis Hicks, prevailed on Army engineers to spend a quarter of a million dollars dredging the river where it parallels Main Street.

At about one o'clock in the morning, a man named Arthur Royer, who lived on the third floor of the Landi block and who had been out visiting friends during the evening, came home. By that time, the river had risen enough so that a couple of inches of water were flowing down Main Street, which slopes to the east. Royer, another of Winsted's numerous French Canadians, tends to be a worrier, and he thought that perhaps

9

before going to bed he should tell the old ladies on the top floor that the river was swollen. He climbed to Miss Brochu's door and knocked. For a very long time there was no answer. "Just anyone banging on your door at one o'clock in the night, would you open?" Yvonne later asked Mrs. Kelley. "And a man's voice! I was glad the door was locked." Royer shouted to Miss Brochu awhile in French, and finally, hearing his words, she roused herself, put on a dressing gown, and answered the door. Royer told her about the water in Main Street and went downstairs.

Yvonne looked out of her window and hurried across the hall into Mrs. Kelley's apartment, and at the door of the bedroom she said, "Jessie! Jessie! Put on the light!"

Mrs. Kelley, awakening, felt concern for her friend. She turned on a bedside lamp. "Yvonne, what is it?" she said. "Don't you feel right? Has something happened to you?"

"The water is coming up," Yvonne said. "You can see it in the street. Come in the front and look out the window."

"Gracious, I don't think I want to do that, Yvonne," Mrs. Kelley said.

Miss Brochu was quite excited, and finally Mrs. Kelley said, "Yvonne, I think we should get dressed."

Miss Brochu went back to her apartment, and both ladies put on their clothes. While they were dressing, at about one-fifteen, they separately heard the sirens of Winsted's Civil Defense alarm system, and Mrs. Kelley relieved her distress at hearing this wailing with the thought that Art Royer, downstairs, had a Civil Defense armband. He would be informed. People would come if there was danger. Later, after she had gone into Miss Brochu's front room and had looked at the glistening, shallow water running down Main Street under the street lights in the rain, she discussed Royer's C.D. brassard with her friend, and Yvonne agreed that help would come if help was needed.

What neither of them could know was that at that very time policemen, firemen, and Civil Defense volunteers were combing all the tenements along Main Street and telling the occupants to leave the buildings and go to higher ground, but that somehow the warners had missed the stairway on which the ladies lived, and that they, together with Art Royer and a woman who was still sleeping like a log on the second floor, Mrs. Peter Placek, had been left stranded in the Landi block.

The next two hours were anxious ones for Jessica Kelley and Yvonne Brochu. They were together, and that was a comfort, but they were very restless. They went out on the back porch that opened off Mrs. Kelley's rooms, where they peered down at the black river, and then they went to the windows in Yvonne's apartment, at the front, and looked down at the street. The water, which was flowing swiftly along Main Street—from left to right as they viewed it—had crept over the sidewalk across the way. They saw three cabs standing in front of the office of Sox's Taxi, two buildings upstreet on the near side; the water eddied around the wheels of the cars. The street seemed deserted. They expected to see some kind of Civil Defense rescue boat in the flooded street, and they kept talking about it. Where was the boat? When would it come? They returned to the porch in the rear, and then went again to Yvonne's window, and so kept uneasily moving back and forth. Finally, Mrs. Kelley felt she must rest her foot, and she took the straight chair from her dressing table and sat in the kitchen.

Then the lights went out. At first, both women had an impulse to scream for help, but they talked it over in trembling voices and decided that that would be useless in the rain-muffled night. There was no telephone in the building. Yvonne remembered that she had some candles, and, groping her way into her rooms, she found them and lit several. The light was a relief.

Mrs. Kelley began by candlelight to gather about her chair a small pile of valuables: her black winter coat, her handbag, her prayer book, a few keepsakes, and the dear little green box that contained her insulin packet. In her handbag were her insurance policies, her old-age-assistance papers, and three cloth purses containing her ready money. For more than twenty years she had lived on the nest eggs her prudent husband and father had left her, and now the money was nearly gone. Only a few weeks before, she had applied to the government for old-age assistance, for which she qualified now that her savings were running out. She had just had word that payments of about a hundred dollars a month, plus, she understood, an extra allowance on account of her diabetes, would begin soon. As she sat there in the kitchen, she thought, for some reason, of a ten-dollar gold piece that C. L. Maloney, an undertaker friend of her husband's, had given them once as a luck piece, as lightly as if it had been no more than a lucky penny. Then she remembered the meerschaum pipe the Winsted Elks had given her husband just before a trip he and she took to Florida in the twenties; he was fussy about that pipe, but it had led to his giving up cigars, thank goodness. Those were the heydays! They had been caught right in the thick of the Florida boom-and-bust. They had had two thousand dollars in traveller's checks with them, and her husband had literally sunk it in some real estate: the land had turned out to be under water. They had had to wait to come home until another thousand dollars could be wired down from Winsted. There had been a time, in the early years of the century, when the Strong Manufacturing Company, the makers of coffin trimmings for whom her husband worked, met its payroll in gold coins. When she and her husband built a new home, at 23 Wetmore Avenue, they had laid the foundations, waited a year till the crisis of 1907 blew over, then resumed building, and paid in gold the stonemasons who laid the front walk. She forgot how many gold coins that had been, but she clearly remembered handing them out. The men had scarcely been able to believe their eyes. For years she had had stocks and bonds galore. Somehow, Connecticut Light & Power and United States Steel had seemed to last the longest. Now there was almost nothing left, and she was watching every penny. Ten dollars a week to Anna Landi for rent; less than that for food; enough for a while in the three purses; a tiny bit in the bank.

Jessica Kelley could not say that she was worth much, but what she was worth was right there in the stiff straight chair in the middle of the kitchen and on the floor around it.

Yvonne Brochu, coming on her surrounded by her little heap of wealth, said, "My goodness, Jessie, where do you think you're going?"

"I don't know, dear," Mrs. Kelley said. "But I'm ready."

At about three-thirty, in a rented room in a building known as the Keywan block, diagonally across and about a hundred yards up the river from the tenement where Mrs. Kelley sat waiting, a young man named Frank Stoklasa was being roused from sleep by the occupant of the next room. If two human beings could be opposites, Jessica Kelley and Frank Stoklasa were those two. Stoklasa was a steeplejack, thirty-two years old. Though slight, he was powerfully built. His hairy arms were covered with tattoos that he himself had applied: a dagger, a snake, the Disney dog called Goofy, a ship, and a death's-head. On the backs of the proximal phalanges of the fingers of his left hand were tattooed the letters L-O-V-E; on those of his right hand, H-A-T-E. He was born in Fort Worth, Texas, and his friends called him Tex. He was part Czech, part Polish, part Indian. His mother died when he was twenty-two months old. As a small boy, he had typhoid, diphtheria, and pneumonia. When he was about six, his father took him, his two brothers, and his sister to Oklahoma, and they became Okies—migrant farm workers who moved with the seasons to California, Arizona, Texas, and back to Oklahoma. Stoklasa went to school through the ninth grade, then left his family and wandered all over the Southwest, earning a bare living as a truck driver, gas-station attendant, and common laborer. He fought in a Golden Gloves tournament once in San Francisco. He was taken into the Army in 1942, and after his training went to North Africa and Germany as an infantryman. In the Rhineland, he was wounded by shrapnel in his upper right arm, and was shipped home and eventually discharged.

Because he liked to get high up on things, and because the money in crazy climbing was good, Stoklasa went to work for the Brown Steeple-Jacking Company, in Norfolk, Virginia. He did welding and painting on water towers, smokestacks, radio towers, and bridges. Once a man has become a seasoned steeple-jack, he hears of every topnotch steeplejacking company in the country, and after two years Stoklasa left Brown's in favor of the Universal Construction Company, in Indianapolis. There he took up, as a hobby, stock-car racing—because it was dangerous —but after some time he dropped it, not because it was *too* dangerous but because of the expense. From Universal, Stoklasa moved to the Kessler Company, in Fremont, Ohio, and he stayed there nearly six years. In Fremont, he married and divorced two young ladies; he was on the road too much to settle down. Several times, Stoklasa had seen men "go off," as steeplejacks speak of falling, but it was not until the year before that he had his first accident. In Youngstown, while climbing with three other Kessler men over the lip of an empty hundred-thousand-gallon water tower a hundred and fifty feet high, to get inside and paint it, he put his weight on the spider rods that braced the top of the cylinder; the rods had been weakened by rust, and he fell through them fifty feet to the bottom of the tank and broke an ankle. He went back to work as soon as it mended. He was then earning three dollars and twenty cents an hour. For a year or so, Stoklasa had buddied with a native of Winsted named Donald Linkovich, and some months ago he had decided to move with him to Connecticut. Tex went to work at a dollar-sixty an hour for a tree man named MacBurnie, and worked with him until MacBurnie fell and hurt his back, about a fortnight before Diane; then he took a job with another local tree man, Nickerson, at two dollars and five cents an hour. Nickerson's crew was clearing a forest pathway on Avon Mountain for high-tension wires. Stoklasa had always had a rough time, and he had liked it that way. He was taciturn to the point of rudeness, for he had learned to keep his mouth shut and enjoy himself. He was cynical; there was no room for sentiment in his life. In his view, the average dog's favorite food is living dog meat.

Wakened by his neighbor, Tex put on his dungarees, a T shirt, a canvas jacket, and his working shoes, and went out of the building to move Donnie Linkovich's brand-new Mercury convertible up to high land near the Winsted railroad station, which is across Willow Street from Capitol Products. Then he went into a bar and had a couple of beers. It struck him as being wet as hell out.

At about four in the morning, the whole Landi tenement began to tremble. Apparently, the river was running through and around its ground floor and was eating at its underpinnings. At first, the motion was barely perceptible, but through the small hours it increased, until it had become a real shaking and heaving, and Jessica Kelley, trying to keep up a cheerful front for Miss Brochu's sake, said to her, "Dear me, Yvonne, this is like being on a rocking horse, isn't it?" Mrs. Kelley moved her chair from place to place, thinking that there might be some part of the building that was still. For a while, she sat out in the hallway, on the theory that the center of the tenement might be solid, but she was disappointed. Each time she moved, she fetched along her little clutter of precious things.

Mrs. Kelley held her prayer book in her hand all the time, even though it was almost impossible to read by the flickering light of candles. She improvised some prayers, particularly requesting the arrival of the Civil Defense rescue boat and, for herself, strength of body and character. She had long thought of herself as physically puny and weak. As an infant, she was plump, she had been told; she was born on Thanksgiving Day, 1879, and, on first seeing her, her father exclaimed, "That's the nicest turkey I ever saw!" By the time she reached high school, however, she had grown thin and jumpy, and for a year or two her family thought she had St. Vitus's dance and put her in a private school on Meadow Street, but she got over the disorder. She had a stillborn baby by Caesarean section in 1905, and from that time on was never able to have children. Her mission in life, even after her marriage, was to care for her parents, and she eventually came to think she had been too close to them for her own well-being. Three months after her mother's death, in the late twenties, she began to have diabetic symptoms; she had never had a trace of them before. Her husband died two years later. After her father died in 1935, at the age of ninety-three, she shut herself up in the house for several weeks, and pulled down the shades, and would not answer the telephone, and became suspicious of all human beings, and ranged from room to room like a wild creature. But she recovered and began a new life alone.

One thing that helped her in all her tribulations was her will power, of which she had enough to dole out to ten strong men. Once, a quarter of a century ago, she read somewhere that tooth infections might have serious consequences for a diabetic, so she called her dentist for an appointment and told the nurse she would tell the dentist what she wanted when she arrived; she seated herself in the dentist's chair a few days later and said, "Take all my teeth out." The dentist said, "Heavens! You have granite teeth. Your teeth are far better than mine, and I wouldn't part with mine for a thousand dollars." It was true that her teeth were sound. Strong and prominent teeth ran in her family. Her father, then pushing ninety, had all his own teeth and could still crack walnuts and untie knots in a clothesline with them. Jessica's teeth had perhaps been too much of a good thing. She had once made the mistake of giving her husband a picture of herself smiling, and every time he looked at it on the bureau he used to say, "Fetch me the toothpaste, Jessie." She told the dentist she had fastened her mind on having the whole set out. He gave her novocain and pulled three teeth, and Mrs. Kelley's jaw began to hurt. By this time, the doctor was perspiring and pale. "That's enough," he said. "You can come back another day." "No, sir," Mrs. Kelley said, speaking with difficulty but firmly through the new gap in her mouth. "I said *all*, and I meant *all*." He pulled them all, using nothing but novocain. That was one of the days in Jessica Kelley's life that helped convince her there was nothing even a weakling woman could not do if she made up her mind to it and held fast.

Some of her tenacity had come, she was sure, from her father, William Gilbert Barnes. He was related to the Gilbert Clock people, and after being in the wooden butter-tub and washtub business in New York State for a few years he had come to Winsted and helped make clocks. He had been foreman of Winsted Volunteer Fire Company No. 2 several times and had been an active fireman well into his eighties. He had magnificent white handle-bar mustaches, but to his dying day his hair was hardly even gray, and he stood as straight and trig as a fence post. Right up until his ninety-third year, he celebrated each birthday by walking the seven miles around Highland Lake.

The building trembled more and more, and Mrs. Kelley began to imagine how pleasant it would be if only she could be whisked somewhere far away—to Meriden, perhaps, or New Britain. If only she could fly! During the three-quarters of a century of her life, aviation had shrunk the earth, but she had never been up in a plane. On their Florida trip, her husband had teased her and teased her to go up in a barnstormer, but she had refused. He had gone off then without telling her and had taken a flight, and later he had said it was awfully nice and airy up there. He *was* a sly one! She hadn't learned until after his death what a proficient cardplayer and billiards player he had been. She had known, of course, that he spent a great deal of time at the Elks Home and at the Winsted Club, but he had never boasted to her about his skills, and she had come to hear of them only when someone brought his cues around to the house after the funeral. His favorite cue, the handle of which was inlaid with mother-of-pearl, she had given as a keepsake to one of his best friends—Billy Phelps, president of the Hurlbut National Bank. The thing her husband liked best in the world was precisely what she wanted in those anxious hours —to get up and go. He loved to travel. He took two trips a year; he never missed an Elks' convention. The year he was Winsted's Past Exalted Ruler, his lodge sent him as a delegate all the way to Dallas, Texas. He slipped off to New York quite a bit, too, especially during inventory time at the casket-trimmings plant.

Mrs. Kelley reflected that, besides flying, one thing she had neglected and would like now to have done was to learn to swim. Just a couple of years before, a man at the Y.M.C.A. had tried to coax her to take lessons, saying that he had succeeded once before in teaching a woman to swim who was over seventy. But she had said then, as she had said to her husband when he tried to get her to fly, "I like the feel of terra firma under my feet." There were times during the early-morning hours in the shaking building when the possibility of drowning in the flood outside had forced itself on her, and she reflected that for some hours—perhaps even for some years—she had had sensations like those of a person slowly going down into the darkness of deep water, with the happy scenes of her lifetime flashing through her mind. The sensations had not been too bad. She had had fortunate years; she considered herself ready for whatever might be her lot.

It was beginning to get light, and Yvonne Brochu came running in from time to time with alarming bits of news. It was still pouring. The water was almost up to the awnings on the stores across Main Street, and it was going down the street awfully fast—maybe thirty miles an hour. Two of Sox's taxis had simply disappeared. The water was coming down in great surges—could it be that the causeway at Highland Lake was giving way? There was something floating down Main Street that looked like a refrigerator. And there was a brand-new car— just being rolled along! There went Sox's other cab! A chair from the hairdresser's was going down the street! There was a whole roof out there floating down!

Worst of all was when, after peering out from the back porch awhile, Yvonne came in crying, "The bridge has gone, Jessie! That bridge has gone!"

Mrs. Kelley spoke in as careful a voice as she could command. The bridge at the Winsted center had been built of steel. "I think you must be mistaken, dear," she said. "It must be that the water's over it and covers it, because it's rising so fast."

"No! No! I saw the bridge go," Yvonne said. "It's gone."

After a good long wait, so as not to be rushing hysterically to check up on a piece of calamitous information, Mrs. Kelley went out on the porch and looked upriver and saw for herself: The bridge was washed away, no mistake. Mrs. Kelley returned to her chair and prayed some more. She wept, too, but she managed to hide her tears from Yvonne.

Not long afterward, there was a terrifying crash out back, and bricks and glass and something very heavy fell. Mrs. Kelley and

Miss Brochu went to the back window and saw that a whole corner of the brick Capitol Products building was sagging and gaping, and a cement floor was hanging down like bent cardboard. Huge machines had slid about, and the fall had probably been that of one or more of them into the river.

Art Royer came running upstairs, and rather wildly he suggested that the ladies leave the building with him. They would go out the front door into Main Street. He would go in the center, he said, and hold the two ladies by the hand. Yvonne Brochu pointed out that automobiles and refrigerators were bobbing downstreet like corks; people wouldn't last thirty seconds in that water. All during the morning, Mr. Royer kept renewing his mad, chivalrous offer.

Some time later, Mrs. Placek joined the others. Mrs. Placek, a solid, phlegmatic woman of sixty-nine, whose husband was away in Waterbury, said she had been sleeping until a few minutes before. "The water woke me up," she said. "It told me, 'Get up, you lazy head.'"

In a calm voice, Mrs. Kelley welcomed Mrs. Placek to her apartment and said, "Things seem to be giving way outside."

"This whole building's going," Mrs. Placek said gloomily.

"Oh, dear, no, I doubt *that*," Mrs. Kelley said.

In just a few minutes, this doubt of Mrs. Kelley's was badly shaken. In full sight of Yvonne and Art Royer and Mrs. Placek —she herself, thank heavens, was not watching—a building across and up the river, the first one this side of the washed-out bridge, slowly twisted and went limp and simply fell in a thousand pieces into the river.

The building that had fallen was the Keywan block, in which Tex Stoklasa had had his room.

It was six o'clock, and the flood had reached its crest, which it was to hold for nearly six hours. The rain continued. Highland Lake was running over its spillways and tearing out threatening gullies right across the macadam road on the causeway on either side of them and causing terrible damage in factories and homes between the lake and the river below. All the way from Norfolk, the Mad River was brimming. Along Main Street, it was fifteen feet above its normal level, and the water was ten feet deep in the street itself. It was literally ripping up Main Street. The pavement and sidewalks were being sliced away and gutted six feet deep. The water had broken the plate-glass windows of most of the stores along the street and had ruined their stocks. Winsted Motors, a Buick showroom and service station that had straddled the river high up the street, had been completely demolished, and its new and used cars were rolling all the way downtown, and its roof had lodged itself in mid-street right in front of the Town Hall. On the second floor of the Town Hall, forty-one policemen and Civil Defense workers and the chairlady of the Winsted Red Cross were marooned. All but two of the town's twelve bridges had collapsed or were about to. A four-story hotel at the foot of the street, the Clifton, had floated off its foundation and into the river and downstream three-quarters of a mile, and had settled on the town ball field, more or less erect but with its two lower floors worn away. The water was doing damage to private property that the town estimated at nearly twenty-eight million dollars—more than the entire grand list of assessed taxable property, for assessments in Winsted, as generally in Connecticut, were considerably under real values.

After Tex had had his drinks, he had returned to the Keywan block and sat up talking with several other men there. From time to time, they had gone outdoors to pick up news and watch the river level. After the bridge went, it appeared to them that the foundations of the Keywan block were threatened, and they had gone up to get the landladies, two elderly maiden sisters known in town as the Garrity girls, to evacuate. But the Garrity girls had long considered the building their home, and to them home had always meant safety, and they had refused to leave. After quite an argument, Tex and a friend had bodily removed the ladies, and within minutes the building had fallen. Tex had not had time to go back for his things, and into the river had gone his climbing and welding equipment: his shield, sleeves, pants, boots, belt—nearly six hundred dollars' worth of gear.

A few minutes after the collapse of the Keywan block, the next building downriver, a fifty-year-old brick structure called the Bannon block, turned half around on its base, partly crumbled at the bottom, and leaned over at a crazy angle away from its downriver neighbor, the Capitol Products building, and toward the Keywan foundations.

Tex joined a crowd of about two hundred people on the higher ground near the railroad station and, through the gap where the Keywan block had been, watched what was now happening on the far—the Main Street—side of the river. It was quite a show.

Mrs. Kelley and her companions were subjected to a series of horrifying wrenches, and the Landi tenement perceptibly heeled toward the river. A large piece of plaster fell from Mrs. Kelley's bedroom ceiling. Mrs. Kelley, who was sitting in the kitchen once more, wanted then to get that room out of sight, but she could not close the door, because the frame had been twisted and the floor was all out of kilter.

The four people in the Landi tenement had no way of knowing that the three buildings upriver from theirs, undermined by the water and battered by descending debris, were crumbling and falling, one by one. First went the four-story Petrunti block, containing Riiska's Taxi Stand, Rocky's Garage, and Luben's

Cleaners; then the two-story building with Pelkey & Simpson's hardware store; then, next door to the Landi block, the two-story building that housed Jimmy's Restaurant.

Terrified by the cataclysmic shaking in Mrs. Kelley's apartment, and seeing the crowd across the way by the railroad station, Art Royer went out on the balcony at the back and waved to the people there and beckoned and held up four fingers, indicating that there were four people in the building to be somehow saved.

Tex Stoklasa saw Royer. He ran into the Capitol Products building and crept out onto the very edge of the sagging concrete floor of the plant's press room and looked the situation over. He was about ten feet above the surface of the Mad River, down which all sorts of heavy debris was swiftly floating. The Landi building was straight across from him. The river was several feet up the wall of the ground floor of the Landi block, and of the buildings below it. At first, Stoklasa thought he might be able to throw a rope across to a balcony, if one of the people could climb down to catch it. Then he saw a double clothesline stretched on pulleys between an upper floor of the fifth building downriver from the Landi block and a wooden building belonging to Capitol Products, adjacent to the one he was in. He ran around into the wooden building and found that the pulley at the near end of the clothesline was attached to its outer wall, right next to a window.

Then, in a tenement two buildings down from the Landi block, over Pete's Barber Shop, he saw a thin young man and a plump young woman standing at a third-floor window and apparently calling for help, though over the rushing of the river, the grinding of lumber in it, the pounding of the rain, and the whistling of the strong wind he could not hear their words. He tried to signal to them to make their way, if possible, down to the building with the clothesline—the Lentini block—but they evidently did not understand.

There were others around Stoklasa now, and someone suggested writing a message on a piece of cardboard and displaying it. Soon Tex was holding up a big card on which was written, " COME DOWN HERE," and he pointed across at the Lentini block. The man disappeared from the window.

Tex told the people around him to try to find a length of half-inch rope and a climbing belt.

The young man and woman in the tenement over Pete's Barber Shop were Billy Fields, a twenty-seven-year-old employee of Hickey's Fur Shop, and his wife. When Fields read the sign, he at once started working his way downriver. On a stair landing of his building he found a long-unused, locked door connecting with the next building, the Serafini block; he broke it down with his shoulder. He went out onto a back porch of the Serafini block and saw that the next building downriver, the Orsi block, was only one story high, with a roof sloping back from Main Street. He ran down the fire escape to the second-story balcony of the Serafini block and there discovered that he could climb around the end wall of the balcony and drop a few feet to the Orsi roof, and he did. At the far end of the Orsi roof, he had a six-foot climb up a wooden wall to a sort of lean-to roof over the back rooms on the second floor of the Lentini block. Once he was on this roof, he was able to make his way up to the balcony from which the clothesline ran.

By this time, someone had produced a rope from the New England Knitting Company factory, across the street and up-river from the former site of Keywan's, and someone else had miraculously procured a belt with a pulley on it. Tex saw that

the rope, while far from new, was a sturdy half-inch line—
regular nine-hundred-pound-test rope, of the sort steeplejacks
are commonly satisfied to use. He tied one end of it to the
upper strand of the clothesline and pulled it across the river.
Fields untied the rope from the clothesline. Tex held up a new
cardboard sign: "TIE ROPE TO POST. KEEP AHOLT OF END." Fields
did as directed. Tex strung the belt pulley onto his end of the
line and took turns of the rope around two stanchions inside
the wooden Capitol Products building and directed men to
hold the free end and keep the whole line taut. He took everything off but his dungarees. He slung the belt outside the window, backed into it, so that he sat in the loose loop of the belt
facing the Capitol Products window, and pulled himself hand
over hand across above the river in the pouring rain.

Stoklasa and Fields dropped to the Orsi roof, swung around
the end wall of the Serafini balcony, then ran along the connected porches. Fields stopped off for his wife; Stoklasa went
on to the Landi block and up the fire escapes to Mrs. Kelley
and her companions. Curtly, Stoklasa directed them to follow
him. Mrs. Kelley put on her winter coat and picked up her
pocketbook and went out on the porch after the young man.
The others came behind.

Stoklasa on one side and Fields on the other pushed and
supported the women past the one dangerous point—out
around the end of the Serafini porch and down onto the Orsi
roof. Mrs. Kelley felt all out of breath, but she trusted the
strong, half-naked young man. At the far end of the Orsi roof,
Tex above and Fields and Royer below raised the women to
the lean-to roof of Lentini's block, and from there to the Lentini
balcony. When they were all assembled, Tex began to explain
how to ride the belt across. The rope sloped downward to
Capitol Products. At its lowest point, it was about fifteen feet
above the water. The lean-to roof provided a good launching
platform. Whoever was going over, Tex said, should sit in the

belt, facing Capitol Products, cross his feet over the rope ahead of the belt pulley, and grasp the rope with his hands and feed himself down the incline. Mrs. Kelley gasped. She hadn't the strength for such work. An argument followed as to who should go first. Tex urged Mrs. Fields to go. She refused. Fields tried to persuade her. She wept, and finally said she would never go.

Then Tex turned to Mrs. Kelley and said, "Come on, lady, I'm taking you over."

"Gracious!" Mrs. Kelley said. "I'm not certain I *want* to go over on that little rope."

"There's no time to lose," Stoklasa disgustedly said to the whole group. "All these buildings may go down."

Mrs. Kelley was surprised to hear herself say, "Tell me what to do. I'll go."

The next thing Mrs. Kelley knew, Stoklasa had lifted her like a doll off the porch and out onto the slanting roof. He was strong!

"What've you got that for, for Christ's sake?" he said, pointing to her pocketbook. "We may go in the river."

"I've got valuables in there, young man," she said. "If I go in the river, that goes with me."

"Throw it on the roof," he said.

"It goes where I go," she said.

"God damn it, throw it on the roof," Stoklasa said. "I'll bring it over. Take that heavy coat off."

"Excuse me, I'm staying dry," Mrs. Kelley said with considerable spirit. But she did put down her bag, with a great deal of reluctance. She had already let herself be separated from her insulin packet, for the first time in many years. And now her money. She kept her coat on.

"O.K., come on," Stoklasa said roughly. "Let's get going."

Stoklasa sat in the belt at the edge of the lean-to roof, put his hands and feet up, and directed Mrs. Kelley to lie supine on him, tucking both legs through the loop of the belt. She found herself with her bad foot lying on the young man's legs and the other up over the rope above his feet. Tex told her to hold the rope with both hands and keep them moving constantly, hand over hand, feeding out rope as they moved.

"Let's go," he said.

"Oh, dear," she said. "I'm so nervous."

"Don't worry, lady, I'll get you over," he said. "Whatever you do, don't look down."

They swung out over the river. They moved terribly slowly. The rope rubbed Mrs. Kelley's right leg. The line swayed in the wind. It was raining.

From the Capitol Products side, the sight of Stoklasa with the little old lady in the black coat on his belly, slowly easing down the swaying line, was so fearful that many people felt ill and some had to look away. The proprietor of the factory had to leave the building and stand on the railroad-station side.

Now someone in Capitol Products spotted an old, old man in a window of one of the buildings upstream from the rope. He had a white stubble on his chin and was wearing a hat in the house. He was watching Stoklasa and Mrs. Kelley and smiling and nodding, apparently oblivious to all peril.

About halfway across, Stoklasa grunted and said, "I got to take a breather. Hold up." He stopped. "This is rough," he said. "We ought to have a block and fall."

Mrs. Kelley, looking steadfastly up at the leaking heavens, felt so agitated that she wondered whether she was going to be able to keep hold of the rope. At last, the young man told her to start moving again. The rope began to burn her leg. They seemed to make steady progress, but about ten feet from the far side Stoklasa stopped for another rest.

"I'm getting out of breath," Mrs. Kelley said. "I feel as if my breathing is going to be shut off."

"Hang on," Stoklasa said. "It's only going to be another minute."

He started again.

At last, the hands of two men named DeLutrie and Shakar grasped Mrs. Kelley, and she heard one of them say, "It's all right. I have you. You're safe now."

"I know it! I believe you!" she said feelingly.

Then she was cradled like a child in a man's arms in the window. "I couldn't have stood much more," she said between gasps for air, and she tried to smile.

Someone drew up a wooden crate and sat her on it. How good it felt to have her feet on a solid floor! Terra firma! She still felt out of breath, and she asked if she could have a sip of water. Someone said there was no water; after a few moments she was handed a bottle of cream soda. Then an office chair with a spring on it was produced, and she was tilted back in it, and someone fanned her with the top of a carton. She began to feel more composed, and she sat up straight. She noticed that a pocket had been sheared off her coat. "Well!" she said cheerfully. "Thank goodness for my coat. I'm dry as a chip, anyway." A woman handed her a cup of hot coffee, and she drank every drop. "That *is* bracing!" she said. Then, all at once, she grew terribly disturbed, for she had thought of Yvonne. "Can you tell me whether someone is about to come over on the rope?" she asked a woman nearby.

By that time, Stoklasa had gone back and both Fields and his wife had crossed safely on the belt, without Stoklasa's help. Fields had gone first, to show his heavy wife how to manage, and she had relented from her determination never to ride that rope. Mrs. Kelley had not seen them lifted into Capitol Products.

Yvonne Brochu was on her way across, solo, when Mrs. Kelley

asked about her, and in a few moments Mrs. Kelley saw her friend being helped into the window. The seventy-five-year-old woman stood up and tottered to her young friend and took her in her arms. "I'm so glad to see you, my dear," she said.

On the other side, Tex helped first Art Royer and then Mrs. Placek onto the rope. Then he scrambled along the buildings to find the old man in the window. This was a seventy-seven-year-old town character named Sam Lane.

"Come on," Stoklasa said. He was getting tired, and he was impatient. The buildings were shaking badly.

"What do you think I am?" Lane said in a cracking voice. "A tightrope walker?" He chuckled.

"You coming or not?" Stoklasa asked.

"I can't leave Queenie," Lane said, shaking his head. Lane had a squat, miscellaneous dog he called Queenie; he used to tell Winsteders she was a Spitz—she chaws tobacco and spits, he would say.

Tex climbed back and rode the rope to Capitol Products, carrying Mrs. Kelley's pocketbook and one belonging to Mrs. Placek. He dropped the pocketbooks on the floor and walked out of the building. Someone tried to shake his hand, but he wouldn't be grabbed. There was a Navy helicopter landing near the parking lot of the Pontiac place downriver, and Tex ran down to it. The pilot asked for a volunteer to be lifted on a harness to rescue a woman from the Burke & Navin building, which was all twisted in the current at the foot of Main Street. Tex said he'd go. The 'copter carried him over and dropped him on the roof. He climbed down and broke a window to speak to the woman. She came at him half-crazed and asked him what he meant by breaking in the windows of a woman's home. He said he was the fellow who had come to save her.

29

She said he wasn't the right person; someone else was coming for her.

"All right, you dumb jerk," Tex said. "Stay there and drown." He waved for the helicopter to come and pick him up.

In the next twelve hours, the flood abated, almost as quickly as it had come up. The building in which Lane had decided to stay with Queenie remained standing; he eventually walked out onto dry land on the arm of a policeman. The Burke & Navin building, where Stoklasa had left the woman who was expecting someone else to come and save her, was frightfully battered, but it did not fall, and she, too, walked away from the wreckage. The Landi block, in which Mrs. Kelley and her friends had lived, sagged further, but it did not collapse. Perhaps she and the others might have stayed safely in it—but who could have foreseen that?

Mrs. Kelley and Mrs. Placek were taken into the home of the man named DeLutrie, who had helped them into the window of Capitol Products. In the next few days, they and friends who visited them talked of little but the flood. Yvonne Brochu, who had been given shelter in the home of some people who lived not far from the DeLutries, went back into the Landi block and fetched, among other things, Mrs. Kelley's green box containing her insulin packet. Often the ladies talked of Tex. Once, Mrs. Kelley spoke of how muscular he had been. "A fine young specimen," she said. "I've never seen a more fearless man." Then, with her hesitant, puzzled smile, she said, "I wonder why he did it. I don't think it was exactly out of the kindness of his heart. He was really quite impatient with us, and, gracious, he used rough language. I guess he just did it to dare the Devil."

FLIGHT

---

*Journey Toward a Sense
of Being Treated Well*

FLIGHT

ONE MEANS *of surviving is to run away. The act of flight does not always connote a lack of courage, and in the case of the Feketes, whose story is told next, it manifestly did not, for the risks of departure from Hungary, after the suppression of the revolt of 1956, were barely out of balance with the horror that staying would have been for this man and his wife and daughters. Vilmos Fekete not only made a dangerous election of a life in freedom; he took all the chances of starting an entirely new life in an unknown world.*

I became acquainted with the Fekete family in Austria, at a teeming refugee camp, a few days after the family's eruption from its homeland, and it was there that the gaunt paterfamilias told me most of this story; I lived parts of its last chapters with him.

Journey Toward a Sense of Being Treated Well

AT ABOUT eight o'clock in the evening of Monday, November 19, 1956, there appeared at the door of a small apartment on the rise of Buda, above the right bank of the Danube at Budapest, a man in a thin, faded blue raincoat, who had an extraordinarily haggard face—all bones, hair, and wires, it seemed. The face had no cheeks—only scoops on either side of a black mustache—and its sharp cheekbones shelved back to conical bumps of bone just in front of big ears, and the ears seemed to have been pulled forward by the wirelike steel bows of a pair of delicate, twisted spectacles. The wire bridge of these glasses had found a resting place a quarter of the way down the man's straight nose, so that the pupils of his sad brown sunken eyes looked out just under the wirelike upper rims; the lenses were tilted up and out at two different angles, making the glasses seem an apparatus for ventilation, or perhaps shelter, rather than for clear examination of the world. Above the eyes were black brows, taut over the bone, and now and then the man shot up these brows, as if to demonstrate that they were not, as they appeared, rooted in his skull, and when he did this, his enormous forehead was gathered up toward his thick black hair in terrible arching creases that told a lot about the years just past. The man was forty, but he looked ageless—simply out of connection with any time of life at all. At that moment, he also looked cold and tired, and, in fact, he was, for it had taken him two hours to walk home from the food-canning plant on the outskirts of Budapest where he worked as a lawyer. As soon as he had opened the door, he said to his wife, who had been waiting for him, "We can go tomorrow."

There were three rooms in the apartment, which the man, whose name was Vilmos Fekete, had rented for twelve years; now he shared them with his wife, his two daughters, his brother-in-law, and his father-in-law. His own father and mother, two brothers, and a sister lived elsewhere in the city. After the family had had some supper, Fekete and his wife, Elvira, prepared for the journey that they, together with their daughters—Klara, who was twelve, and Magdalena, who was nine—planned to take. They told the girls merely that they were all going to a city called Veszprém, near Lake Balaton, to visit some friends—the truth, though only part of the whole truth, for the Feketes intended to make Veszprém their first stop on a longer journey westward. Fekete did not know how dangerous the trip might be. He had learned caution at a high cost during the children's lifetime, and he felt sure that if the Avo, the Hungarian secret police, were to take him and his family into custody along the way, they would question the children separately, and in case that unthinkable thing should happen, he wanted the children to have the strength of truth-telling on their side. The girls were thrilled, because in the past they had had carefree vacations at Lake Balaton.

There was really almost nothing to be done to get ready for the trip. Packing anything was out of the question. Fekete knew that it would be impossible to take any baggage, because parts of the trip would have to be made on foot. Elvira baked some biscuits and wrapped them up, along with a crucifix on which she had given her wedding oath fourteen years before, and some toilet articles, into a small parcel. Fekete put in a box his most important documents, such as his school and university diplomas and his favorite photographs of his family. He next called on the superintendent of the apartment building, who kept the official register of tenants, and told him that because of the disorganization of life in Budapest since the October uprising, he and his family were going to live in Veszprém, and that a friend and his family, who had been shelled out of their home during the Russian counterattack, would move into the flat in the Feketes' places, if the authorities approved. Then Fekete took the box of papers to this same friend, for later delivery to Fekete's father.

Fekete borrowed some money from his friend. His salary from the factory had been a thousand forints a month. At the official rate of exchange, this was about ninety dollars; at the black-market rate, it was only twenty dollars. Fekete had no savings. On the previous day, he had drawn his salary for the second half of November, and he actually had about a hundred forints left over from the first half, because it had been impossible to buy anything during the worst of the fighting; his factory director had given him and the other employees four pounds of flour, two pounds of sugar, and a pound of salt to tide them over while the shops were closed. Altogether, counting his own money and some that he had been able to borrow from his father and what he now borrowed from his friend, he found himself with about two thousand forints for his journey. Fekete returned home and went to bed at about ten o'clock.

The family arose at five in the morning, drank some tea, and started out. As they left, Fekete turned on the landing and looked back into the apartment. This was the only home he and his wife had ever had, and in abandoning it he felt a sense of loss, not over the possessions he was leaving behind—the thread-bare furniture his godfather had given him, a Telefunken radio with a short-wave band he had bought after saving for many months—but over the words said and the things done in these rooms in twelve years of the prime of his life. The one material thing he hated to leave was his stamp collection, which repre-sented thousands of hours of deep absorption scattered over twenty-six years. Elvira, seeing tears behind the tilted spectacles, stood on the landing silently waiting, her close-set eyes hooded and dry. She had always been a more practical person than Vilmos; a question she often asked was "For what?" To her this small apartment had been a center of hard work and crowded living.

It was barely getting light as the Fekete family walked down the hill toward the railroad station. It was a ghostly hour in an exhausted city. Signs of bombardment were plentiful; the streets were cluttered with fallen bricks. The day was going to be gray, and it was cold. There was no traffic at all. A general strike was in progress, and few people were out. In Szena Place, the family walked past two railroad cars that the Freedom Fighters had rolled up from the station on streetcar tracks and overturned for barricades; in Moscow Place there was a similar barricade. Half an hour's walk took the Feketes to the station.

Trains had started running from Budapest the day before, for the first time in a month, but, as Fekete had explained to his wife, he had wanted to wait one day before leaving, to make sure that the tracks out in the countryside had not been mined by Freedom Fighters to inhibit deportations to the Soviet Un-ion. The previous afternoon, he had sent a friend to scout the station for him, and this explorer had reported that the trains had gone through safely and that the Avo did not seem to be watching the station.

Fekete walked up to a window and bought four third-class tickets to Veszprém, for eighty-four forints. At a few minutes before seven, the family boarded their train. Nobody asked any questions. The Feketes made their way to a section of a third-class coach that was partly cut off from the rest of the car—a coupé, with wooden benches for about ten passengers. Shortly after they had entered, two young couples joined them in the coupé. The Feketes inspected the newcomers; the newcomers glanced at them. These people, Fekete observed, were warmly dressed, carried no luggage, and had small parcels under their arms. He said with his eyes to his wife, "Their destination is the same as ours."

That train went only about thirty miles, to a place called Székesfehérvár, and there, in a station jammed with warmly clad people who had no baggage, the Feketes bought tea and bread. In the afternoon, a train was announced for Veszprém. The Feketes, on boarding it, found places on benches; the aisles were soon crowded with standees. The travellers were silent until a conductor, entering the car as the train started, said in a loud voice, "Nobody remains in Budapest? *Everyone* comes out?" This seemed to be a joke, and all the people laughed.

As the cars went through a cold countryside of low hills and eroded scarps of limestone, Fekete sat still and looked out, enjoying the swift motion of the train. He had long dreamed of this journey. He had lived the four decades of his life under a warring Emperor, a Communist leader who established his reforms by bathing the country in blood, a ruthless Fascist regent who called himself an admiral in a landlocked country, a German dictator who regarded Hungary as a pawn, and another Communist regime, this one sustained by Russian-controlled secret police. For a brief, dreamlike moment between the last two of these political numbings, he had experienced democratic parliamentary government—at first hand, for he himself had been elected a member of the Hungarian Parliament in 1947. He had quickly paid, and expensively, for this honor, and the payment was the nightmare memory of his life. Yes, he had long wished for the sensation of momentum this crowded train gave him.

Late in the afternoon, Fekete saw the forested mound of Mount Bakony off to the right, and at its foot a number of bauxite mines and factories; then the train arrived in Veszprém. Fekete led his wife and children to the home of an old friend, a lady schoolteacher, and because she had no spare food, she took the Feketes to a hotel to eat. There two other families, friends of the teacher, joined the group—among them a physician and a member of the local county council. At first, Fekete, who wanted to find out how best to go forward on his journey, felt impatient at having strangers at the table. For a long time, he had made it a practice to speak not a word to people he did not know. But he trusted the teacher's judgment, and the waiter who came for their order took Fekete's breath away by saying quite openly, "You can talk about anything you want. The people at the next table are all right."

At once, the guests began asking Fekete questions about the revolt in Budapest. Was it true, one asked, that though shop windows had been broken in the fighting there had been no looting?

Feketes said that one day he had passed a shop with a smashed window, and inside, on the broken fragments of glass, within easy reach of the sidewalk, he had seen a box heaped with coins and paper money, with a sign on it reading, "We are praying for money for the relatives of those dead in the revolution. In this revolution we can leave this box here, and tonight we will get it."

Another guest asked: What of the assertion by the Kádár regime that the revolution had been the work of Fascists?

Fekete, a Catholic, said he considered anti-Semitism the worst manifestation of the kind of Fascism that Hungary had had under Admiral Horthy before the war; for him anti-Semitism was the badge of Fascism. One day early in the revolt, he said, while walking home from his factory, he had heard a man on a street corner make a remark about the Jews. Two young men with rifles who were standing nearby had turned on the man, and one had slapped him in the face and said that the Freedom Fighters would not stand for that kind of talk.

A little later, Magdalena, the Feketes' nine-year-old, a restless child with a broad face and huge eyes, announced with satisfaction, "There is a big shell hole in our school."

The teacher asked Fekete what the schools in Budapest had been like during the last couple of years.

Not too bad, Fekete said. One day, a friend of his, the director of an elementary school, had said to him, "I'm very glad that among the teachers in my school are some members of the Party but no Communists." Such teachers, Fekete said, had joined the Party only for food cards. They had taught the children how to answer questions on dialectics when the inspector came around, but they had made it clear that all those things were only for the inspector.

One of the men asked: Had Fekete seen any actual fighting?

Fekete was now experiencing for the first time in several years the pleasurable sensation of a loose tongue in his mouth. He had, he said. On the third day of the revolution, October 25th, in the afternoon, while he was dodging along the streets on his way home from the factory, he had seen a boy not more than fourteen years old jump on a tank and open the lid and drop in a bottle full of benzine. And very near his factory were situated the Kilian Barracks, where General Pál Maléter, the commander of the Freedom Fighters in the city, had held out for several days with nine hundred men. And on October 26th and the two days following, when there was fighting around his home and his wife wouldn't let him go to the factory, he

4 1

had looked down on the square below their windows and had seen the young men hiding in doorways and shooting, and he had seen a barricade being made of two railway cars.

He had been only a witness, he said. This had been a young people's fight.

It had all started, he said, on October 23rd, in the evening, when the man who was then Premier, Ernö Gerö, announced on the radio that the students' demonstration that afternoon, in favor of the Gomulka liberalization in Poland, had been staged by Fascists and criminals. Fekete said that he had heard the speech, and that it had made him angry. The students had been very angry, and they had marched to the radio station to demand time to answer Gerö, and the guards had become excited and at ten o'clock in the evening had fired shots into the crowd of young people. That was the first thing that had made it a real revolution, Fekete said. He had heard shots during that night. The next morning, the twenty-fourth, he had started out for his office and had found the streets practically deserted. He had walked all the way to the factory both that day and the next, in order that he might be where he could telephone his father and find out how he was.

In the very first days of the revolution, Fekete had begun to hear that Hungarians who lived near the Austrian border were going into exile, and he talked over with his wife the question of whether they should try to go, too. Maybe they could even get to the United States, he said.

On the twenty-ninth, the fighting had died down. Imre Nagy was Premier, and in his Cabinet was a member of the non-Communist Smallholders' Party, Béla Kovács, whom Fekete had known since the time when he himself was a Smallholder. On the thirty-first—a day of great illusory joy in Budapest, as Soviet tanks withdrew from the city and it seemed that a few boys with rifles and bottles of flammables had set back a great military power—Fekete had gone to see Kovács and had talked with him about a possible rejuvenation of the Smallholders' Party.

Then, on the following days, there were ominous rumors of Russian reinforcements. Fekete heard on the radio that Nagy had taken Hungary out of the Warsaw Pact and had proclaimed the nation's neutrality, and that he had appealed to the United Nations for protection.

On the morning of Sunday, November 4th, at five o'clock, the Feketes awoke to sounds of heavy bombardment. Hundreds of Russian tanks were pouring into the city. Nagy took asylum in the Yugoslav Embassy, and the Feketes took refuge in the cellar of their apartment house. There the family stayed, off and on, for a full week, and there, for the first time, they made the acquaintance of the people who had been living in the same building with them for years. The rule of Fekete's life had been: Tranquillity lies in isolation, in saying nothing, in living like a wild beast in the love and protection of one's immediate family. At the factory, everyone had known who the tiny handful of hard-core Communists were, and everyone had kept them, as the expression went, "three steps of air away." No one had taken seriously the pathetic group of food-card Communists, who were pushed into all the front positions and given all the titles. But in the apartment building there had been no way of knowing who thought what; the Avo penetrated everywhere. Now, in the cellar, where someone had set up a radio, it was a staggering revelation to see tears in every eye when, on November 6th, the rebel radio said farewell to the world in defeat. All those in the building whom Fekete had feared had felt the same way as he!

For an hour or so each day, during lulls in the fighting, the Feketes went up to their apartment, and had a meal. They carried a sofa down to the cellar for the girls; the parents slept on the basement floor. Twice that week, Fekete risked going out into the streets, in order to visit his father and make sure he was all right. The wreckage along the streets was appalling.

By Sunday, November 11th, most of the fighting was over. The next day, Fekete walked to the factory. He felt obliged to do this, because he was running low on money and food for his family. He was given his emergency rations that day. He walked to the plant all that week. Everyone there was deeply depressed. The Kádár government was announcing repressive measures; the hopes of late October had proved false; there were reports of wholesale deportations of young men to the Soviet Union; the wreckage in the city was far greater than it had been during the entire war; people had no energy, no desire for work. The official radio and the papers were saying that Soviet troops were guarding the border with Austria, and that the people who had fled to that country were being held as prisoners in camps or made to work in mines, and were given but one piece of bread a day.

On Monday, November 18th, Fekete heard at the factory that trains were going to start running again the next day, and he decided that the time had come to try to escape.

Fekete's new acquaintances in the hotel in Veszprém were so open and warm, and they listened to him with such visible emotion, that he felt once again, as he had in the cellar at home, a poignant shock of emergence from isolation. These people had confidence in him! And he trusted them! One of the men said that he admired and envied Fekete for his courage in attempting to leave the country—that only the dangers of the frontier and fear of a Russian prison held him back—and others agreed.

Now Fekete felt safe in asking what these people had been hearing about the frontier.

The consensus of their opinion, based on reports that had

drifted back from the border, was that the best region in which to try an escape was around a town called Kapuvár, about eighty miles northwest of Veszprém. Here the worst dangers were natural: It would be necessary to go through swampy land in cold weather.

The Feketes rested a full day in Veszprém. The schoolteacher suggested that they go to Celldömölk, the first large town on the way to the Kapuvár swamps, by automobile. She said she had in her class the son of a taxidriver whom she knew to be an honest man; the Feketes could ride with him. Fekete asked her to arrange this, and she did. Early in the morning of November 22nd, the Feketes were picked up by the driver, a taciturn man of about fifty, in a black Russian-built Pobeda. Fekete considered trying to arrange the fare in advance, but he decided that this might be embarrassing; after all, the schoolteacher had said the man was honest.

The black taxi set out across flat farm country on a broad paved highway, one of the main arteries of Hungary, which was bordered in places with rows of poplars and locusts. It was a lonely drive through an empty land, for there was hardly any traffic—not a single car, and only a few trucks—and the farmers were not in the fields. Fekete, who had travelled widely in the country as a lawyer and a politician, in war and peace, had never seen a crisis before that had caused the farmers to stop work. Nowhere had winter rye or wheat or cover crops been planted.

The drive to Celldömölk took two and a half hours, and when the driver set the Feketes down in the center of town, he asked for eight hundred and eighty-two forints. From his former trips, Fekete knew that this fare was quite normal for the distance, and he gave the driver nine hundred forints and told him to keep the change—a tip that Fekete would have thought twice about if money and budgets had meant anything to him any more.

Now Fekete had no idea what to do. He took his family to the railway station, simply for shelter; no trains were running in the direction of Kapuvár. Then he walked out in the town alone. Near a market place, he saw an open farm truck, an old three-ton Hungarian diesel with a cloth canopy over the back; the driver, a peasant, was standing by the cab. Fekete approached him and said, "Which direction do you take?"

"Your direction," the peasant said. "I know where you want to go. Hop in. Let's go."

Fekete said that the farmer was very kind but that his wife and children were at the station.

The man told Fekete to go and get them and any others who might be waiting to go toward Kapuvár.

Fekete ran off to the station, and there he found, besides his family, two coal miners who wanted to leave the country.

When the Feketes and the miners reached the truck, the driver was in the cab, and the motor was running, and in the back were a number of villagers who had been to market. Fekete's party got aboard, and the truck left Celldömölk. The villagers said they were from a collective farm about twelve miles north of Celldömölk, and were heading back there now. They estimated that it was twenty miles to Kapuvár from their farm. There is a perfectly good Hungarian word for collective farm, *szövetkezet*, but to Fekete's surprise these peasants used the Russian term *kolkhoz*, and used it with the same contemptuous force that Fekete's friends in the city gave it. In Budapest, the lawyers' groups set up by the Communists were also widely called "collective farms," with this same Russian word, for laughs.

At the farm, the truck dropped the Feketes and the miners. Fekete reached for his wallet, but the driver waved him off and said, "Good luck." He was about to drive away when he turned back and beckoned to Fekete, and said, "Don't let them forget us out where you're going."

The Feketes and the miners walked through a cold noon hour as far as the next village, which was called Kenyeri. As they walked, the miners told Fekete that this was their second try. They had been caught by Russian soldiers in their first attempt to cross the border, near Szombathely, farther south. The Russians had turned them over to Hungarian frontier guards, and these Hungarians had taken them a few miles back from the border and set them free, and one of the guards had said, "Be more careful next time."

As the group entered Kenyeri, a woman accosted them in the main street and said, "You must hurry. The milk truck from Répcelak is unloading. It can take you farther."

Fekete was disconcerted at the thought that his group could be so easily recognized for what it was. The truck was about three hundred yards up the street, and he and one of the miners started to run toward it. All at once, Fekete saw in the street, on the near side of the truck, a policeman holding a bicycle and talking with two armed civilians. At the sight of the uniform and the guns, he was suddenly afraid, and he pulled the miner with him into the front yard of a house that was surrounded by a high board fence. The two men were standing there, unsure of what to do, when a peasant woman came out of the house and asked what the matter was. Fekete said, "We saw a policeman. We don't want to be caught."

The woman went to her front gate and looked up the street, and then said, "Dear God! That's *our* policeman. He wouldn't hurt a flea. It's perfectly safe to go on. Ask him how to get to the border. You'll see."

Fekete and the miner went on up the street, at a walk. The policeman nodded benignly to them. They asked the driver of the milk truck if he would give the party a lift, and he said he would be glad to, but he was not quite ready to go, and he suggested that they wait for him on a street corner about a hundred yards ahead.

Fekete went back for the others and took them to the corner. It was cold. In a few minutes, a peasant woman came out of her house and invited them inside to get warm. In her house, she fed them all soup and bread, and when it came time to leave, Fekete wanted to pay her for the food, but she refused the money. Indeed, when they were in the street and about to board the truck, one of the miners told Fekete that the woman had drawn him aside and pushed a hundred-forint note into his pocket. He had fished it out and tried to make her take it back, but she had said that he and his friends would need it up the line.

The driver took the two little girls in the cab with him; the others climbed up into the back and sat on empty milk cans there. Suddenly, Fekete felt tears well up.

Elvira Fekete asked her husband reproachfully, as if he were a small boy, what his trouble was.

He leaned toward her and said, in a low voice, "Everybody wants to help us. I never thought the whole Hungarian people could be so equal. These miners are really our friends. Everybody is together. Why did that woman want to give us food and money? She never saw us before, and she'll never see us again! It's all amazing!"

In the summer of 1933, in his seventeenth year, having finished grammar school, Vilmos Fekete attended a Boy Scout World Jamboree in Budapest, and in talking with English and German Scouts he found that he had pretty well mastered the second and third languages he had studied in school. After the Jamboree, he sent his name around to the various hotels in the city with notice that he would be glad to serve as a tourist guide for English- and German-speaking visitors. That autumn, he began studying law at Peter Pazmany University, in Budapest, and from then on for several years he earned spending money by working as a guide and, later, as a clerk in his father's law office. In 1938, when the International Eucharistic Congress was held in Budapest, Fekete had his last big fling as a guide, because after Hitler entered the Sudetenland few tourists ventured into Central Europe. Fekete received his law baccalaureate in 1939 and his doctorate in 1941. He entered private practice with his father, and because he served as counsel to an association of small leather-goods tradesmen who sold holsters, belts, and saddlery to the Hungarian Army, his military service was at first deferred, but on October 7, 1942—four days after his marriage to Elvira, whom he had met at a law-school party —he was drafted, and was assigned to desk work in Szeged, near the Yugoslav border. Army life disagreed with him, and he developed asthma, and in February, 1944, he was given a medical discharge. He resumed his law practice. The Soviet Army entered Pest in January, 1945, and Buda the next month, and at once rounded up, as prisoners of war, all the Hungarian men it could find who were or had been soldiers. Fekete was picked up on February 17, 1945. He was interned with five thousand men of various nationalities in a school on the Pest side of the river until mid-March, when he heard that a Czech mission had arrived in Hungary, and that everyone who claimed Czech nationality was being assigned to the mission, which promptly turned all pseudo-Czechs loose. Upon being asked his nationality by a Russian in an interview on March 16, Fekete knew what to say: He was a Czech. Where were his documents? Sorry, he said—taken from him by a Russian soldier. The Russian sent him to join a band of seventeen men for delivery to the Czech mission; five of them were real Czechs. Two days later, he was at home with his wife, who was seven months pregnant.

Fekete, a liberal idealist who had always considered himself mild, gentle, and sickly, was surprised to find during this experience that his nerves were steady under stress.

Fekete entered politics as a member of the Smallholders' Party. This party, a holdover from before the war, had a long record of representing the peasants' interests against the landlords. In the first postwar election, in November, 1945, which was altogether open and free, it received fifty-seven per cent of the popular vote, while the Communists received only seventeen per cent. The Soviet Army and secret police were still in Hungary, however, and during the next two years, as Fekete gradually rose to membership in the central committee of the Smallholders' Party, he saw many of the men he regarded as the best in the Party pushed out, discredited, or arrested, while by infiltration and pressure the Communists drove the surviving Smallholders further and further to the Left. Fekete was one of a group that broke with the Smallholders' leadership in the summer of 1947, and just a month before the second postwar election, he and his friends set up a new party, the Independents, and Fekete was elected to Parliament with forty-seven of his colleagues—a large number, considering the shortness of their campaign. The Communists, who by then had an efficient machine, seated a hundred members of Parliament, the Smallholders about seventy.

So wildly and quickly had the Independents' fire spread that it was clear to the Communists that the new party would have to be suppressed, and the job of liquidating it was given to the secret police. This was when Fekete fell into his nightmare time; somehow he survived it sane. For five years afterward, he tried to resume private law practice, but nothing came of that. In 1953, discriminatory taxes were levied against private businessmen and professional men, and Fekete, who was earning about twelve hundred forints a month, found himself obliged to pay six hundred and fifty forints of his earnings in taxes.

He dropped his practice and took what he could get—a job at a cannery in the Ferencváros section of Budapest, where he was mostly engaged in arranging contracts with shopping centers and restaurants. He worked surrounded by food and got thinner and thinner.

There was no cover over the back of the milk truck, and it was bitterly cold. Along the way, the driver stopped to pick up three men and three women who were also headed for the border. Two of the men were in filthy, sooty clothes, and wore a kind of harness over their shoulders; as soon as they were settled on the cans, the miners and Fekete congratulated each other and touched them, for they were chimney sweeps, symbols of good luck. Each New Year's Eve in Budapest before the war, chimney sweeps used to go from restaurant to restaurant, often carrying suckling pigs under their arms, and people would rush to touch them for luck. Now the miners laughed and said the trip across the border would be easy.

The truck arrived at a milk-and-cheese plant in Répcelak at a little after four in the afternoon. The village was about twenty-five miles from the border, the driver said, and it was obvious that the Feketes and their friends would not be able to cross the frontier that night; they would have to find a place to sleep. Fekete, who still had a fair amount of money, asked a passer-by in the street whether there was an inn in Répcelak. The stranger was friendly; like everyone else along the way, he knew, without being told, where these people were going, and he said that they had better not stay in Répcelak overnight, because there were quite a few hard-core Communists in the village, who might make trouble for them.

Fekete remembered seeing along the highway, not far back, a signpost pointing to a village called Vamoscsalad, and he also remembered that in Budapest the father of a schoolmate of one of his daughters had once spoken of having relatives in that village. This was a rather tenuous connection, but on the strength of it the Feketes and their friends the miners walked four miles through the twilight to Vamoscsalad. They found a village of farmers' houses, round about which were ranged, in scattered strips, the lands the people worked. Fekete knocked at the door of the first house the party came to, and asked the farmer who answered if he knew such a name as that of his daughter's classmate's father.

"Do I know it?" the farmer said. "Three quarters of the village has that name."

Fekete then asked if the farmer knew of a family, among the three quarters, that owned a young man who was now working in Budapest and had a little daughter.

Why, the farmer said, directly across the street!

The Feketes and the miners received cordial shelter that night from the mother and father of a man who was a virtual stranger to Fekete. The farmer and his wife gave their guests a hot supper—and, better than that, they gave them advice. They said there had been numerous reports in recent days of a strongly reinforced Russian border guard on this side of the swampland around Kapuvár. There were said to have been some shootings. It would be best, the hosts thought, to take a local train that paralleled the border, and attempt their crossing farther along, where the frontier was said to be much less carefully guarded.

At one point during the evening, Fekete said that as far as he could observe, few farmers seemed to be leaving the country. "Almost none," the old farmer said. Fekete asked why that was. "Because they cannot leave the land," the old man said. "They used to say we peasants were slaves of landowners. No, it's deeper. We are slaves of the land."

There were three beds in the farmhouse, and the Fekete

family was given two of them. The miners slept out in a barn.

The next morning, when it came time to leave, Fekete offered the farmer money for the family's and the miners' food and lodging. The farmer refused it, and, gripping Fekete's slender hand with his hard one, he said with great earnestness, "No, I owe you a debt. You will risk your life to get out. You are of the intelligentsia. You must explain to them in the other countries everything that has happened. Tell them not to forget us!"

At seven o'clock, the Feketes and the miners caught a local train, consisting of only four cars, from Vamoscsalad. There was nobody else aboard who seemed to be border-bound. The passengers were workers and peasants. The train went for only about half an hour, as far as a place called Hegyfalu. There the group had a three-hour wait for the next train. More and more people gathered in the station to take it, and among them were about forty who appeared to be headed for the border. Peasants and railway officials talked freely with them about the frontier, and confirmed what the old farmer had said the night before. At the moment, the best place to cross seemed to be near a village named Repcevis, some distance up the line. In that sector, the border patrols were Russian and Hungarian troops working together. Every few hundred yards, one Russian walked with one Hungarian. In the last few nights, there had been wholesale crossings near Repcevis, with no loss of life.

Somebody warned Fekete not to let himself be cheated at the frontier. He told a story about a border guide who had accepted two thousand forints in advance to take a party into Austria and who, on hearing shooting, had run away, abandoning even women and children. Hungarian soldiers had found the group. Things had turned out well, however. The soldiers had finished the guide's work—led the people to the border and sent them across with good wishes.

Was there any danger of secret police along the way? Yes.

The Avo had been setting up check points at various railway stations—a different one each day—but the stationmasters were in constant communication with each other by telegraph, and the conductors would warn the passengers ahead of time if there was any danger.

At last, the train came. It was five cars long and was already packed. There seemed to be many travellers to foreign lands. The Feketes and the miners had to stand in an aisle. At each station, conductors and trainmen went along the platform, stopping at the doors of the cars and quietly speaking to the passengers inside: "The next station is clear. Go forward." The railway officials did this, that is, until the train reached a place called Bö, five stations before Repcevis. There, as they went from door to door, they said, "Avo at the next station. You will need documents at the next station."

Three hundred passengers got off the train, and it went lightly on. Vilmos Fekete was among the most eager to get off, for he never wanted to see the Avo again.

On the evening of September 16, 1947, two weeks after Fekete had been elected a member of Parliament, he and his wife paid a visit to his father. While they were talking, there came a knock on the door. As a kind of reflex, the Feketes went into a bedroom and shut themselves in. Fekete's father, opening the door, found two plainclothes policemen on the landing, and Fekete could hear one of them ask the father whether his son was with him. Quite calmly, the older man said that his son lived on Logodi Street, as doubtless the gentlemen already knew; perhaps the gentlemen would find his son there. The Avo men left without making a search. Fekete and his wife spent the night in the apartment of a friend.

Fekete knew why the Avo wanted him. About two months

before, on July 22nd, two hundred members of the central committee of the Smallholders' Party had convened in Budapest to discuss the national election that was to be held at the end of August. Many of the delegates were worried because the Party's incumbent leaders had been going further to the Left than the membership wanted, or even knew about. The committee sent a delegation of twenty men to call on Zoltan Tildy, the President of Hungary, who was the titular head of the Smallholders' Party. The single representative from Budapest in that delegation, and its spokesman, was Vilmos Fekete, who told the President that the central committee felt that the Party's leaders had drifted far from its rank and file, and that the committee was afraid the Smallholders had lost the confidence of the public and would lose the election. Tildy said he did not see things so dark; he believed the Party leaders were taking the proper course. The delegation returned to the committee, and Fekete, after reporting Tildy's words, proposed a resolution censuring the Party leaders. Some of those leaders, including several Cabinet Ministers, appealed to the central committee not to take this action, and it adjourned without voting on the resolution. But the next day more than half the central committee resigned, and the dissidents formed the Hungarian Independence Party.

With only a month to go before the election, the Independents set up a slate of candidates, all of whom had the official approval of the elections board, dominated by the four principal parties—the Communists, the Smallholders, the Social Democrats, and the Peasants. Fekete and his friends began to campaign in the countryside; because Fekete had exercised his English and German during his days as a tourist guide, he was given charge of the Party's relations with the foreign press. On Election Day, the Independents discovered that the Communists were making wholesale fraudulent use of blue forms that had been issued for absentee voting—driving in cars from town to town and voting over and over. In the days after the election, the Independence Party gathered proof of these frauds, and Fekete had the evidence in his apartment.

The morning after the visit from the two Avo men, Fekete sent his wife home, instructing her to take the vote-fraud material to a friend's house. He himself went to the headquarters of the Independents. On the way, he bought a newspaper and read the surprising news that he had been arrested the night before, along with seventy others, all designated as Fascists. At the Independents' headquarters, he learned that most of the seventy had only been held overnight. One of the Party leaders telephoned the Avo on Fekete's behalf and asked what the police wanted of him. The chief of the Avo himself got on the phone, and said he simply wanted a brief interview with Fekete; he gave his personal word of honor that the man would be free within an hour.

On the strength of that promise, Fekete voluntarily went to the headquarters of the secret police, at 60 Stalin Street. The interview lasted six weeks, and Fekete was set free a little less than a year later.

That morning, the chief of the Avo told Fekete that he wanted only two things of him—admission that the Independence Party had perpetrated vote frauds during the election and that through his contacts with the foreign press Fekete and the Independence Party had received funds and instructions from outside the country. Upon hearing this, and realizing that he was in for something far more serious than an hour's chat, Fekete made three important decisions: to speak only the truth as he understood it, and never to make anything up; to shut his lips firmly rather than say anything that might be dangerous to his friends or his family; and never to speak another person's name.

As for the first question, Fekete replied to the Avo chief, it was not true that the Independents had been guilty of vote frauds; it was, in fact, the Communist Party that had perpetrated such frauds, and the Independents had proof of them. As for the second, he had been merely a press-relations officer for the Independents. He could speak a little English and German, so he had been given the job of interpreting to the foreign correspondents what the leaders of the Party said. That was all.

The chief pressed his questions, and elaborated them, and when he grew tired he turned the interview over to three subordinates, and when they grew tired they were replaced by three others, and they by three others, and this went on for three days and three nights, with an hour off now and then. Fekete clung to his three rules. Finally, this first question period ended, and Fekete was taken to a small, damp room in the cellar, which contained nothing but a bed and a bare two-hundred-watt bulb hanging from the ceiling directly above the bed. There was no window. There was a peephole in the strong door.

Fekete, who had heard about such things, understood that he was to be honored with the breakdown treatment. This form of slow torture, which was based on the empirical observation that nervous breakdowns often follow periods of severe insomnia, consisted simply of keeping the victim awake until, on the verge of a breakdown, he would be ready for even the most bizarre variants of that well-known form of therapy, confession. The brilliant bulb in Fekete's cell was kept on all the time, day and night. Whenever a passing guard, peeping through the hole in the door, saw Fekete asleep, he woke him up. From time to time, Fekete was taken upstairs for relays of questioning.

Fekete kept his sanity during the following weeks by concentrating on his three rules as if they were all that a human mind was supposed to contain. He did not let his thoughts ramble in daydreams and memories. He learned to sleep deeply for five or ten minutes at a time. He dozed standing up. As the days passed, he began to derive more and more courage from his interviews. Telling only the truth as he saw it meant that his answers never changed, and that he never gave his inquisitors openings to force inconsistencies from him. They grew angry with him now and then, and he took this as a sign that they were breaking down, not he. He grew thinner than ever, and physically weak, but his nerves and mind remained sound.

One day toward the end of his sixth week in prison, during questioning by the chief himself, who had often threatened Fekete with a thrashing if he didn't co-operate, Fekete was amazed to hear himself say, in his quiet voice, "If it would make you feel better to beat me, why don't you?" It was perfectly clear to Fekete that the moment the chief began to beat his body, Fekete would have got the better of the chief's mind. The chief did, in fact, fly into a rage, and he beat Fekete into a bloody, unconscious heap.

The next two sessions, which followed periods of recuperation, were also beatings.

The day after the third beating, the chief summoned Fekete to his office and said, "You are no longer important to us. Your party has no more influence. You understand, of course, that a powerful organ of the state cannot now simply release you and say it has made a mistake. But we are willing to change your charge from a political crime to a civil crime. You will sign a document saying you falsified a document for a friend."

Fekete said he would sign the statement and then would say in court that he had been forced to sign it—that he had been beaten just before signing it.

The chief said he wouldn't dare.

Fekete signed the statement, and in the civil tribunal on Marko Street, a few days later, he told exactly what had happened in the secret-police building. The court acquitted him.

But Fekete was in for a new shock. He was told that prisoners who had been acquitted in civil trials initiated by the secret police had to be remanded to the Avo building for their release. Fekete was taken back to 60 Stalin Street. He was not released; he was returned to his dazzling cell. Three weeks later, in December, the chief instructed him to sign a paper reiterating his previous admission and repudiating his repudiation of it. Fekete said he could not sign such lies. The chief said he would find ways to make him sign. Fekete said, "What would be the use of that when you know I would say in court all over again that you made me sign it?"

The chief then asked Fekete how he would feel about starting afresh—signing a statement to the effect that he had not actually falsified the document but that he knew it was false?

Fekete signed this statement. He was transferred to the civil prison and was held for eight months awaiting his second trial.

During this time, Elvira Fekete, who had been notified that her husband was alive but who did not know whether he would ever be freed, went to work as a bookkeeper to support her children. She was obliged to sell many of the family's belongings, including some of her husband's most precious stamps.

At Fekete's second trial, in August, he told the court that he had been forced to sign the new Avo paper. By that time, the court knew its duty better than it had back in November, and it found Fekete guilty and sentenced him to ten months in prison. Since he had already spent more time than that in jail, he was to be set free—and he finally was, after one more night in the bright room in the cellar of 60 Stalin Street.

Fekete immediately appealed his case. The appellate judges heard his appeal in 1950; they summoned and questioned a number of witnesses. It was by then all too evident that the case of this one man was unimportant to the government. The Independence Party had been wiped out. What was more, the

59

Smallholders' Party, the Social Democratic Party, and the Peasants' Party were practically defunct. Zoltan Tildy, the former President and leader of the Smallholders, who had been so sanguine before the 1947 elections, had been ousted in disgrace. There was no longer any problem about vote frauds, for Hungary had long since had its last multiple-choice election. At any rate, the appellate court—a Communist court—reversed the judgment of the civil tribunal and declared Vilmos Fekete innocent of all he had been charged with.

Such a crowd of people bound for the border had detrained at Bö that for a long time there was the utmost confusion. It was about noon. No one seemed to know what to do. Soon the crowd began to sway and stretch, and small groups split away from it, and after a while Fekete and his family and the faithful miners found themselves on a side street of the town, in a cluster of about thirty people surrounding a farm boy of seventeen or eighteen, a native of Bö. The boy told the travellers that the border was something like fourteen miles from the town, and that there was no natural frontier here; the border simply ran through open fields. It was best to cross at night; very many people were crossing the border every night. Someone asked the boy if he could lead this group of thirty to the border, and he said he could, but he thought they should wait until the early afternoon to leave Bö, since there was to be a funeral that afternoon at two and the whole village would be at it; while the funeral was in progress, it would be easy to go off unnoticed through the fields behind the houses. In the meanwhile, he said, the people—all thirty of them—were welcome to come and wait in his family's home, and he took them there. They quite filled the small farmhouse. The boy's family gave the people bread and tea and milk; they said they had been doing this every day for two weeks. When Fekete and one or two others offered money for the food, the peasants, with stoic generosity, refused to accept it, saying that the escapees might have to give money to the border guards or be turned back. The peasants changed into their best clothes for the funeral and left.

Then the boy took his charges out the back door of his house and led them across fields on which could be seen the dead stubble of autumn grains. The country was unremittingly flat. Near the villages that the party passed, and along the roads, stood bare locusts and poplars. The land looked grim under a gray sky. There were occasional flurries of delicate snow. In one way, the extreme cold was a blessing: the ground was firm and not muddy.

More than half the group of which the Feketes and the miners were a part consisted of young men in their late teens and early twenties—Freedom Fighters and youths who were fleeing because they had heard that the Russians were indiscriminately deporting able-bodied men to the Soviet Union. There were six children in the group, the oldest of whom was Klara Fekete and the youngest a baby about three months old that two men carried in a blanket slung from a pole. Mostly, the people were of the laboring class; a few were white-collar workers. Nobody spoke to anyone else. The party moved in a long file, and every head was down as the walkers watched their footing on the furrowed ground.

As dusk fell, the young guide's course seemed to grow erratic, and Fekete had a feeling that the boy was lost. During the last of the light, the party approached a road that lay across their way, and saw the headlights of an automobile coming from the left. Someone in the group shouted in alarm that it might be a carful of soldiers, and everybody threw himself on the ground. Almost at that moment, the car stopped and turned off its lights. Fekete and the others lay silent on the frozen ground for what seemed a very long time—probably about a quarter of an hour, in fact—during which it became entirely dark. Finally, the people heard the car's motor start up, and it moved slowly along the road without turning on its lights. When it was certainly gone, the party moved on.

Now that it was dark, the guide passed word back along the line that there should be no smoking. He also informed his followers that some lights they could see not far away were those of a village called Szakon; he was not lost, after all. In the darkness, the walking was hard over the rough fields. Two by two, the young men began to help the women and children.

At about seven o'clock, the group approached another village, Gyaloka, which the guide said was the last big settlement before the border and was about three and a half miles from it. He led the party straight to the village, and at one of the first houses they reached he said he would go in and arrange for everybody to have a rest. Someone asked if he knew the people who lived in the house. He said that he didn't, but that there was nothing to worry about, because in the villages along the frontier every Hungarian, without exception, helped his fellow-Hungarians on their way.

The house belonged to a tradesman, who, with unemotional hospitality, led the whole party into the capacious kitchen of his home. His guests had been walking for five hours in freezing weather. The tradesman's wife prepared hot tea. The children took off their shoes and hung their socks by the kitchen stove. The guide went out in the village to get information, and in a few minutes he came back with three men and a story.

The story was that some people headed for the border had driven into Gyaloka in a car about an hour before, and had told of seeing a troop of soldiers in the dusk in a field near

Szakon. They had stopped their car and turned out their lights; the soldiers had deployed by the road. After dark, the driver of the car had started it up and got away safely without turning on his lights. The guide had put the villagers' minds at rest about the troop of soldiers.

The three men were peasants, about thirty years old, wearing waterproof coats and cloth caps. They said they lived in a cluster of houses right on the border and knew the countryside well; in fact, they had already taken three parties across to Austria during broad daylight that very day, and they would take this group across, too. The young man who had led the party from Bö whispered to Fekete that he would start out with the three to see that they were going in the right direction, and Fekete, remembering the story of the runaway guide, was glad to hear this. He took up a collection of about two thousand forints from the party in the kitchen and offered it to the boy, who refused it, saying he was not a professional guide; he had only been doing what he felt was right. But Fekete said that refugees would have no use for forints in Austria, and finally the boy took the money.

One of the three men now gave the party a briefing. Between here and the border was the zone of danger. Nobody was to speak from this point on, or smoke, and if anyone had to sneeze or cough, he should do it into cupped gloves, as quietly as possible. The party would walk very fast—almost run. No one should lag behind, because it would be easy to get lost.

During this speech, the Feketes' nine-year-old, Magdalena, began to weep, and afterward, when her mother tried to get her to put on her shoes and socks, the child said she didn't want to go out in the night. Couldn't they wait until the next morning? Magdalena grew increasingly frightened, and finally Fekete gave her a sedative called Legatin; a doctor whom the Feketes had met in the basement of their apartment during

63

the fighting had given him some for the children, to tide them over the bombardments. Magdalena soon became calm.

At eight-thirty, the party started out on the final leg. The three men led the group at very nearly a dogtrot. The young man from Bö went with them for about a mile, and then, quite satisfied that the guides were trustworthy, he turned back for home. For Elvira Fekete, who was wearing heavy overshoes, the pace was trying, and before long she began to have palpitations of the heart, but she could not stop to rest. Two strong young men gripped her arms and at times almost carried her.

It took better than an hour to reach the constellation of houses at the border where the three men lived. The party halted while one of the three ran into the hamlet to find out where, at the moment, the Hungarian soldier and his Russian sidekick were who had been assigned to the few hundred yards along the frontier at this point. He discovered them supping at a tavern that stood among the houses. He ran back to the group and said that if someone would give him a hundred forints, he thought he might be able to make good use of the money. A collection was taken. The guide returned to the tavern, managed to get the Hungarian soldier aside just before the pair set out to renew their patrol, and, in return for the money, got an assurance from the soldier that he would take his Russian colleague westward for their first sweep, leaving the area to the east of the houses free for the guides and their party. The Hungarian told the guide, furthermore, that his party should not be alarmed at the sound of shooting; he had to demonstrate to his officer that he was being vigilant, and he would do a little shooting at nothing—certainly not in the direction of the party.

The guide returned and whispered the good news, and the

group set out on their last dash. Soon there was indeed some shooting off to the left. The people came to a dry ditch in a flat field, and one of the guides said, in what seemed a startlingly loud voice, that the ditch marked the line between Hungary and Austria.

Upon crossing the ditch, Fekete felt empty of emotion. He consciously told himself that he ought to have grand feelings, but all he felt was weariness and cold.

The guides took the refugees a hundred yards farther and then told them they could stop to rest in perfect safety. They could smoke now. There were some lights about five hundred yards ahead, and a church tower with an illuminated clock, and Fekete, who had not owned a watch since 1945, read and announced to his wife the time of their arrival at that place: twenty minutes past ten on the evening of November 23, 1956.

One of the guides told the refugees to go straight to the lights, where they would find people waiting to help them. Again Fekete took up a collection, and the thirty people gave the three guides a thousand forints apiece. When it was all over, Fekete had about eight hundred forints left, and he was sorry he had them.

As the party approached the Austrian village of Lutzmannsburg, Fekete could see many people on the roads that converged on the place—some with children, a few carrying small suitcases. All these walking people, and Fekete's group, too, made their way to a school near the church. The school building was already crowded with something like three hundred refugees, and still more were pouring in.

In the school, the Feketes were fed a hot meal of stew, bread, and tea, and then they were taken to a classroom on the second floor, which contained a teacher's table and several straight

65

wooden benches for scholars. On the walls were pictures of animals, a relief map of Austria, and a map of Burgenland, the province of Austria that adjoins Hungary. Within a few minutes of the Feketes' arrival, there were more than fifty refugees in the room. A party of Austrians brought in some straw-filled mattresses for the children to sleep on.

The director of the school, a brisk, short man in a black hat and coat, entered the room and made a stiff but affecting speech of welcome. The Red Cross, he said, had offered to send a harvest of food and a regiment of staff to this negligible village, to receive the refugees from Hungary, but the people of Lutzmannsburg had not wanted to accept help from the outside world; they had wanted to give their guests from Hungary food from their own cupboards and greetings with their own hands, and this they had been doing day and night for two weeks now, and they were glad that they could do it but sorry that what they did was so crude and so poor.

After the schoolmaster left the room, the exhausted refugees settled down to sleep. The room was so crowded that Fekete had to sit up on the floor with his back against a wall. Suddenly, as the room grew quiet, one of the refugees, a young man, began to sing the Hungarian national anthem, and at the sound Fekete felt all the emotions surge up in him that he had expected to feel at the moment he crossed the border. He struggled to his feet and saw men and women and children getting up all the room, and they all stood and sang and wept together.

At eight o'clock the next morning, November 24th, the refugees at the Lutzmannsburg school, and some who had spent the night in a movie theatre down the street, were loaded into a caravan of buses and driven for three hours through gently rolling farm country, where winter cover crops had been planted, and through a number of small towns, whose shop windows seemed bursting with richness, to a huge, gloomy gray stucco barracks at Eisenstadt, close to the former Esterházy estate, where Josef Haydn once wrote music. Here the Austrian police registered the names, ages, and home addresses of the single men and the heads of families while the women and children were taken off to wash and eat. Afterward, with the other heads of families, Fekete was given a blue nylon bag— like the bags that some airlines give passengers on overnight trips—marked, in English, UNITED STATES ESCAPEE PROGRAM, and containing a bar of soap, three handkerchiefs, a razor and a shaving stick, a toothbrush and toothpaste, a towel, a comb, a mirror, and several packs of Hungarian cigarettes.

At noon, the crowd of refugees was loaded into buses again and taken to a train waiting at a railway station, and the Feketes were directed to a coach at the front that was reserved for families with children. At the entrance to the coach, an Austrian policeman in a gray uniform bent over Magdalena, frightening her at first, but then he smiled and put his big hands on her waist and lifted her up into the car and patted her on the bottom. It was warm in the car. The train stood on a siding for two hours. An Austrian came to the door of the car and announced that the train was headed for Vienna. At last, it moved.

On the way, at the station in Bruck an der Leitha, a lady Red Cross worker came through the car giving out fruit and candy. As she passed along the aisle, Fekete saw several parents begin to cry, but it was only when the lady in uniform held her basket out to his own children, and they asked him a question, and tears came to his own eyes, that he realized what was causing the distress: His children, and all the Hungarian children in the car, had no idea what oranges and bananas were, for they had never seen them before.

67

The train stopped at Schwechat, near Vienna's airport, and a Red Cross man announced in the car that there was no more room for refugees in Vienna; the train would have to wait here until someone higher up decided where it should go. For twenty-four hours, the refugees sat in the cars. From time to time, volunteers brought goulash, cheese, wurst, sardines, lemons, hot milk, tea, bread, and a surfeit of candy. Now the car was overheated. It was nearly impossible to sleep in it. Finally, late the following afternoon, November 25th, the people were told that their train would go to a refugee camp at a place called Traiskirchen. It started to move through the dark at about seven, and two hours later it stopped at a country station.

Three weeks earlier, on the chilly Sunday morning of November 4th, Dr. Viktor Wlach, an official of the Austrian Ministry of the Interior, received a telephone call as he was shaving. He was summoned to the Ministry by that call, and there, at noon, he was directed to take three men—named, as it happened, Sturm, Litchka, and Spitchka—to Traiskirchen to organize some kind of habitation for about a thousand refugees who were expected to cross the border from Hungary that night.

Traiskirchen had been the seat, in Austria's more martial days, of the country's West Point—a vast compound of a dozen buildings, named after Mozart, Beethoven, and other former residents, temporary or permanent, of Austria. The place was dominated by an enormous imitation palace, decked with baroque shells and spilling cornucopias and round female torsos —a nightmare of pretentiousness, whose every great apparent stone had been carefully shaped in cement veneer over cheap underlying bricks. All this, when Wlach and his team reached it, was a set of roofed ruins. After the end of the Second World War, the place had been used as a barracks by Soviet Occupation troops, who, on retiring from Austria, had been careful to break every window, rip out most of the plumbing, remove every trace of kitchen equipment, and generally scorch the earth of the grounds. Some of the roofs had later been used for sheltering a huge waste of furniture that had once been requisitioned for military use and was supposed to be awaiting return to its myriad owners. The sewage system of the academy had long since broken down, and soil pipes in the main building were backed up to the third floor. Wlach, a man of explosive energy and tongue, commanded Sturm, Litchka, and Spitchka to arrange illumination, build a roomy latrine, and gather straw to spread on the floors for temporary bedding. Wlach shouted all day, both into a telephone and into the open air. He called the gendarmerie, the local police, student organizations, the Red Cross, and even the Boy Scouts and Girl Scouts. As it was Sunday, places of business were closed; nevertheless, things soon began to happen. Three electricians appeared from somewhere with nearly a mile of wire. Farmers all around gave their winter's hay, and a neighboring monastery called Heiligenkreuz contributed several stacks of it, too. A trailer truck brought milk for three hundred babies. Bread came by the carload from bakeries and restaurants in Vienna. A start was made at removing the congestion of furniture. Eight young ladies showed up with typewriters. Nobody was paid, or expected to be, because Wlach had not been given a single schilling of money, and toward dark, when the wrecked academy swarmed with volunteers carrying contributed goods here and there, Wlach roared to a man standing near him, "Do you see all this? Man is not as bad as he appears!"

The first refugees arrived at midnight. By five o'clock the next morning, the Traiskirchen Refugee Camp had fed, registered, and bedded four thousand six hundred dead-tired Hungarians.

In the days that followed, the bare shell of a camp was gradually improved. The Austrian government, which at the moment

69

could ill afford the cash, devoted two hundred and eighty thousand dollars to its repair and furbishing. Windowpanes were installed, toilets put in order, a local telephone exchange set up, and double-decked beds imported—first, old Army ones of iron, and then better ones of wood. Someone devised a chapel that could readily be converted into a movie theatre. Agencies of mercy descended on the place: Caritas, an Austrian Catholic charitable organization, took over the reception of new refugees, as well as camp welfare; the Intergovernmental Committee for European Migration, abbreviated for the tongues of Central Europe to ICEM—an international agency with headquarters in Geneva, which for several years had been shunting the Continent's homeless wanderers back and forth—took over the task of moving refugees on for relocation in other countries; the Swedish Red Cross, liltingly multilingual (but Hungarian was not one of the languages; no one at the camp save the Hungarians could speak Hungarian), took over the kitchen and, eventually, other administrative functions; officials representing the United Nations High Commissioner for Refugees came to co-ordinate and placate and keep things on a high plane. Most inspiring of all was the generosity of several nations, which kept draining Traiskirchen's supply of refugees as new ones came. Switzerland set an example in the very first days by declaring that its territory should be regarded as an extension of the area of asylum, rather than as a begrudged haven for selected refugees; in other words, Switzerland would take any comers, just as Austria was being obliged to do. The Swiss simply sent trains and told the Austrians to fill them. This was an unprecedented act in the history of refugee movements. Other nations, perhaps spurred by this example, broke other old rules of the refugee trade. Britain and France announced that they would take unlimited numbers of refugees. Norway began taking tubercular patients. And even the glacier in the commodious halls of the United States Consulate in

Vienna, consisting of visas frozen solid by the McCarran-Walter Immigration Act, showed signs of thawing, drop by drop.

Because Traiskirchen had only five buses with which to unload the trainful of refugees that arrived on the evening of November 25th, the Feketes had to spend a long final hour in their car, with its steam-fogged windows. During the wait, Fekete was given some green cards, two for each member of his family, to fill out. Then, at last, the family was taken to the camp.

Getting out of the bus, the Feketes were received and checked off by a tall, stick-thin, middle-aged woman who was dressed in what could only have been a Girl Scout uniform and whose plain, maidenly face was touched by something that looked to Fekete suspiciously like saintliness. Just as his children had been given far too much candy in Austria, and were getting pale on it, so he felt he had had his fill in two days of charitable grins, but *this* face struck him as offering the true welcome of love. He saw, too, in the receiving force a priest with a different sort of face—of a kind that barely tolerates the pain of being alive.

The Feketes were lucky; they were sent to a room with only eight bunks—in a small building called the Steltzhammerhaus, where families with children were being housed just then—and were spared the huge bunkrooms of the main buildings, where up to a hundred men and women, mostly total strangers to one another, were stacked two deep in bedroom intimacy. The Feketes were given blankets and a bucket of coal for the stove in their room, and, in company with a mother and two children they had never seen before, they went to bed at midnight.

Early the next morning, after cleaning themselves and their clothes as best they could, the Feketes went out to see the camp. Fekete's first impression was that there were too many people in it; the second thing he noticed was the predominance of youth. More than half the refugees were very young men— either workers or students—of the sort who had staged the revolution, and Fekete wondered: How had they, who had lived so long under strict indoctrination, developed notions about freedom for which they were willing to die? Then he thought: A political system is nothing more, in the end, than a system of human relationships, and what these boys understood of politics was simply that they—and all the Hungarians they knew—were being treated badly as individuals by other individuals who had taken charge of things, and they had come to believe that freedom is the sense of being treated well and that life without that sense is not worth living.

Fekete learned that he and his family could draw any clothing they needed at a distribution center in the camp that was run by the British Friends Ambulance Service. He said to Elvira, "Those should go first who haven't anything. We can wait." Fekete also learned that he could send free cablegrams or telegrams, of not more than fifteen words each, anywhere in the world, and he sent three. The first, to his father in Budapest, said, "WE ARE WELL. GIVE US A SIGN OF LIFE." He had no idea whether that one would get through. The second was to a brother of Fekete's father who had emigrated from Hungary to Neukirchen, near Salzburg, at the end of the Second World War, and it said, "WE ARE WELL. COME AND SEE US." And the third, to a sister of Fekete's mother who had gone to Buenos Aires many years before, said, "WE ARE WELL. GIVE HELP. SEND MOTHER MESSAGE." All three gave the Traiskirchen camp as the Feketes' address. That day, Fekete also sent home an eighteen-page letter, enclosing his eight hundred forints; he had little hope that the letter would reach his family—and it never did.

The next day, November 27th, the Feketes went to the Quakers' clothing warehouse, and among mountains of wool and seas of linen and beaches of shoes they found the things they needed most—decent overcoats and underwear for the whole family. There were clothes in the Quakers' great hall from all over the world. The givers of the world had sent what looked like several years' supply of overcoats for the entire population of Hungary, but it had apparently not occurred to them that Hungarians wear underclothing. Of this there was a desperate want, for the refugees had come across the border without baggage. The underwear at Traiskirchen was largely brand-new—store-bought by the Red Cross and other agencies.

In the clothing warehouse, Fekete heard English spoken, and German, and poor German, and he perceived that the young helpers, like the clothing, had come from the corners of the earth. There had gathered at Traiskirchen, indeed, as at other refugee camps and at border shelters all through Burgenland, a New Bohemia of camp helpers—young, rootless idealists. There were bearded boys from art schools and the merchant marine, girls who had been trying to write in Paris, rich kids on grand tours, students from Oxford and the Sorbonne and Rome on vacation or simply out on hooky, conscientious European nobility, and some naturally noble but poverty-stricken youths, themselves former refugees, from Europe's deep pool of wanderers. The young man in charge of the clothing distribution, Joseph Nold, was a Canadian schoolteacher who, crossing the Channel from Dover to Dunkirk on his way to a job in a private school in India, had met some Quakers who said they were going to Austria to lend a hand; he had decided to join them and had simply cabled the school in India that he would be one term tardy. His tact and energy and his even temperament had eventually made him the head of the clothing warehouse. Among the helpers in the clothing hall and elsewhere in the camp were a girl who had been a stenographer in the Philadelphia law firm of Montgomery, McCracken, Walker & Rhoads, and had decided she would like to see a wider world than *that*, and had been dutifully touring Europe's museums when she suddenly found herself in an American consulate saying she wanted to go and help the Hungarians; a German countess; a big, bearded East Prussian of twenty-three who as a child had walked to West Germany and, after some time in a refugee camp, had escaped, apprenticed himself as a printer's compositor, and worked at that trade three years in Germany, then had gone on to work as a printer in Helsinki, a lumberjack in Lapland, a carpenter in Norway, a poultry farmer's helper in England, and a work camper in France and Germany, and between times had spent his earnings on quite elegant skiing holidays in Switzerland and Norway and Austria; and a New York girl who had once earned an M.A. in primary-school teaching at the Bank Street College of Education and who, though she couldn't speak a word of Hungarian, was now in the process of setting up a wildly progressive kindergarten for Hungarian children, with free painting and unstructured play and a healthy concern for such things as the attention span and major muscular motility.

Going to bed that night, Fekete said to Elvira that he would be surprised if his uncle from Neukirchen didn't show up soon. Two hours later, he was awakened from a deep sleep and, looking up, saw a policeman. He had a moment's sleepy terror, but the policeman said gently, in German, that Fekete had a visitor. Fekete went to the gate of the camp and found his uncle there, with a carful of friends. The uncle, a middle-man for Austrian dairy products, had not spoken with any member of his family in twelve years, and for a feverish fifteen minutes he questioned Vilmos; then he went off to Vienna.

The uncle was back early the next morning. Vilmos got a pass from camp headquarters and accompanied his uncle to the capital to see what could be done to get the family started toward the United States. They drove to the American Consulate, where a clerk told Fekete that the quota of regular United States visas, sixty-five hundred, had already been heavily oversubscribed, but that it might help in the long run if Fekete could get a sponsor in the United States. Fekete remembered an elderly American who had worked in the United States Consulate in Budapest just after the war and who had married a Hungarian lady—a neighbor of the Feketes, and a woman they had liked. This man had gone home to retire from the consular service ten years before. Fekete asked if he could send a message to him through the State Department, which would doubtless know where he was, and the clerk told him to write a letter; it would go to the States by diplomatic pouch. The clerk also told Fekete to register for emigration with the ICEM office at the camp. Fekete wrote the letter, and his uncle took him out and bought him a Wiener schnitzel.

Early the next morning, Fekete went to the ICEM office, and after standing in a line for a long time he was admitted. The office was under the sweet, yet firm, command of a tiny, fragile-looking girl, half French and half Chinese, named Rose Clémann, who had been a mere stenographer in the ICEM headquarters in Geneva and was now suddenly in charge of the destinies of several thousand homeless people. She sat Fekete down at a small table, opposite a Hungarian woman with frizzy yellow hair and thick glasses, herself an émigré from Budapest to Vienna a few years back, who had volunteered to help with the new wave of refugees. Not many days before, this woman's brother had completed a heroic double escape from Hungary. He had carried his wife, a victim of polio, in his arms over the last several miles of Hungarian farmland and across the border into Austria, and then, having deposited her at his sister's pension in Vienna, he himself, bitterly exhausted, had returned to Budapest and fled the country all over again, this time with his two small daughters. The woman registered Fekete for emigration to the United States.

Soon Fekete's registration got lost. Of course, he did not know this. Not long after the Hungarian revolt, the process of screening and sponsoring refugees for emigration to the United States had been placed in the hands of a number of religious welfare agencies, the most important of which were the National Catholic Welfare Conference, the World Council of (Protestant) Churches, and the Hebrew Immigrant Aid Society. In practice, this assignment of such an important part of the exodus to religious welfare organizations proved to be something of a mistake. The N.C.W.C. office in Vienna was badly undermanned and inefficiently administered, and in time the suspicion arose that the Catholic hierarchy in Austria, which evidently did not want a shortage of vigorous young Catholic men to develop in southeastern Europe, was in no hurry to ship off wholesale the fine specimens from Hungary. The Protestants and Jews quickly filled and moved their quotas, and the Catholics who were left behind in the camps came to the conclusion that Western freedom, about which they had heard such inviting details from Radio Free Europe, was a Protestant and probably, in the last analysis, a Jewish monopoly. At any rate, Fekete's registration was sent to the N.C.W.C. office in Vienna and apparently was soon mislaid there, in a wrong pile of forms.

Fekete decided that while he was waiting for a visa he should make himself as useful as he could, and, hearing that the Austrians in the various offices under Herr Doktor Wlach, who was now *Lagerleiter*, or director of the camp, were badly in need of interpreters, he volunteered for work. For one day, he worked at the top of the seemingly endless line of campers applying for passes to Vienna. Word had already spread through the camp that the refugees who were getting away to the countries of their choice were not the patient people in camps but the so-called free-livers—people with money or connections, who could stay in Vienna and murmur in the lobbies of the consulates until, perhaps just to get rid of them, the authorities sent them flying to distant places. The second day, Fekete interpreted in the camp's office of information—a commodity of which, from the campers' point of view, there was far too little. The third day, he worked in a room where campers could try to trace relatives who were also presumed to be refugees in Austria. And on the fourth day he was assigned to the office of Caritas, where, seeing miracles happen and finding the personification of all he had hoped to find when he left Hungary, he decided he would like to stay.

The person in charge of Caritas was the strange, tall woman in the Girl Scout uniform whom Fekete had seen on his arrival at Traiskirchen. Her name was Frau Doktor Charlotte Teuber, and, among other remarkable things, she turned out to be indeed the Chief of the St. George's Scouts, a country-wide Girl Scout movement in Austria. She had been at a Girl Scout meeting in Graz when the flood of refugees began to cross the border, and she had offered her services to Caritas and had wound up in command of the agency at Traiskirchen, with hardly time to change her clothes. She was a Doctor of Philosophy from the University of Innsbruck, in the field of archaeology, with a specialty in Byzantine art; she was an old hand at digging in Greece and Turkey. She had long had a habit of wintering in Italy, and studying there. Before she landed at Traiskirchen, she had been making plans to attend Princeton for a year or two, to further her researches. She was, as well, on the waiting list for a post with the Austrian diplomatic service.

As Dr. Teuber's interpreter, Fekete had his eyes opened to camp existence. Dr. Teuber worked twenty-one hours a day, and she did everything. She fetched toilet paper when it was needed. She talked would-be suicides out of the notion over a cup of tea. She took supplicants for scraps of string for parcels quite seriously. Fekete watched her spend all one day on the telephone trying to trace for a camper two children who had been lost at the border, one of them an adolescent boy who had been wounded as a Freedom Fighter and who turned up in a distant hospital. She arranged buses for campers to go to see plays and the opera in Vienna, and she persuaded a textile factory, Wöslauer Kammgarnfabrik, to let whole busloads of women come to its plant and take showers. She could spot a lie from a very appreciable distance. She told Fekete that she was a convert to Catholicism and therefore, as she put it, "a very hectic Catholic," but she struck up a close working relationship with the head of the Socialist welfare agency that worked in the camp, and quite often she trotted into his office and saucily asked if his supply of rosaries was holding up all right. One day, a grave British journalist asked her to define her job, and she said, "It's nothing but trying to explain all day that this person or that person is, after all, an angel." Gloom and hysteria could not survive near her. "Isn't this gay?" she exclaimed one day to a morose American volunteer. "Soap problems and soul problems!" Fekete saw her accosted, during the arrival of a fleet of buses with new campers, by a young Austrian helper who was violently furious over some minor mistake that another volunteer had made. As he poured out a stream of abuse and complaint, Charlotte Teuber simply put her hand on his cheek and held it there. His tirade faded like a mist burned off by the sun. After that, for a few minutes, Dr. Teuber seemed melancholy, but when the young man went off, she said at once to Fekete, "I couldn't do things like that if I weren't the camp poodle. I get my cold little nose into everything! And people don't mind. They just say, 'There's that darling poodle knocking the furniture over again.'"

Under Dr. Teuber's frivolity Fekete apprehended that there was a deep well of sadness and strength. Her sworn enemy was Father Gombos, the priest with the sour face. This man poured a malignant zeal into safeguarding the morals of the campers.

He had a system of spies and informers to tell him of cases of adultery and thievery; Dr. Teuber called this little police force the Gavot—Gombos' Avo at Traiskirchen. She found out that the priest had a jail, with an inch of water on the floor, in the cellar of the main building, and she went to him and said, with blazing eyes, "Are these people refugees? Are they prisoners? What are they? If you make prisoners of them, you make criminals of them." Another time, after a member of the Gavot had struck a girl in the face for flirting with another woman's husband, Dr. Teuber said to the priest, "Ah, Father, the less power and the more love, the better we'll catch the youth."

Once she intercepted the priest as he was taking a drunk down to his jail. She said, "Aren't you at least going to give the man a blanket down there?"

"Drunks feel warm," the priest said.

"But it is a well-known medical fact that the moment of sobering up is most dangerous," Dr. Teuber said. "All sorts of germs enter the body then."

"He deserves a few germs."

"Can you really blame him? He's probably seen plenty of Austrians drunk around here."

"The Austrians are not my concern. The Austrians are in Austria. They have a right to behave as they wish."

"But maybe," Dr. Teuber said, "the Hungarians have better reason than the Austrians to be drunk just now."

A few days later, Dr. Teuber was notified that Father Gombos had filed with the bishop a written complaint that Charlotte Teuber was corrupting the morals of the campers of Traiskirchen. Dr. Teuber had to take a day off to go to Vienna and see the bishop. She was able to persuade him that corruption takes varying forms. He blessed her and sent her back to work.

Young lovers in the camp came to Charlotte Teuber for advice, and on December 8 she made the arrangements for the camp's first wedding. The couples were of different religions, so it was a civil ceremony, held in the *Rathaus* of the town of Traiskirchen; Dr. Teuber and a German student were witnesses, and Fekete was the official interpreter. After the vows, Fekete translated a heartfelt speech by the official of the *Standesamt* who had married the young people. "We are happy," he said, "that this greatest festival of life could have been held in a free country. This is a small country but a free one. I hope that this event will never be forgotten. I bring you dear ones wishes— in the name of the town and its people and its leaders, and the *Bürgermeister*, and on my own behalf—for a good life, and a happy new life, and freedom!"

Having had no word of his visa for two weeks, Fekete became a little worried. He had begun to hear from the outside world. One message, a telegram from Budapest, had made him very happy: "WE ARE ALL WELL. FATHER." From Washington, D.C., from his retired consular friend, he had received a prompt and generous offer of sponsorship, money, a home, and a job. His aunt in Buenos Aires had cabled him some money. But no word came of his visa.

An American volunteer at the camp, learning of Fekete's worry from Dr. Teuber, offered to take him in to the American Consulate again. A vice-consul told them that there was nothing the Consulate could do. The letter from Washington was of no use. Since Fekete was a Catholic, it was up to the N.C.W.C. to sponsor him. By chance, a representative of N.C.W.C. walked into the Consulate just then, and Fekete's American friend appealed to him. The N.C.W.C. man called his office; the phone call lasted fifteen minutes. There was no sign of Fekete's registration, the man finally reported, but since this American vouched for him, they would take his word for it that the papers had been sent in, and then and there the man wrote a note authorizing Fekete and his family to be processed to go to the United States as parolees.

The Feketes returned to Vienna the next day for a physical examination, and again, two days later, for an interview. On December 22nd, they were taken by bus to a transit camp at Korneuburg, north of Vienna, where for three days there seemed to be nothing but Christmas parties, given by Austrian students, a sugar refinery, a shipbuilding plant, and a labor union. The children were presented with at least three months' supply of candy. On December 27th, the family was put on a train for Munich, and the next afternoon the Feketes boarded one of six United States Air Force transport planes at Munich Airport. The Feketes' plane took off at five minutes after four o'clock. The day was clear; the ascent was at a remarkable angle. Fekete had never flown before, and he decided that he had never seen anything so pure as the sky above the misty atmosphere of Europe.

A SENSE
OF COMMUNITY

Survival

A SENSE
OF COMMUNITY

S URVIVAL" *tells the story of a crucial episode in the life of* John F. Kennedy, *who, seventeen years after these events, be- came President of the United States.*

It is a tale of a young man's discovery of his inner funds of resourcefulness, optimism, and stamina, and it exemplifies, bet- ter than any other story in this book, the courage-giving force of a sense of community. Here the community was a small crew, Kennedy's own; as commanding officer of a Patrol Torpedo boat, he was responsible for the ten of his twelve who survived the precipitating accident, and the extent to which he grasped his duty toward them—so that his thoughts and anxieties and actions were all turned outward from himself—may well have been what saved both him and them.

The time of these occurrences was August, 1943. I wrote the account a few months later, when Kennedy had been returned

85

to the United States for recuperation and for separation, in due course, from the service. He told me the story one afternoon when I visited him in the New England Baptist Hospital, in Boston, where the disc between his fifth lumbar vertebra and his sacrum, ruptured in his crash in the Solomons, had been operated upon; and I asked if I might write it down. He asked me if I wouldn't talk first with some of his crew, so I went to the Motor Torpedo Boat Training Centre at Melville, Rhode Island, and there, under the curving iron of a Quonset Hut, three enlisted men named Johnston, McMahon, and McGuire filled in the gaps.

Survival

I T SEEMS that Kennedy's PT, the 109, was out one night with a squadron patrolling Blackett Strait, in mid-Solomons. Blackett Strait is a patch of water bounded on the northeast by the volcano called Kolombangara, on the west by the island of Vella Lavella, on the south by the island of Gizo and a string of coral-fringed islets, and on the east by the bulk of New Georgia. The boats were working about forty miles away from their base on the island of Rendova, on the south side of New Georgia. They had entered Blackett Strait, as was their habit, through Ferguson Passage, between the coral islets and New Georgia.

The night was a starless black and Japanese destroyers were around. It was about two-thirty. The 109, with three officers and ten enlisted men aboard, was leading three boats on a sweep for a target. An officer named George Ross was up on the bow, magnifying the void with binoculars. Kennedy was at the wheel and he saw Ross turn and point into the darkness. The man in the forward machine-gun turret shouted, "Ship at two o'clock!" Kennedy saw a shape and spun the wheel to turn for an attack, but the 109 answered sluggishly. She was running slowly on only one of her three engines, so as to make a minimum wake and avoid detection from the air. The shape became a Japanese destroyer, cutting through the night at forty knots and heading straight for the 109. The thirteen men on the PT hardly had time to brace themselves. Those who saw the Japanese ship coming were paralyzed by fear in a curious way: they could move their hands but not their feet. Kennedy whirled the wheel to the left, but again the 109 did not respond. Ross went through the gallant but futile motions of slamming a shell into the breach of the 37-millimetre anti-tank gun which had been temporarily mounted that very day, wheels and all, on the foredeck. The urge to bolt and dive over the side was terribly strong, but still no one was able to move; all hands froze to their battle stations. Then the Japanese crashed into the 109 and cut her right in two. The sharp enemy forefoot struck the PT on the starboard side about fifteen feet from the bow and crunched diagonally across with a racking noise. The PT's wooden hull hardly even delayed the destroyer. Kennedy was thrown hard to the left in the cockpit, and he thought, "This is how it feels to be killed." In a moment he found himself on his back on the deck, looking up at the destroyer as it passed through his boat. There was another loud noise and a huge flash of yellow-red light, and the destroyer glowed. Its peculiar, raked, inverted-Y stack stood out in the brilliant light and, later, in Kennedy's memory.

There was only one man below decks at the moment of collision. That was McMahon, engineer. He had no idea what was up. He was just reaching forward to wrench the starboard engine into gear when a ship came into his engine room. He was lifted from the narrow passage between two of the engines and thrown painfully against the starboard bulkhead aft of the boat's auxiliary generator. He landed in a sitting position. A tremendous burst of flame came back at him from the day room, where some of the gas tanks were. He put his hands over his face, drew his legs up tight, and waited to die. But he felt water hit him after the fire, and he was sucked far downward as his half of the PT sank. He began to struggle upward through the water. He had held his breath since the impact, so his lungs were tight and they hurt. He looked up through the water. Over his head he saw a yellow glow—gasoline burning on the water. He broke the surface and was in fire again. He splashed hard to keep a little island of water around him.

Johnston, another engineer, had been asleep on deck when the collision came. It lifted him and dropped him overboard. He saw the flame and the destroyer for a moment. Then a huge propeller pounded by near him and the awful turbulence of the destroyer's wake took him down, turned him over and over, held him down, shook him, and drubbed on his ribs. He hung on and came up in water that was like a river rapids. The next day his body turned black and blue from the beating.

Kennedy's half of the PT stayed afloat. The bulkheads were sealed, so the undamaged watertight compartments up forward kept the half hull floating. The destroyer rushed off into the dark. There was an awful quiet: only the sound of gasoline burning.

Kennedy shouted, "Who's aboard?"

Feeble answers came from three of the enlisted men, McGuire, Mauer, and Albert; and from one of the officers, Thom.

Kennedy saw the fire only ten feet from the boat. He thought it might reach her and explode the remaining gas tanks, so he shouted, "Over the side!"

The five men slid into the water. But the wake of the destroyer swept the fire away from the PT, so after a few minutes Kennedy and the others crawled back aboard. Kennedy shouted for survivors in the water. One by one they answered: Ross, the third officer; Harris, McMahon, Johnston, Zinsser, Starkey, enlisted men. Two did not answer: Kirksey and Marney, enlisted men. Since the last bombing at base, Kirksey had been sure he would die. He had huddled at his battle station by the fantail gun, with his kapok life jacket tied tight up to his cheeks. No one knows what happened to him or to Marney.

Harris shouted from the darkness, "Mr. Kennedy! Mr. Kennedy! McMahon is badly hurt." Kennedy took his shoes, his shirt, and his sidearms off, told Mauer to blink a light so that the men in the water would know where the half hull was, then dived in and swam toward the voice. The survivors were widely scattered. McMahon and Harris were a hundred yards away.

When Kennedy reached McMahon, he asked, "How are you, Mac?"

McMahon said, "I'm all right. I'm kind of burnt."

Kennedy shouted out, "How are the others?"

Harris said softly, "I hurt my leg."

Kennedy, who had been on the Harvard swimming team five years before, took McMahon in tow and headed for the PT. A gentle breeze kept blowing the boat away from the swimmers. It took forty-five minutes to make what had been an easy hundred yards. On the way in, Harris said, "I can't go any farther." Kennedy, of the Boston Kennedys, said to Harris, of the same home town, "For a guy from Boston, you're certainly putting up a great exhibition out here, Harris." Harris made it all right and didn't complain any more. Then Kennedy swam from man to man, to see how they were doing. All who had survived the crash were able to stay afloat, since they were wearing life preservers—kapok jackets shaped like overstuffed vests, aviators' yellow Mae Wests, or air-filled belts like small inner tubes. But those who couldn't swim had to be towed back to the wreckage by those who could. One of the men screamed for help. When Ross reached him, he found that the screaming man had two life jackets on. Johnston was treading water in a film of gasoline which did not catch fire. The fumes filled his lungs and he fainted. Thom towed him in. The others got in under their own power. It was now after 5 a.m., but still dark. It had taken nearly three hours to get everyone aboard.

The men stretched out on the tilted deck of the PT. Johnston, McMahon, and Ross collapsed into sleep. The men talked about how wonderful it was to be alive and speculated on when the other PT's would come back to rescue them. Mauer kept blinking the light to point their way. But the other boats had no idea of coming back. They had seen a collision, a sheet of flame, and a slow burning on the water. When the skipper of one of the boats saw the sight, he put his hands over his face and sobbed, "My God! My God!" He and the others turned away. Back at the base, after a couple of days, the squadron held services for the souls of the thirteen men, and one of the officers wrote his mother, "George Ross lost his life for a cause that he believed in stronger than any one of us, because he was an idealist in the purest sense. Jack Kennedy, the Ambassador's son, was on the same boat and also lost his life. The man that said the cream of a nation is lost in war can never be accused of making an overstatement of a very cruel fact. . . ."

When day broke, the men on the remains of the 109 stirred and looked around. To the northeast, three miles off, they saw the monumental cone of Kolombangara; there, the men knew, ten thousand Japanese swarmed. To the west, five miles away, they saw Vella Lavella; more Japs. To the south, only a mile or so away, they actually could see a Japanese camp on Gizo. Kennedy ordered his men to keep as low as possible, so that no moving silhouettes would show against the sky. The listing hulk was gurgling and gradually settling. Kennedy said, "What do you want to do if the Japs come out? Fight or surrender?" One said, "Fight with what?" So they took an inventory of their armament. The 37-millimetre gun had flopped over the side and was hanging there by a chain. They had one tommy gun, six 45-calibre automatics, and one .38. Not much.

"Well," Kennedy said, "what do you want to do?"

One said, "Anything you say, Mr. Kennedy. You're the boss."

Kennedy said, "There's nothing in the book about a situation like this. Seems to me we're not a military organization any more. Let's just talk this over."

They talked it over, and pretty soon they argued, and Kennedy could see that they would never survive in anarchy. So he took command again.

It was vital that McMahon and Johnston should have room to lie down. McMahon's face, neck, hands, wrists, and feet were horribly burned. Johnston was pale and he coughed continually. There was scarcely space for everyone, so Kennedy ordered the other men into the water to make room, and went in himself. All morning they clung to the hulk and talked about how incredible it was that no one had come to rescue them. All morning they watched for the plane which they thought would be looking for them. They cursed war in general and PT's in particular. At about ten o'clock the hulk heaved a moist sigh and turned turtle. McMahon and Johnston had to hang on as best they could. It was clear that the remains of the 109 would soon sink. When the sun had passed the meridian, Kennedy said, "We will swim to that small island," pointing to one of a group three miles to the southeast. "We have less chance of making it than some of these other islands here, but there'll be less chance of Japs, too." Those who could not swim well grouped themselves around a long two-by-six timber with which carpenters had braced the 37-millimetre cannon on deck and which had been knocked overboard by the force of the collision. They tied several pairs of shoes to the timber, as well as the ship's lantern, wrapped in a life jacket to keep it afloat. Thom took charge of this unwieldy group. Kennedy took McMahon in tow again. He cut loose one end of a long strap on McMahon's Mae West and took the end in his teeth. He swam breast stroke, pulling the helpless McMahon along on his back. It took over five hours to reach the island. Water lapped into Kennedy's mouth through his clenched teeth, and he swallowed a lot. The salt water cut into McMahon's awful burns, but he did not complain. Every few minutes, when Kennedy stopped to rest, taking the strap out of his mouth and holding it in his hand, McMahon would simply say, "How far do we have to go?"

Kennedy would reply, "We're going good." Then he would ask, "How do you feel, Mac?"

McMahon always answered, "I'm O.K., Mr. Kennedy. How about you?"

In spite of his burden, Kennedy beat the other men to the reef that surrounded the island. He left McMahon on the reef and told him to keep low, so as not to be spotted by Japs. Kennedy went ahead and explored the island. It was only a hundred yards in diameter; coconuts on the trees but none on the ground; no visible Japs. Just as the others reached the island, one of them spotted a Japanese barge chugging along close to shore. They all lay low. The barge went on. Johnston, who was very pale and weak and who was still coughing a lot, said, "They wouldn't come here. What'd they be walking around here for? It's too small." Kennedy lay in some bushes, exhausted by his effort, his stomach heavy with the water he had swallowed. He had been in the sea, except for short intervals on the hulk, for fifteen and a half hours. Now he started thinking. Every night for several nights the PT's had cut through Ferguson Passage on their way to action. Ferguson Passage was just beyond the next little island. Maybe . . .

He stood up. He took one of the pairs of shoes. He put one of the rubber life belts around his waist. He hung the .38 around his neck on a lanyard. He took his pants off. He picked up the ship's lantern, a heavy battery affair ten inches by ten inches, still wrapped in the kapok jacket. He said, "If I find a boat, I'll flash the lantern twice. The password will be 'Roger,' the answer will be 'Willco.' " He walked toward the water. After fifteen paces he was dizzy, but in the water he felt all right.

93

It was early evening. It took half an hour to swim to the reef around the next island. Just as he planted his feet on the reef, which lay about four feet under the surface, he saw the shape of a very big fish in the clear water. He flashed the light at it and splashed hard. The fish went away. Kennedy remembered what one of his men had said a few days before, "These barracuda will come up under a swimming man and eat his testicles." He had many occasions to think of that remark in the next few hours.

Now it was dark. Kennedy blundered along the uneven reef in water up to his waist. Sometimes he would reach forward with his leg and cut one of his shins or ankles on sharp coral. Other times he would step forward onto emptiness. He made his way like a slow-motion drunk, hugging the lantern. At about nine o'clock he came to the end of the reef, alongside Ferguson Passage. He took his shoes off and tied them to the life jacket, then struck out into open water. He swam about an hour, until he felt he was far enough out to intercept the PT's. Treading water, he listened for the muffled roar of motors, getting chilled, waiting, holding the lamp. Once he looked west and saw flares and the false gaiety of an action. The lights were far beyond the little islands, even beyond Gizo, ten miles away. Kennedy realized that the PT boats had chosen, for the first night in many, to go around Gizo instead of through Ferguson Passage. There was no hope. He started back. He made the same painful promenade of the reef and struck out for the tiny island where his friends were. But this swim was different. He was very tired and now the current was running fast, carrying him to the right. He saw that he could not make the island, so he flashed the light once and shouted "Roger! Roger!" to identify himself.

On the beach the men were hopefully vigilant. They saw the light and heard the shouts. They were very happy, because they thought that Kennedy had found a PT. They walked out onto the reef, sometimes up to their waists in water, and waited. It was very painful for those who had no shoes. The men shouted, but not much, because they were afraid of Japanese.

One said, "There's another flash."

A few minutes later a second said, "There's a light over there."

A third said, "We're seeing things in this dark."

They waited a long time, but they saw nothing except phosphorescence and heard nothing but the sound of waves. They went back, very discouraged.

One said despairingly, "We're going to die."

Johnston said, "Aw, shut up. You can't die. Only the good die young."

Kennedy had drifted right by the little island. He thought he had never known such deep trouble, but something he did shows that unconsciously he had not given up hope. He dropped his shoes, but he held onto the heavy lantern, his symbol of contact with his fellows. He stopped trying to swim. He seemed to stop caring. His body drifted through the wet hours, and he was very cold. His mind was a jumble. A few hours before he had wanted desperately to get to the base at Rendova. Now he only wanted to get back to the little island he had left that night, but he didn't try to get there; he just wanted to. His mind seemed to float away from his body. Darkness and time took the place of a mind in his skull. For a long time he slept, or was crazy, or floated in a chill trance.

The currents of the Solomon Islands are queer. The tide shoves and sucks through the islands and makes the currents curl in odd patterns. It was a fateful pattern into which Jack Kennedy drifted. He drifted in it all night. His mind was blank, but his fist was tightly clenched on the kapok around the lantern. The current moved in a huge circle—west past Gizo, then north and east past Kolombangara, then south into Ferguson Passage. Early in the morning the sky turned from black to gray, and so did Kennedy's mind. Light came to both at about six. Kennedy looked around and saw that he was exactly where he had been the night before when he saw the flares beyond Gizo. For a second time, he started home. He thought for a while that he had lost his mind and that he only imagined that he was repeating his attempt to reach the island. But the chill of the water was real enough, the lantern was real, his progress was measurable. He made the reef, crossed the lagoon, and got to the first island. He lay on the beach awhile. He found that his lantern did not work any more, so he left it and started back to the next island, where his men were. This time the trip along the reef was awful. He had discarded his shoes, and every step on the coral was painful. This time the swim across the gap where the current had caught him the night before seemed endless. But the current had changed; he made the island. He crawled up on the beach. He was vomiting when his men came up to him. He said, "Ross, you try it tonight." Then he passed out.

Ross, seeing Kennedy so sick, did not look forward to the execution of the order. He distracted himself by complaining about his hunger. There were a few coconuts on the trees, but the men were too weak to climb up for them. One of the men thought of sea food, stirred his tired body, and found a snail on the beach. He said, "If we were desperate, we could eat these." Ross said, "Desperate, hell. Give me that. I'll eat that." He took it in his hand and looked at it. The snail put its head out and looked at him. Ross was startled, but he shelled the snail and ate it, making faces because it was bitter.

In the afternoon, Ross swam across to the next island. He took a pistol to signal with, and he spent the night watching

Ferguson Passage from the reef around the island. Nothing came through. Kennedy slept badly that night; he was cold and sick.

The next morning everyone felt wretched. Planes which the men were unable to identify flew overhead and there were dogfights. That meant Japs as well as friends, so the men dragged themselves into the bushes and lay low. Some prayed. Johnston said, "You guys make me sore. You didn't spend ten cents in church in ten years, then all of a sudden you're in trouble and you see the light." Kennedy felt a little better now. When Ross came back, Kennedy decided that the group should move to another, larger island to the southeast, where there seemed to be more coconut trees and where the party would be nearer Ferguson Passage. Again Kennedy took McMahon in tow with the strap in his teeth, and the nine others grouped themselves around the timber.

This swim took three hours. The nine around the timber were caught by the current and barely made the far tip of the island. Kennedy found walking the quarter mile across to them much harder than the three-hour swim. The cuts on his bare feet were festered and looked like small balloons. The men were suffering most from thirst, and they broke open some coconuts lying on the ground and avidly drank the milk. Kennedy and McMahon, the first to drink, were sickened, and Thom told the others to drink sparingly. In the middle of the night it rained, and someone suggested moving into the underbrush and licking water off the leaves. Ross and McMahon kept contact at first by touching feet as they licked. Somehow they got separated, and, being uncertain whether there were any Japs on the island, they became frightened. McMahon, trying to make his way back to the beach, bumped into someone and

97

froze. It turned out to be Johnston, licking leaves on his own. In the morning the group saw that all the leaves were covered with droppings. Bitterly, they named the place Bird Island.

On this fourth day, the men were low. Even Johnston was low. He had changed his mind about praying. McGuire had a rosary around his neck, and Johnston said, "McGuire, give that necklace a working over." McGuire said quietly, "Yes, I'll take care of all you fellows." Kennedy was still unwilling to admit that things were hopeless. He asked Ross if he would swim with him to an island called Naru, to the southeast and even nearer Ferguson Passage. They were very weak indeed by now, but after an hour's swim they made it.

They walked painfully across Naru to the Ferguson Passage side, where they saw a Japanese barge aground on the reef. There were two men by the barge—possibly Japs. They apparently spotted Kennedy and Ross, for they got into a dugout canoe and hurriedly paddled to the other side of the island. Kennedy and Ross moved up the beach. They came upon an unopened rope-bound box and, back in the trees, a little shelter containing a keg of water, a Japanese gas mask, and a crude wooden fetish shaped like a fish. There were Japanese hardtack and candy in the box and the two had a wary feast. Down by the water they found a one-man canoe. They hid from imagined Japs all day. When night fell, Kennedy left Ross and took the canoe, with some hardtack and a can of water from the keg, out into Ferguson Passage. But no PT's came, so he paddled to Bird Island. The men there told him that the two men he had spotted by the barge that morning were natives, who had paddled to Bird Island. The natives had said that there were Japs on Naru and the men had given Kennedy and Ross up for lost. Then the natives had gone away. Kennedy gave out small rations of crackers, and water, and the men went to sleep. During the night, one man, who kept himself awake until the rest were asleep, drank all the water in the can Kennedy had brought back. In the morning the others figured out which was the guilty one. They swore at him and found it hard to forgive him.

Before dawn, Kennedy started out in the canoe to rejoin Ross on Naru, but when day broke a wind arose and the canoe was swamped. Some natives appeared from nowhere in a canoe, rescued Kennedy, and took him to Naru. There they showed him where a two-man canoe was cached. Kennedy picked up a coconut with a smooth shell and scratched a message on it with a jackknife: "ELEVEN ALIVE NATIVE KNOWS POSIT AND REEFS NAURO ISLAND KENNEDY." Then he said to the natives, "Rendova, Rendova."

One of the natives seemed to understand. They took the coconut and paddled off.

Ross and Kennedy lay in a sickly daze all day. Toward evening it rained and they crawled under a bush. When it got dark, conscience took hold of Kennedy and he persuaded Ross to go out into Ferguson Passage with him in the two-man canoe. Ross argued against it. Kennedy insisted. The two started out in the canoe. They had shaped paddles from the boards of the Japanese box, and they took a coconut shell to bail with. As they got out into the Passage, the wind rose again and the water became choppy. The canoe began to fill. Ross bailed and Kennedy kept the bow into the wind. The waves grew until they were five or six feet high. Kennedy shouted, "Better turn around and go back!" As soon as the canoe was broadside to the waves, the water poured in and the dugout was swamped. The two clung to it, Kennedy at the bow, Ross at the stern. The tide carried them southward toward the open sea, so they kicked and tugged the canoe, aiming northwest. They struggled that way for two hours, not knowing whether they would hit the small island or drift into the endless open.

The weather got worse; rain poured down and they couldn't see more than ten feet. Kennedy shouted, "Sorry I got you out here, Barney!" Ross shouted back, "This would be a great time to say I told you so, but I won't!"

Soon the two could see a white line ahead and could hear a frightening roar—waves crashing on a reef. They had got out of the tidal current and were approaching the island all right, but now they realized that the wind and the waves were carrying them toward the reef. But it was too late to do anything, now that their canoe was swamped, except hang on and wait.

When they were near the reef, a wave broke Kennedy's hold, ripped him away from the canoe, turned him head over heels, and spun him in a violent rush. His ears roared and his eyes pinwheeled, and for the third time since the collision he thought he was dying. Somehow he was not thrown against the coral but floated into a kind of eddy. Suddenly he felt the reef under his feet. Steadying himself so that he would not be swept off it, he shouted, "Barney!" There was no reply. Kennedy thought of how he had insisted on going out in the canoe, and he screamed, "Barney!" This time Ross answered. He, too, had been thrown on the reef. He had not been as lucky as Kennedy; his right arm and shoulder had been cruelly lacerated by the coral, and his feet, which were already infected from earlier wounds, were cut some more.

The procession of Kennedy and Ross from reef to beach was a crazy one. Ross's feet hurt so much that Kennedy would hold one paddle on the bottom while Ross put a foot on it, then the other paddle forward for another step, then the first paddle forward again, until they reached sand. They fell on the beach and slept.

Kennedy and Ross were wakened early in the morning by a noise. They looked up and saw four husky natives. One walked up to them and said in an excellent English accent, "I have a letter for you, sir." Kennedy tore the note open. It said, "On His Majesty's Service. To the Senior Officer, Naru Island. I have just learned of your presence on Naru Is. I am in command of a New Zealand infantry patrol operating in conjunction with U.S. Army troops on New Georgia. I strongly advise that you come with these natives to me. Meanwhile I shall be in radio communication with your authorities at Rendova, and we can finalize plans to collect balance of your party. Lt. Wincote. P. S. Will warn aviation of your crossing Ferguson Passage." [1]

Everyone shook hands and the four natives took Ross and Kennedy in their war canoe across to Bird Island to tell the others the good news. There the natives broke out a spirit stove and cooked a feast of yams and C ration. Then they built a lean-to for McMahon, whose burns had begun to rot and stink, and for Ross, whose arm had swelled to the size of a thigh because of the coral cuts. The natives put Kennedy in the bottom of their canoe and covered him with sacking and palm fronds, in case Japanese planes should buzz them. The long trip was

---

[1] The wording and signature of this message are as Kennedy gave them to me in Boston in 1944. The message was in fact slightly, though not substantially, different; and many years later, after Kennedy had become President, the identity of the actual signer was uncovered—A. Reginald Evans. Wherever the name Wincote appears in the rest of this story, the reader will understand that that of Lieutenant Evans should be substituted.

fun for the natives. They stopped once to try to grab a turtle, and laughed at the sport they were having. Thirty Japanese planes went over low toward Rendova, and the natives waved and shouted gaily. They rowed with a strange rhythm, pounding paddles on the gunwales between strokes. At last they reached a censored place. Lieutenant Wincote came to the water's edge and said formally, "How do you do. Leftenant Wincote."

Kennedy said, "Hello. I'm Kennedy."

Wincote said, "Come up to my tent and have a cup of tea."

In the middle of the night, after several radio conversations between Wincote's outfit and the PT base, Kennedy sat in the war canoe waiting at an arranged rendezvous for a PT. The moon went down at eleven-twenty. Shortly afterward Kennedy heard the signal he was waiting for—four shots. Kennedy fired four answering shots.

A voice shouted to him, "Hey, Jack!"

Kennedy said, "Where the hell you been?"

The voice said, "We got some food for you."

Kennedy said bitterly, "No, thanks, I just had a coconut."

A moment later a PT came alongside. Kennedy jumped onto it and hugged the men aboard—his friends. In the American tradition, Kennedy held under his arm a couple of souvenirs: one of the improvised paddles and the Japanese gas mask.

With the help of the natives, the PT made its way to Bird Island. A skiff went in and picked up the men. In the deep of the night, the PT and its happy cargo roared back toward base. The squadron medic had sent some brandy along to revive the weakened men. Johnston felt the need of a little revival. In fact, he felt he needed quite a bit of revival. After taking care of that, he retired topside and sat with his arms around a couple of roly-poly, mission-trained natives. And in the fresh breeze on the way home they sang together a hymn all three happened to know:

> *Jesus loves me, this I know,*
> *For the Bible tells me so;*
> *Little ones to him belong,*
> *They are weak, but He is strong.*
> *Yes, Jesus loves me; yes, Jesus loves me . . .*

STRENGTH
FROM WITHOUT

Joe Is Home Now

STRENGTH
FROM WITHOUT

This is *a story of a man evading a living death—of how an American G.I., crippled by war and discharged from uniform while hostilities continued, tried to grope his way back to some kind of civilian survival. Joe Souczak's strength, such as he had, was drawn from without, from a loyal friend; love can be a mortal enemy of death, especially of living death.*

Something needs to be said about the reportorial technique used in this story and the one that follows. These two accounts, unlike the orthodox journalistic tales that constitute the rest of the book, are dovetailings, in each case, of the actual experiences of a number of men. In the spring of 1944, a year before the end of the Second World War, by which time a million and a quarter soldiers of the United States, casualties of the world-wide fighting, had been turned back into civilian clothes, so that the problem of human reconversion had already become a

*heavy one, I drove up through the valleys of New York State
and gleaned the first of these two accounts from long talks with
forty-three discharged wounded soldiers. The story of this veteran's struggles is not "fictionalized," because nothing was invented; it is a report. Joe does and says things that were actually
said and done by various of the men with whom I talked; I
simply arranged the materials. Let us say that the story was "can-
nibalized"—the expression our mechanics use for the process
of putting together one flyable airplane from the parts of several. The reason—an ample one at the time—for employing this
technique was to protect individual veterans of the war, who
were as yet by no means sure of their ability to survive whole in
a civilian world, from an exposure through publication that
might have made their trials more severe than they already
were.*

Joe Is Home Now

THE BOY with one arm stood in the Rochester station and looked around. He was on his way to Onteoga, New York, and he was full of going home.

He glanced up at the iron clock—five fifteen, it said. Above the clock he saw the service flag showing that the railroad had sent 25,602 men to the wars. Jeepers, the boy thought, more than a division.

A middle-aged civilian came up to him and said: "You're in the First Division. I seen your shoulder patch."

Joe Souczak said, "Yeah."

"Where'd you get hurt?"

"Africa."

"God, I got hurt myself."

"Yeah?"

"I was in the First in the other war. Company H, Eighteenth Regiment."

"No kidding, I was in G Company of the Eighteenth. Neighbors, huh?"

"God," the older man said, "where you headed?"

"Home," Joe said. "I got thirty days' leave. They're going to discharge me later, only they given me thirty days first. I'm going to hit this town before I catch the train on home. I don't know how my mother will take it. About the arm. I'm going to hit the town first, you know, get a little happy for my mother's sake."

"God, what are we waiting for?"

They went to the Seneca Grille. Joe ordered whisky with beer for a chaser. He found out the civilian came from Auburn and was a policeman off duty. The cop had a Purple Heart ribbon with him and some small articles he had picked up off Germans in the First World War. Joe said he was sorry, but he had checked his souvenirs in his barracks bag at the station. The cop asked, "How you feel about getting home?"

Joe said, "I'm almost as scared as I'm happy. I don't know how it's going to be."

They had several, then went across the street to Odenback's. The cop kept telling about his experiences; he told about chasing Pancho Villa in Mexico before the other war. He called Joe "my old regiment pal."

The cop said, "I'm going to ride out home with you. Least a guy can do for an old regiment pal. Maybe I can help out with your old lady."

Joe had had enough drinks to think that was a fine idea. They bought a quart of whisky to take along, and went to the station, and Joe called home and arranged for his sisters to meet him. Then the pair caught the last train for Onteoga. After pulling on the bottle for a while, the cop fell asleep.

Joe moved across the aisle and started talking with a girl. It turned out that she worked in a Rochester camera factory. Joe said, "Among my souvenirs I got this French camera, I wonder could you look at it and inspect it all the way through and find out does any American film go in it?"

She looked it over and said, "A three-twenty would fit it perfect." She promised to put in a priority and send Joe some film. After they got more friendly, she said, "Sometime you're in Rochester come down to my house for Sunday dinner and all that."

Joe said, "Thanks just the same, only I'm interested in getting home and I got a girl there. I don't know how she's going to take to the one-arm idea."

"Oh, she won't care," the girl said.

Joe said, "I don't look so good to see her tomorrow. I'm kind of disgusted on the point of view my clothes don't fit me. I don't have any others, they're used uniforms they hand out to us at the hospital."

"You'll do all right," the girl said.

When the train was nearly due, Joe wrote a note and pinned it on the lapel of the cop's coat, using the Purple Heart ribbon to pin it on with. The note said, "Figure I'll make out all right with my mom. Thanks for everything, regiment pal, Joe."

Joe left the cop sleeping and got off the train. His sisters Anna and Mickey were waiting for him in the old car. Joe was excited and he said, "Well, after so long a journey I'm almost home, I only got nine miles to go. How's the car run? It still running? Those girls you taught driving lessons to ruin it? Can we get any gas?"

Anna said, "We waited a long time for this. You're gone a long time from home. We've been praying every day you'd come home."

Mickey said, "We hated to hear about the arm."

They all started out with a crying jag and wound up laughing.

They drove out to Onteoga, and as they crossed the tracks into town, Mickey said, "I'm sorry we don't have the brass band out for you."

Joe said, "Let the band go to hell; I don't need the band. Riding up Genesee Street, that's all the welcome I ever wanted. This is my home-coming, the streets are out to greet me." And he said, "Hello, streets."

The first stop was home, naturally, 143 Front Street. By this time it was nearly four in the morning, and Joe was rather drunk. He had only meant to have a couple so as to be cheery when he first saw his mother, but now he was pretty far gone.

He walked up to the front door and banged on it. His father shouted from bed upstairs, "Who is it?"

Joe Souczak shouted, "Does Joe Souczak live here?"

His father shouted, "He ain't home yet."

Joe shouted, "Who you think this is, dad? It's me."

Right away Joe's father and mother came downstairs together in their night things. The two kid brothers, Anthony and Sam, came crashing down after.

Joe's mother went straight to him and embraced him. All she said at first was, "My boy."

She held him and moved her hands up and down his back. She said, "You're all one piece, I'm so glad they didn't molest your face at any point, you're very thin, my Joey." She did not speak of the arm.

Joe's father stood by smiling and said to Anna, "Looks like mother took first choice at embracing the boy."

Finally Joe's mother let go. She smelled the alcohol on his breath and started crying.

Joe's father stepped up and said, "Son, a good many days I wished our Lord that if you could only come back, our Lord could take me then, only I wanted to see you just one time." Joe's father was fifty-three, a railroad worker.

Joe could not think of anything except to reach out the bottle to his father and say, "Take a drink." His father took the bottle and drank. That only made the mother cry harder.

Joe broke into a temper in spite of himself and said to his mother savagely, "What's the sense of crying, for God's sake, I'm home now, ain't I?"

His father said, "Come in the house, son."

They turned on the lights and sat in the living room formally. The father said, "How was it in this war, son?"

Joe said, "I don't know, but it's rougher than the last."

Joe's young brother Anthony said, "How many Germans you kill, Joe?"

Joe said, "Nobody who is a soldier answers that, Tony. You don't like to talk about it, mostly you don't even know, the range is big."

Anthony went over and touched Joe's empty left sleeve and said, "What happened, Joe?"

Joe said, "I remember it was nighttime, doing a patrol action, well, that's when I got hit. It was a rifle bullet."

"Sniper, son?"

"That I couldn't say, maybe it could've been a sniper. They took me to the Thirty-eighth Evac, that's a hospital. They took the arm in Algiers. . . . Could I have something to eat?"

Anna asked, "What you want?"

"Could I have some eggs, plenty of eggs anyhow? Then they started bringing me home, see." Joe looked at his mother crying, and talked fast, feeling bad because he had spoken sharply to her. "I stood in Gibraltar couple days. I took an English boat, what was it, the *Jervis*. I went to near Bristol, I stood there till I had three more operations. From there I left in June, it was on a Canadian boat, the *Nova Scotia*, that was the second trip she took, she went to Halifax. I stood a while at Fort Devens in Lowell General, then it was Walter Reed. Now I come home."

They sat talking till it got light. Joe asked about different things that had happened at home, who was married and so on. No one volunteered any information about Mary Ellard, his girl. Joe's voice was shaky and his one hand trembled. At one point someone said maybe Joe was tired, but he said, "Let sleep go to hell, sleep is a luxury."

When it was day Mrs. Souczak stopped crying and went to the telephone. She dialed a number and said, "Joe is home now," and hung up. She dialed many numbers and all she

113

would say was: "Joe is home now." Then she would hang up.

Pretty soon the people she had called started coming, uncles, cousins, Mrs. Souczak's neighbors, and friends of the family. Mr. Shaughnessy, president of the Onteoga Knitting Mills, where Joe had worked before the war, came, and he said never to worry about a job, just worry about getting well. "The factory is there waiting for you, Joe," he said. "Come over this afternoon and see us." Joe agreed to go at two o'clock.

At each knock at the door, Joe jumped up and went to see who it was. It was about ten o'clock before Mary Ellard came.

Joe reached out his hand. She couldn't seem to say anything. Joe had decided to be cold toward her, for defensive reasons. He just said, "Hello, Mary," and led her right into the living room. They couldn't kiss because of all the company.

Everyone talked busily, but Mary just sat there looking at Joe. He pretended not to see her. After a while she stood up and said, "My brother, he's in from the Pacific, only he has to go back this afternoon, his leave's up. Three o'clock. I better go see him."

Joe went out on the porch with her.

Mary said, "Our first meeting wasn't too personal together, Joey."

"It couldn't be. Didn't you see all those people?"

"I'm so excited, I been biting my fingernail right off."

Joe said, "I'll be seeing you," and he went back in the house. He was trembling all over. He ran upstairs and looked at himself in the mirror: the sleeve was quite neat in his pocket, but his face looked sickly, and the uniform was too big.

At about two o'clock Joe reached the factory. He went up on the second floor, where he found the whole mill waiting for him in a large room. Mr. Shaughnessy said, "We've shut off the wheels of progress for thirty minutes, we want you to make us a little speech."

Joe stood up and said, "I'm glad to be back, and I can say

that I'm very lucky to be back. I remember a good many times when Mr. Shaughnessy used to talk to us on production, that if we didn't produce, the soldiers wouldn't have anything. That is so because I went three months without underwear over there. There wasn't any. It was pretty wicked up there in those mountains."

Then Mr. Shaughnessy and Joe presented each other with gifts. The factory gave Joe a twenty-one-jewel Lord Elgin wrist watch, plus $161 purse. Joe gave Mr. Shaughnessy a green French pocketbook. "On here," Joe said, "is the inscription in silver thread made by the Ayrabs, it says ORAN. I carried this through all the battles, even the worst ones. I had you in mind, Mr. Shaughnessy."

Afterward Joe went out and shook hands around the town. Everyone wanted to shake his one hand, and he felt like quite a hero. He stopped in at the barbershop and was very glad to see Charley the barber again, his old friend. When he got home late in the afternoon his mother asked him what he had been doing and he said, "People been patting me on the back and offering me lifetime jobs."

After a couple more days of callers at 143 Front Street, a crowd of fellows came after Joe and said, "Let's hit the road and do some hell-raising. Let's have a doings among ourselves."

So the boys began going out. The first night they planned to make all the rounds, but the first place was as far as they got. Joe had such a good time that he persuaded the crowd to repeat, night after night.

One day toward the end of his leave Joe went in to see Charley the barber, who was twice Joe's age. Joe had always come to Charley for advice and sometimes Charley gave advice without being asked. Charley said, "You're raising too much hell."

"It's fun, I earned some fun."

"People beginning to talk."

"Let people go to hell, they didn't fight."

"Why don't you see Mary?"

Now Joe tumbled out the words that had been rolling around inside him all through his leave, "Hell, I'm no use to myself with the one arm. What use would I be to any girl?"

Charley said, "I'll be glad when you're discharged. What you need is the right job and the right girl."

Joe did not have the courage, though he had plenty of desire, to see Mary before his leave was finished. He kept telling himself he would be home for good soon; that would be the time to see her. The film for his French camera came from the Rochester girl a couple of days before his leave was up, and he kidded himself that he would go collect that Sunday lunch.

When he reported back to Walter Reed the doctor said, "You look better. Want thirty days more?"

Joe said, "No thanks. My friend told me, he said, 'Joe, I seen you twenty-seven days and I seen you drunk twenty-seven days.' I could use thirty days to rest, doctor."

After a few days they brought an artificial arm and strapped it on. From the first Joe disliked it. He told the nurse, "It hurts my—the upper part of my arm that's left." He never could learn to say stump. But they taught him to use the arm.

In January his honorable discharge came. This time Joe got a uniform that fit better, and he thought he looked pretty well as he started out on the train. He had left off his fake arm, because he liked the empty sleeve in his pocket. The arm was in his suitcase. He had on his ribbons—African Theater, Purple Heart, Before Pearl Harbor. On the way a second lieutenant came over to Joe's seat. You could see the lieutenant had just won his bars and was full of authority. He apparently did not notice Joe's empty sleeve.

"Private," the lieutenant said, "what do you think you're doing, wearing all those ribbons? Do you think you're some kind of a lousy hero?"

Joe stood up and controlled himself. "Sir," he said, "I served eighteen months' foreign duty, I given my left arm, they told me I earned these ribbons."

The lieutenant, horribly embarrassed, stared at Joe's limp sleeve and said, "I'm awful sorry, fellow, I didn't realize." Trying to make it all right, he said, "What's that end ribbon for?"

Joe said in the politest tones, "Sir, I think if you want to go around and make remarks about people's ribbons, you ought to know what the ribbons stand for."

Joe sat down. When the lieutenant went away the man sitting next to Joe said, "Lousy shavetail."

Joe expressed the enlisted man's universal complaint. "They've made this into a two-man army," he said. "They've made it an officer's army and an enlisted man's army. The two of them eat in different pots, bathe in different pots, and pee in different pots. Now the looey don't want me wearing my ribbons. Aw, let him go to hell, I'm out of uniform in a few days anyway."

But when he first got home, Joe found that it was not at all easy to get out of uniform. He was authorized to wear the uniform for ninety days. He felt better in uniform. The khaki sleeve in the khaki pocket was very neat, and his stump felt a lot better in a uniform sleeve.

For a long time Joe just lay around the house. He told his parents he figured he'd earned a month's vacation, and that when the month was up he would choose one of these high-paying defense jobs. "In the meantime," he said, "don't bother me, I'm all geared up ahead of everyone else around me. I'm looking for a slowdown."

But the more Joe tried to rest, the more restless he got. He got feeling disgusted with himself, and he began to think he was not worth anything and never would be again. He tried walking out in the town, but he felt like a beaten dog; he would not speak to a civilian.

He tried working around the house, but whatever he did, he ended in a rage. His father had been a frequent fisherman once, and Joe got out some of his tackle one day, but trying to oil the reel and feed the line through the little leader holes on the rod with one hand made him more and more nervous, and he wound up putting his fist through his closet door. That was the way it went.

About ten days went by before he took Mary out, and then he persuaded two other fellows to take their wives along as cover-up for his embarrassment and uneasiness. They went to Charter's and ate steaks and tried to talk above the jukebox noise. Mary was pathetically eager to please Joe, but on the way home he said, "I don't want you to be nice to me just because you're sorry for me."

"It doesn't matter, Joe, I'm just glad to see you."

"I don't want nobody sorry for me. Nobody." And when they got home Joe shook hands coolly and drove right off, leaving Mary crying.

The vacation was not panning out. One day he found he was getting low on cash, and at lunch he asked his family, "Where's my allotment money I sent you? In the bank?"

Joe's father and mother looked at each other, and his mother said, "We had to spend it when your father was in the hospital having his hernia."

Joe said, "You spent it. All I can say is it's quite discouraging to think you can't trust the ones you ought to trust most. Jeepers, you spent my lifeblood savings." He got up from the table and left the house in disgust.

He went down to the barbershop. There were no customers. Charley the barber said, "How's it go, Joe?"

Joe said, "Like hell. In the money department I'm worried,

Charley. The family spent my allotment money. Looks like I worn my welcome out with my folks. I'll get the hell out, I guess."

"That doesn't sound right, Joe."

"Well, you don't wear your welcome out with your folks, they're dear to you, I guess, but you wear your welcome out with yourself. I feel funny as heck, it makes me nervous and twitchy around their house, you get thinking too much when you sit down."

"You better get a job."

"Maybe you got something there. Seems like the more I stand fast and wait, the more nervouser I get. I tell you, Charley, you put yourself on a pedestal when you first come home, you figure you're a kind of hero, you feel proud of yourself, you've accomplished something, you feel good about fighting for your country. But after about two weeks you know you're just another fellow, only you haven't got your left arm below the elbow."

"You better get a job," Charley said. "And I know just the one, if we could only work it. You know Seraviglia's Bakery? Well, the old man died a couple months ago and the shop's idle. You'd make a good baker, Joe." Joe said, "With one arm?" Charley said, "Why not?"

He decided to try a war job. Out in the field he had heard all about the high wages in defense industries. Now it was his turn for some of the gravy. No more Onteoga Knitting for him.

He went first to the Principo Company—small makers of safety razors before the war, aircraft self-starters now. He was introduced to a Mr. Fenner in the personnel department.

Fenner said, "We'd be glad to take you on, Mr. Souczak, any day you can start."

Joe said, "What do I get?"

Fenner said, "We'll start you at seventy-three cents an hour, that'll come to about $48.50 if you work a good week."

Joe said, "That don't sound like a lot of tin to me. I read in *Stars and Stripes* over the other side about these $150 a week positions in defense plants. I don't go for that $48.50."

Fenner said, "That's our starting rate, Mr. Souczak."

In the following days Joe tried three other small war shops and got the same story at each. Then one afternoon he came home and found a telegram waiting for him. It was from Mr. Shaughnessy of Onteoga Knitting. It said:

HEAR YOU ARE LOOKING FOR JOB. REPORT TOMORROW MORN-
ING FOR PHOTOGRAPH AND INTERVIEW PLANT NEWSPAPER AND
GO TO WORK EIGHTY CENTS HOUR PLUS FIVE CENTS EXTRA FOR
NIGHT WORK. REGARDS.

Joe knew he would take his old job back, but he did not bother to show up the next morning, nor for four mornings after it. "Let the damn job wait for me," he said, as if it were an imposition to ask him to go to work.

On the fifth morning he strapped his artificial arm on for the first time in two weeks and reported at the plant. All the people there were very kind to him. The personnel manager said, "We start most at sixty-five cents an hour and five cents extra for night work. We're going to make an exception in your case and start you at eighty and five.

Joe said, "I don't want any personal favors."

The personnel man said, "It's not because of your handicap, Mr. Souczak. After all, you're one of our old hands around here." He gave Joe an advance on his first week's wages.

Joe could not handle his previous job at the yarn-winder with one arm, so they put him on oiling and cleaning the machines.

At the end of the first day's work Joe was very tired but also happier than he had been for a long time. The advance payment felt nice and crisp in his pocket. He joked at supper, and his family was glad to see him perked up.

The job seemed to go well, and day by day Joe felt more and more like himself. He went to work in khaki pants and shirt, with an old basketball sweater on top. After a few days he discarded his artificial arm. The men in the plant fixed up a special harness for him to carry the oil can and waste around with, so he could leave off the arm.

He felt like going out with Mary again, and he did. They went the rounds and ended up at The Siding. It was like old times for a change. They laughed all night.

On the way home Joe stopped the car. He said, "I don't know what to say, Mary, I'm kind of stumbling in my words."

She said, "That's all right, Joe." Then she added, "In case you've been wondering, it doesn't matter to me."

He knew that she meant about the arm. He was able to say, "I'm not much use to a girl, I only got one hand."

"Love comes from the heart, not from the hand, Joe."

"Yeah," Joe said, "that's right, I never thought of that."

"Everything's the same."

Joe put his arm around her and kissed her. After a while he said, "I don't want to rush into anything."

"You haven't been in any rush so far. I been waiting so long for this."

"Hugging you with one arm is kind of strange," Joe said, "but the kissing is just the same as it ever was."

She said again, "Everything's the same."

Joe said, "Yeah."

After that it was one good day after another. The days just flew.

Joe got all his appetites back. He couldn't seem to get caught up on food. He was always buying an ice-cream cone on the way home from work or stopping for a hamburger late at night. He found he wanted to do many of the old things, and found he could do them. He joined the plant bowling team. He went roller skating. He even went swimming in an indoor pool and found he could pull himself along lying on his right side in the water.

One night he walked with Mary down to Seraviglia's Bakery, and they put their faces against the plate glass and looked in. They saw the mixer, a long table, some racks, a roll-top desk, and, in the back, the big oven.

"Looks nice, don't it, Joey?" Mary said.

"Yeah," Joe said, "but not for a one-arm man."

Three weeks after he went to work he heard about a badge for honorably discharged soldiers—a little gold-plated plastic button with an eagle on it, for the lapel buttonhole. He went over to Camp Prestley with his discharge certificate and got one. That helped with getting out of uniform, and for a while he wore khaki pants and shirt and a civilian coat with the badge on it. No one knew what the badge meant, but he was glad to explain.

Then he bought a whole new set of civilian clothes. He blew a lot of money on the outfit: a suit for $42, topcoat for $50, shoes for $10.50, and a hat for $10. The things were just made to his taste. Everybody made remarks about his showing up in civilian clothes. His brother Tony said he looked like a preacher. Charley the barber said he looked like an undertaker. Mary said, "You look like Joey." Joe passed off the remarks with a joke which was only half a joke, "I got me a spruce outfit in case opportunity comes my way."

One night when he was out at Charter's with Mary and the gang, he was introduced to a boy who was just about to be drafted. Whoever brought the boy up said, "Joe's an old veteran here. You better get some low-down."

Joe laughed and said to the boy, "When you're over there, don't believe nothing of what you hear and half of what you see, and you'll be O.K."

The boy said, "They told me you was sore about the whole thing. They told me you was sorry you went."

Joe might have answered bitterly in his first ten days at home, but now he said, "Who told you that? To me, it was a privilege to fight for my country. I didn't go in for sergeant's stripes and dough to save up, or a pension. It was and it always will be a privilege, the biggest privilege and honor a man will ever get."

"I guess it is," the boy who was about to be drafted said.

"I figure you and I and every other American, we got a lovely home, haven't we, we got a nice girl or maybe a wife, we got our mother and dad, we got complete freedom to shoot our mouth off, haven't we?"

"Yeah," the boy said.

"There always comes a time, the same as if you're out with a crowd on a party, it's the same thing, there comes a time when you got to pay the check, and in the world of today, in the things we've had in the past, I don't think the check's too high, even if it comes to giving your life for your country. That's the way I'm always telling 'em at the plant, they're always squawking about how they have to do so damn much, that's what I tell 'em."

Joe had fun that night at Charter's, and he had fun many nights with Mary. And Sundays especially were fine as springtime came on.

Joe and Mary discovered the countryside together. They would drive out in the Souczak car and then leave it and walk across the farmlands. They would take off their shoes and socks and wade in streams, and Mary would pick bunches of violets, snowdrops, and arbutus. They would lie on their backs in the grass and play cloud games and funny-name games. And Joe would point at a blossoming tree and say, "What's that? I forget the name of that one." Mary would say, "That's the shad tree, Joey. That's the one the farmers say, 'When the shad blows, bullheads will bite and time to plant corn.'" They went fishing a couple of times, and Mary was very good about hooking the bait and taking the fish off the barb. And sometimes they kissed until it was hard to stop. Those were very happy days.

One night they went to the movies. The picture was *Bombardier*, and everything was fine until a bomb came down on a Japanese; the Japanese was running toward the camera, the bomb went off, the concussion exploded a big oil drum and blew the Japanese to Japanese hell. Joe felt the blows and the pain all through his body and his heart began pounding. He said, "Excuse me," to Mary, and he got up abruptly and left. She followed him out as quickly as she could, but he had already hurried home.

Joe felt sick and upset all that night, and from the next day on things seemed to go badly. Joe began to be touchy all the time. People bothered him.

A veteran of the first war came into the barbershop one day when Joe was talking with Charley, and began shooting his face off. He said, "It's going to happen the same thing in this war that it did the last—after the war England will take all the gravy."

Joe got angry and said, "We are American citizens, we give a square deal and we get back a square deal, save criticisms till after."

The veteran said, "I think it's rather stupid sending lend-lease to Russia. Russia will declare war on us, she'll be looking for us in the future."

Joe was very angry. "Those Russians can fight," he said. "Let 'em win this war first."

Very soon afterward he was riding out to the plant on a bus and an elderly woman sat down next to him and said, "You poor boy." Joe's face got red. She asked, "Where did you get maimed like that?"

Joe said, "Tunisia."

The sympathetic lady said, "Dear me." Then she added with genuine interest, "Are those little Japs as bad as people say?"

Joe lost his temper wildly. "Damn it, lady," he said, "they don't have Japs in Africa."

She was alarmed at his outburst, and she said, "My goodness, son."

Joe said, "I'm sorry, lady, but you people get me all nerved up. A person has gambled with their life, it's wrong soldiers should have to listen to such ignorance."

Each day Joe seemed to get more and more out of control. Someone made a perfectly innocent remark in the drugstore about rationing, and Joe turned and said, "We should all have our food cut in two by fifty per cent, and we'd still be in luxury compared with those occupied countries, hell, they was eating grape leaves over there." And when a girl at the mill, thinking she was kidding Joe, called him a privileged character, he said loudly, "I don't ask for any privileges. I can take care of myself."

But the worst blow-up was his fight.

The fight took place in the Depot Lunch. Joe stopped in there for a drink one night with Charley. Charley was sitting on Joe's left at one of the tables against the wall. A sergeant from Camp Prestley came in and sat on Joe's right, where he could not see Joe's left arm. The sergeant had two privates with him, and all three were half cut on beer.

The sergeant said, "Too many healthy-looking guys around here in civilian clothes. They ought to be in uniform." Joe pretended not to hear.

When the sergeant spoke again it was obvious he was trying to bait Joe and Charley. He said, "Must be Four-F."

Joe said very quietly, "Take it easy there."

The sergeant turned and grabbed Joe's right arm and began to shove. He said, "Get into uniform, Four-F."

Joe said sharply, "Quit bulldozing me around."

The sergeant said, "Trying to dodge the draft?"

Joe said, "Listen, you dance-hall Ranger, you're talking to an old trooper here."

The sergeant didn't get the point. He went on, "Four-F."

Joe said, "Listen, I had more bad time in this Army than you had good time in it."

The sergeant was too drunk or too stupid to understand. He still had not seen Joe's left arm. He stood up. Joe stood up and was in a tearing red mood. He clenched his right fist and his stump felt queer because he wanted to clench his left fist too. The stump made some little left jabs and then the right arm came around in a haymaker.

Charley ran around the table and picked the sergeant up off the floor and said, "Stand up and shut up. Don't say a thing or else you'll get thrown out of here."

But the other two soldiers jumped on Joe and Charley, and the sergeant came back in. Then several others, thinking this an ordinary soldier-civilian brawl, jumped in too. Joe stood in the middle of it all, swinging hard with his one arm, trying to learn very quickly how to balance a one-armed blow with a little swing of the hips. Some of his blows landed, some missed. He took some around the chest. His stump hurt sharply.

One by one the brawlers noticed Joe's empty sleeve. One by one they pulled out of the fight, until there was no fight left. All the soldiers except the sergeant walked out of the place. The Depot Lunch grew quiet. The sergeant went to the bar and drank alone.

After a while he walked soberly to Joe's table. He stretched out his hand. Joe shook it.

The sergeant said, "I made a bad mistake. I want to buy you a round of drinks."

Joe thought a moment and then said, "No, I want to buy you

a round." Then he smiled and said, "Since I'm a Four-F, I got a good job, I can afford a round, and you can't."

In the next few days people kept asking Joe about the fight, and that upset him more than the fight itself. Finally he went to Charley and said, "Charley, why can't these people lay off? I thought I traded part of my body for a clean conscience, but they keep bothering me. A bunch of these older folks, these barroom quartets or what-you-call-'em, they got the whole war situation solved on one glass of beer, they size it all up, they keep arguing with me. All I want to do is stay around myself and think it over."

Charley said, "Why argue with them?"

Joe said, "You've broken a commandment, you've had the supreme thrill, you've killed somebody. It makes you restless, you get so you got to pick a fight."

He grew increasingly irritable. In the mill one day his foreman, who had some kind of inferiority complex about not having been to the war, told Joe he was spending too much time in the toilet.

Joe said, "I can't handle these little gidgets and gadgets. It makes my hand nervous. I have to have a smoke."

The foreman said something about not having to smoke all day, and Joe blew up and quit.

A couple of days later he moved out of his family's house into an unfurnished room. He said he didn't want to sponge any longer. He also said, "I don't like this neighborhood, too many trucks and buses, it's just like before an action, they're all going somewhere, you never know where but they're all going like hell. You can't sleep."

Joe's family loaned him an iron bed. He found it just as hard to sleep in the bare room as it had been at home. One night he would lie awake reliving his experiences, the next night he would do the same thing, only imagining himself more heroic than he had actually been: he would save his battalion, he would capture slews of Germans, he would end up walking the floor and smoking.

It was at this period that Joe joined both the Veterans of Foreign Wars and the Disabled American Veterans. Joe took comfort from the meetings, where members talked over all the problems of returned soldiers.

But all through his unhappy days, Mary was Joe's greatest support. She went walking with him every evening; they must have walked a hundred miles in those days. She sided with him in almost everything he did. She kept saying he ought to go into business for himself. He asked how she expected him to do that, when he had no money and was no use.

She urged him at least to go and inquire about the bakery. Joe went to Seraviglia's cousins, and they said the bank owned the bakery now. Joe went to the bank, and they told him there that the bakery was for sale, but there was a $4,900 mortgage on it. Joe told Mary it was hopeless. She said to take a job—but not to forget that someday he would be his own boss.

He took a job as a clerk in a local grocery store, Maturo Brothers. It was hard on his feet, and all the reaching with his right arm made his stump hurt. He quit after three days. He signed on with John B. North, riggers and haulers, supposedly doing desk work in the office. On the fourth day the company fell shorthanded, and Mr. North asked Joe if he'd mind riding out on a job. The job involved moving an upright piano down some porch steps. That was no work for a one-armed man; Joe quit on the spot. He took a job with Moley, the line contractor, as a lineman's assistant. He understood he would merely be handling tools and cutting and unreeling wire, and he thought he would enjoy the outdoor work. But they made him help set up poles, lifting and tugging at the heavy logs, propping them into deep holes. He quit there, too.

The night after he quit Moley's he went out with Mary. He talked about his jobs. He said, "Is this what we laid in slit trenches for? Is this what we stood those bullets for? I'm going around talking to myself, Mary, I tell myself everything's going to be O.K., then I get the real picture, I can't do much at all, there's no hope for me here in this lousy town."

"It's not that bad."

"I tell you how bad it is: sometimes I think I'd rather be out there fighting again, that's how bad."

"What seems to be the trouble, Joey?"

"It's a lot of things," Joe said. "One thing, out there a man is proud, he's in the best damn unit in the whole frigging army, he's got buddies who would gladly die for him, he's got something to do all day, a routine. He's got responsibility. If he flops, somebody's going to die. Back here, I'm not busy, I got no buddies, nobody's interested in giving me responsibility. I'm just burning up my days."

Mary said, "God doesn't punish people, Joe. People punish themselves. You got to do something about this."

"Wish to God I could."

"Would you be fed up if I gave you some advice?"

"I've took so much advice and orders for two years, I'm still in the habit."

"Don't try to earn a million dollars the first job you take."

"I don't care if King Solomon himself advised you along those lines. Out in the field you've heard all these stories about the gravy train back home, you get so you believe them."

"Don't try to be a bank president, Joe. Don't try to earn a thousand bucks a week. Be satisfied with what's coming to you."

Joe thought a little, then said, "I guess you're right, Mary. I got thousand-buck ambitions and forty-five-buck ability."

"It's all right to have ambitions," Mary said, "and maybe when you have a chain of baker shops you'll get a thousand a week."

"That damn bakery again."

Mary said, "I just thought of something, Joe. Why don't you go see Mr. Shaughnessy about the bakery?"

"What use he got for a guy that quit his mill? What would I say to him?"

"He likes you, Joey, maybe he could figure out some way for you to pick up the property."

After a couple of days of winding up his courage, Joe did go to see Mr. Shaughnessy. He told Mr. Shaughnessy about the bakery, how nice it looked from the outside. He spoke of the mortgage, and he asked, "What can a man do to beat a mortgage?"

Mr. Shaughnessy was noncommittal. He said he'd think it over, and asked Joe to leave his address. Joe couldn't figure out whether Mr. Shaughnessy was still sore at him for having left the knitting mill. Joe was discouraged by the conversation.

Four days later a messenger from the knitting mill came to Joe's room and told Joe to report to Mr. Shaughnessy's office. When Joe got there Mr. Shaughnessy had a lawyer with him. He told Joe to come with them, and they went out to Mr. Shaughnessy's Packard and drove off. Joe didn't know what it was all about.

Mr. Shaughnessy pulled up in front of the bakery. He and the lawyer and Joe got out. Mr. Shaughnessy went up and unlocked the door and motioned the others in.

Joe said, "How come you got the key to the bakery?"

Mr. Shaughnessy said, "It's yours, Joe."

Joe said, "You wouldn't pull my leg, Mr. Shaughnessy."

Mr. Shaughnessy said, "We got together a small syndicate of men here in Onteoga who have confidence in you, Joe. We've bought out the mortgage on the bakery and we want you to run it."

Then the lawyer went into a long song and dance about common stock, forty per cent for Joe, sixty per cent for "the syndicate," a lot of stuff Joe didn't understand. All he could think about was that he wanted to tell Mary. He hurried off to tell her as soon as he could get away.

Mr. Shaughnessy had arranged to send Joe to a bakery in Binghamton to learn the trade. Joe spent three weeks there as an apprentice and then came back to be his own boss.

In those first days Joe Souczak was a proud baker. He worked like a slave. He loved the smell of the dough in the proofing box as the bread came up, and his one hand, growing strong now, soon became expert at knocking the gas off and rounding the loaves. He kept his oven at exactly 400°, he pinched off his loaves and scaled them at exactly eighteen ounces. He reached the peel into the deep oven and scooped out the loaves like an old hand. He ruined some loaves, but they had told him in Binghamton that the only way to learn was to have a few bad batches. One day he left the salt out, and what his teachers said was true: "Bread without salt tastes like dirt." After that he always measured the salt into the dough mixer first of all the ingredients. Salt, then flour, then water, then yeast and enriching tablets in lukewarm water. The mixing, the rising, the rounding, the scaling, the proofing, the slitting, the baking, the cooling—it was all a daily rite, and Joe in his white baker's robe felt like some high-and-mighty priest of bread.

Mary came in every morning and helped for a while. She was just as proud as Joe. Joe could see her pride, and he knew it was about time to speak his mind to her. He still was not sure of his right to ask for her, but he was positive of the need and he certainly had the urge.

One night he borrowed the family car and took Mary to Charter's. They had a fine meal and quite a few drinks. Joe was not particular about drinks; he would toss off anything that passed under his nose. The evening was fast and happy, and on the way home Joe stopped the car.

"I'm on the up-and-up," he said. "We taken in $64.85 this week." He always said "we" when he talked with Mary about the bakery.

"That's wonderful, Joe."

"Of course," Joe said, "we're not going to have as much in our pocket while we're building up our stocks of ingredients and things as we would have."

"That doesn't matter, Joey."

"I got a pension coming," Joe said. "A sixty-per-cent disability means sixty bucks a month, plus another thirty-five because I lost the arm. I'm grabbing that mustered-out pay: I'm expecting a check for three hundred smackers any day from the Army. I'm doing fine."

"You're doing very good, Joe."

"You understand, I won't ever be rich. I'm too good-hearted, I could never get rich."

"Who wants to be rich?"

"I don't know how it is with you."

"It's the same as it always was, Joe."

Joe pulled out a cigarette and said, "I'm great stuff for these butts. I got started like a chimney on that invasion over there." He fiddled with the cigarette.

Mary said, "I want to marry you in spite of the arm, Joe. I like your strong right arm."

Joe was quiet for a long time. Finally he said, "How's June? June O.K.?"

"June would be good, Joe. June would be very good."

For a couple of days Joe was wildly happy. He now had what Charley had said he needed: the right job and the right girl.

Everything, he thought, was going to be hunky-dory. But then Joe found out that his serenity was neither permanent nor even real.

It rained on the third day after he and Mary became engaged. On the way to the bakery, walking through the rain, Joe saw a new war poster in a store window. It was a lurid picture of death on a battlefield, with a young man pointing an accusing finger at passers-by. The young man looked like one of Joe's friends in Company G who had been killed. The poster shocked Joe. He felt a little dizzy as he went to the bakery. Joe forgot to put flour on the cloths in the proofing box, so when the bread came up it was all stuck to the cloth. The dampness crept into his stump and it began to ache; then his head did, too.

Mary came into the bakery at about noon and found Joe slumped at the roll-top desk with his hand over his eyes. She said, "What's the matter, Joe?"

He looked up and said, "I got me a scare this morning." And he told her what he had seen.

Mary said, "The only person who can help Joe Souczak is Joe Souczak."

"Mary, I don't want to be a wreck, nobody wants to be a wreck from this war."

"You're no wreck, you're going good, Joey. Look at this bakery."

"You're the only thing that keeps me going any good at all." Then Joe thought about the war again, and he frowned and said, "I got to concentrate on my business, got to concentrate my mind, that's what I got to do. God, I wish I could forget a lot of these past incidents. That's the way I'd like to do if I only could. God, if I could." Joe leaned forward and put his hand back over his face. "If only I could," he said.

Mary said, "You can't do it overnight, Joe, you can't do everything all at once. It takes time."

FUNK

A Short Talk with Erlanger

FUNK

This is *a story of a failure of nerve that sheds some light, by reflection, as it were, on courage.*

It cannot be said that the soldier of this tale survived because of an act of cowardice, for, as the colonel points out, the mortars that night simply may not have had Erlanger's number on them. Indeed, in some ways this man acted bravely. The moral of the tale is that survival in high-explosive warfare sometimes depends upon strength, courage, endurance, patriotism, or a nourishing belief in a righteous cause, but very often it does not, for fate can be blind, sardonic, and witless.

By 1945, when this piece was written, the United States Army had admitted to its hospitals more than a million cases of men suffering from what was popularly, but not quite accurately, called combat fatigue. Erlanger was one such. The treatment he receives in this tale, one of many therapeutic devices that were invented or adapted to meet the critical conditions of wartime, was called narcosynthesis. Basically the administering of a so-called truth drug for hypnotic effect, it had what a few doctors considered a short-cutting value in at least one type of disability, in which a "hysterical conversion symptom" is manifested—a paralyzed limb, a heavy tic or twitch, loss of speech, a digestive disturbance, or some other physical failing for which there is no physical cause. The treatment was never a cure but only a possible step toward one. I witnessed many sessions of narcosynthesis at Mason General Hospital, in Brentwood, New York, and while a few achieved immediate outward results, like those in this account, others were unsuccessful. At any rate, the point of this tale is obviously not the therapy that is used, but the substance of Erlanger's brush with fate.

A Short Talk with
Erlanger

THE PATIENT rode in on a wheel chair.

A lieutenant colonel, an Army psychiatrist, standing in the room, said, "Good morning, Erlanger."

The patient said, "Morning, doctor."

"How do you feel this morning?"

"I feel fine. Except my leg. It won't carry me to walk. It hurts here. It worries me, my leg, sir."

"All right," the colonel said. "We're going to try to help that leg."

An attendant, a nurse, and Erlanger's ward officer helped Erlanger to hop on his left leg from the wheel chair to the edge of an iron cot. The patient was a huge man, but he seemed to want aid in everything he did. The nurse helped him take off his red hospital jacket, eased him down on the cot, and straightened his limp right leg. The colonel pulled up a wooden folding chair and sat beside the bed.

Erlanger asked, "What are you going to do to me this morning?"

The colonel said, "We're going to give you an injection that will make you feel good."

Erlanger said, "Shots. I got enough shots in me since I come in the Army. I got everything. I got typhoid, yellow fever, I don't know what all I got."

The nurse handed the doctor a hypodermic needle, a pad of alcohol-soaked gauze, and a rubber tourniquet tube.

Erlanger said, "You got enough in that needle for a horse."

The colonel said, "It'll make you feel good."

"I mean a very big horse."

The colonel pulled the tourniquet tube tight around Erlanger's husky upper arm, cleaned the hollow place at the bend of his arm with the gauze pad, and stuck the needle into the antecubital vein. As soon as the needle was in, the nurse pulled the shade down over the window and drew a curtain across the door. The crippled man lay in semidarkness.

The nurse snapped the tourniquet tube loose, and the doctor slowly pushed one cubic centimeter of ten-per-cent sodium Amytal solution into the vein, left the needle's point still embedded, and said, "Count backwards from one hundred."

Erlanger said, "That I can do." And he began, "A hundred, ninety-nine, ninety-eight, ninety-seven, ninety-six, ninety-five, ninety-four . . ."

Everything the colonel knew about Pfc. Fred M. Erlanger was contained in a manila folder that lay next to the nurse's white instrument tray on the table across the room. This was Erlanger's medical record, which the colonel had studied carefully before the patient came in. The first item in it was simply a beaten-up slip of rough paper with a notation on it that after a night patrol action near Nürnberg, Private Erlanger had been admitted to the 109th Field Hospital incapable of walking and claiming that blast from nearby mortar explosions was responsible for his condition. On the same slip there was a second note, that two days later, after examinations had failed to turn up any wounds, lesions, bruises, or degeneration of tissue that might have been caused by concussion, he was sent on to the 182nd Evacuation Hospital. There, according to succeeding papers, he had been given further tests, which showed no disturbance in the structure of muscle or nerve or bone such as might have been caused by blast, indicated that he was not suffering from infantile paralysis, that he had not had a stroke, and showed nothing clinically except fatigue and slightly higher-than-normal blood pressure. He was, so far as science could tell, sound of wind and limb. Yet he could not walk. The hospital tried a fortnight's rest, with massage and heat therapy, but the leg did not get better. Erlanger was, therefore, referred for neuropsychiatric examination. The most important document in the record was the form filled out by the evacuation hospital's psychiatrist. It read as follows:

Chief Complaint: Weakness, simulating paralysis, of right leg. Pain, centering in thigh.

History of Present Illness: The patient states that he felt well and was not bothered by excessive anxiety before April 16, when, during a patrol skirmish at night, his best friend was killed, and he himself was under severe mortar fire for some time. First began to notice weakness in leg while withdrawing from patrol. Next day could not walk. Patient insists that his condition must have been caused by concussive effect of mortar fire.

Military History: Inducted into Army as selectee Nov. 10, 1943. To England September 1944. Received grade of private first class November 1944. Joined division in Germany as replacement January 1945; saw 46 days continuous front-line action Seventh Army front in reconnaissance combat team. Understands he has been recommended for Bronze Star as result of action in which he was "injured."

Past Medical History: Mumps, measles, chicken pox, whooping cough as child. T & A age 7. Appendectomy age 17. No serious accidents. VD denied.

Social History: Born in Skaneateles, N.Y., Sept. 17, 1924. Lived for 16 years on his father's dairy farm, then left family to go to Syracuse, N.Y., where he worked as truck driver delivering bottled gas, as electrician's helper, road-construction laborer, and grocery delivery boy and clerk. Unmarried, says he could not afford it; had several girls and wanted to marry one just before he was drafted but has since given up idea. Does not write to this girl. Corresponds seldom with his family. Smokes, moderate social drinker. States he gets on well with people and dislikes being alone. Enjoys hunting and fishing; has not participated in team sports despite powerful physique.

Family History: Father, age 54, living and well; described as being "strong"; "wouldn't stand for any nonsense." Mother, 51, living, a calm, quiet person. Siblings: one older brother, two younger sisters—one sister "nervous."

Psychiatric Examination: Patient describes his symptoms with classic *belle indifference* but insists on their crippling effect. Has no insight into possibility that they may have been related to situation anxiety. Describes himself as being rather conscientious and says he always wanted to do the best he could in everything he tried. Wishes he had had more education. Says he is sick of army life. Speech is badly blocked when he tries to tell about night patrol of April 16, and he gets quite upset when talking about loss of friend in that action. No psychotic symptoms.

Impression: Anxiety state, severe, with hysterical conversion symptoms manifested by paralysis of right leg.

Disposition: Since action has ended in this theater and since patient's division has orders for redeployment to Pacific theater, it is recommended that patient be boarded for return to Z.I.

Next in the folder came the order which took Erlanger home from Europe: ". . . The board, having carefully examined Pfc.

F. M. Erlanger and the clinical records pertaining to his case, find that he is unfit for further duty in ETO, U.S. Army, because of: anxiety-hysteria state, severe, following combat. Line of Duty: Yes. In view of the above findings the board recommends that this patient be transferred to the Zone of the Interior for further hospitalization and treatment."

The last pages in the history had to do with Erlanger's admission and orientation to Whittier General Hospital. There were reports on further physical examinations, nurses' notes on the patient's daily routine, and the summary of an exploratory interview that the lieutenant colonel had had with the patient. All these things put together said the same thing. There was nothing physically wrong with Erlanger's leg. The paralysis was a "hysterical conversion"—a device contrived in the hidden caverns of his spirit. Erlanger had no conscious knowledge of the true causes of his paralysis; he could not, therefore, be classified as a malingerer.

On the basis of this history, the lieutenant colonel had decided to have a talk with Erlanger while the man's conscious mind was off guard. He would do this with the help of a trickle of a barbiturate drug, which would disarm Erlanger's inner censors and allow him, for a few minutes before the drug put him to sleep, to pour out in their full intensity some of the overwhelming emotions that underlay his sickness. Now, as Erlanger counted, the Amytal began to take effect.

When in his counting Erlanger reached the number eighty-four, he raised his head off the pillow and, without stopping his recital, blinked and looked around. He said, "Eighty-three, eighty-two, eighty-one, eighty, seventy-nine . . ."

He dropped his head back on the pillow. His voice had become thick. The sibilants of the seventies fell off his tongue blunted, as if he were drunk. The numbers came slowly,

"Seventy-eight, seventy-seven, seventy-six . . . seventy-six . . ."

Erlanger stopped counting. He lay still for a moment. His head rolled twice from side to side. His eyes grew big and looked frightened, and he closed them with a frown but opened them quickly again, as if the shadows moving across the insides of his eyelids were unbearable.

He said, "O-o-oh," and the breath rushed out of his throat as he pronounced the syllable.

The colonel said, "What's the matter?"

Erlanger said, "I don't like the dark."

"Why."

"O-o-oh, those God-damn patrols."

"Tell me about the last one you went on."

"No, I don't like to remember."

"Remember it," the colonel said firmly. "Tell me about it."

Erlanger began at once, with a rather surprising calmness at first, to tell about the patrol. "We were dug in there, we were dug in on a hill. Not exactly a hill, a kind of a rise with some of those terraces, had grapevines on them. I remember Ting, we were trying to eat, Ting said something about, 'Write my mother I was a brave boy.' He meant it funny. So there we were dug in on that hill, and the captain told us we would jump off around ten o'clock.

"I was pooped. I hadn't been sleeping so good at that particular time. So Ting said he'd take the point. It was my turn to take the point, but Ting knew I was played out and pooped so he said he'd trade the point for four butts. The thing I'm glad of, he smoked all four butts I gave him before we started—I'm very glad of that, anyhow.

"However, time came to get up off our duff and go. The idea, what the captain said the idea was, we were supposed to find out where the Jerries were so the division could go through where they weren't; that was the idea. There were some woods up ahead off to the right and some of these small farms with stone walls to the left. Most probably the Jerries were in the woods, or maybe the farms, or maybe both. We didn't know, we were going to find out, we were so God-damn smart we were going to find out.

"So Ting assumed the point of our platoon, he was the first man and cracking wise the whole time. I was about twenty yards behind him, I guess I was that much. If our lieutenant had been any good, he would have taken the point up there; however, he was chicken, he led us from where he could watch our shoulder blades. That is why, also me being pooped, is why Ting was way out in front.

"Up over this rise. Barking your shins on the grapevines.

"Near the top of this first rise, I got very scared. It was so quiet that night you could hear the worms eating the grape leaves—that was what Ting said before we started—so I shouted to Ting in a whisper, I said, 'Ting, for Christ's sake let me take the point.'

"All he said, he whispered, 'Shhh, you want to get us all killed?' "

In telling this much, Erlanger had been showing increasing signs of agitation. Now, however, he broke off and lay calm, as if he had begun to think of something else, something tolerable.

To stimulate him the colonel said, "Who is Ting?"

Erlanger said, "Ting? You didn't know Ting? He was my friend."

The colonel waited.

Erlanger said again, "He was my friend." After another pause he said, "He was a little guy and look at me, I'm a great big horse, and he could do ten times as much as me. Hell, he used to look out for me. 'Did you remember to draw your PX ration?' 'Have you got your grenades?' 'You better eat something, Fred.' Always after me. Always jumping on me."

A shadow of a smile disturbed Erlanger's lips. "Why," he said, "he was the worst God-damn robber. He would rob your last sheet of paper, right when you had a dose of the trots. Son of a bitch. Lazy son of a bitch. Whenever the work came around, very sorry, he was busy, something important to do."

Erlanger paused again. Then, with a sudden flood of intense emotion, he said, "He took the best care of me."

The colonel said urgently, "All right. You were on that hill." As he said this, he rearranged the needle, which still lay pricked into Erlanger's vein, and forced a second cubic centimeter of Amytal into the arm.

Erlanger began to speak in a low, urgent voice. "Ting should've let me come up in front there, it was my turn, he should've let me. . . . I was glad I wasn't up there. I didn't want him to lead us into the woods. Christ, it was light, I never thought a quarter of a moon could make it like that. We came to this road, they'd told us in the briefing it might have mines. The thing was to follow Ting. I was thinking we ought to stay out of the woods. Oh, I liked the grass where we came to it, on the other side of the road; you could hide in it. They should've mowed it, I remember I thought they should've taken the hay in before that. We could've stayed there in the grass. I didn't want Ting for goodness sake to take us in the woods. That grass smelled so good.

"Ting, he was sensible, he bore off. They'd told us, go in the woods, but he was exactly right, I would've done the same; those farms looked better, less dangerous.

"Oh, I was so scared. The farms had some stone walls; these walls were nice. Built good. You could hide there pretty good. We went over a couple and across this plowed-up land.

"I wanted Ting should look out. He was going too near a house there; they could see us out there in that damn moonshine.

"Oh my God, I heard a dog barking. I wondered how far

away it was. I wondered could it smell us out. I couldn't tell anything at night.

"We got past one farm, one farm behind us. I looked back and I could see some dumb bastards back there standing up against the sky. Get down, you dopes, get down, I wanted to shout.

"Then we went through a terrible place to go through. Couldn't Ting have stayed away from undergrowth like that, bushes like that? You couldn't tell anything in there, where you were, even. You just hoped you'd come out right.

"Whew, then it was better, in the open. . . . Those barns didn't look so good. . . . *Skirt around, Ting!"*

Erlanger started, as if someone had jabbed a pin deep into him.

An electrifying change took place. His eyes closed. Some gear shifted in his mind, and he began speaking in the present tense. He was evidently transported back to the very situation and had heard in his skull a dim echo of a shot.

He said, "Oh my gosh, who did that?"

Suddenly Erlanger loosed a series of ejaculations and twitched and grimaced in fear. He stopped talking coherently.

The colonel asked, "What is happening?"

For a few moments, in answer to this question, which recalled him part way from his real-seeming memory, Erlanger hovered on the edge of speech; then, shivering, he whispered, "The Jerries have opened fire. I think they're behind that stone fence —in around those barns in there. Oh, they've got us. They got cross angles on us. I got to work over toward that side wall."

Again Erlanger broke off and grunted mere syllables of surprise and fear. He was now gripping both sides of the bed with his hands. His face was pale and his breath came fast.

The colonel asked, "What's that?"

"Ting. He's hollering. He's hollering and screaming my name. They must have hit him with a grenade, there was some grenades went off right near. Oh Jesus, Ting. . . . Stop that screaming. I hear you; everyone can hear you. . . ."

Now Erlanger broke into a halting, shuddering laugh.

The colonel said, "What's the joke?"

Erlanger was immediately drained of his false humor and looked frightened again. "Bronze Star," he said. "I'm in for the Bronze Star. How do you like that, for what I did on the field of battle? Huh? How do you like it? First I kill my best friend, then he saves my life, so I get in for a Bronze Star." He paused, and then the manifestations of cold fear seemed subtly to be translated into those of cold hate and fury. He continued with bitter sarcasm. "My father will be pleased. Oh, yeah, I can see him, yeah, the old man will be very proud. He's a wonderful man and all that, doctor, but for years he's been after me with his God-damn D. S. M., always telling me, always writing me, 'Well, any day now our rural free delivery is looking for your citation.' Needn't to come home without some kind of decoration, he didn't want me back, except if I was a hero. Now I'm a hero, I can go home, he'll pound me and slap me on the back and tell me I did good. . . ."

The colonel interrupted—and injected a third cubic centimeter of Amytal. "Tell me about Ting. What did you do?"

"Well, I crawled up there where he was screaming. More grenades, of course. The Jerries wanted him to shut up just like I did. It's natural; nobody wants a grown-up man to make a noise like that. So I crawled up there, and the first thing I did, I reached out and grabbed his hand and I figured to pull him back by the hand and so I pulled on it, and the hand came along and a piece of the arm came along and the whole thing didn't weigh more than a small kitten; it came right off him. That was what I was dragging off the field of battle, Ting's hand up to the elbow. So of course I had to go back for the rest of him. The grenades were not close enough, only by luck. This time I got onto the solid part of him, and I jerked and yanked at him, and I got him back a ways. I had to leave the hand out there, I had no place to put it. So I kind of shinnied under him and pried him onto my back, and I crawled on back to near a wall. I was damn near dead then from being scared. So I just lay down there while Ting passed out. At least I figure he did, because he didn't sound off like before.

"And then they started slinging these mortars in."

This memory, slipping out into the open so suddenly, cracked Erlanger's sense of time and threw him back again into the actual situation. He gave a full minute's exhibition of naked, unashamed, uninhibited terror; exactly what he had felt inwardly that night by the stone wall in Germany. He was, for a time, a man in the sharply recollected presence of death.

He ripped his arm out from under the needle, wrenched himself away from the outer side of the bed, and huddled abjectly against the wall. His face turned white, then greenish-gray. He began to tremble violently, and his body suffered gross jolts when the memory of each mortar flash dazzled his brain. A fine perspiration broke out on his upper lip, forehead, and neck. His breath came faster and faster, until he sounded like a panting, shivering puppy.

He turned back toward the open bed, flung out an arm, grabbed his pillow, put it over his shoulders, got up on his knees, scrabbled at the wall of the room for a moment as if he were trying to climb over an obstacle, sank back, made himself as small as possible in the angle between bed and wall, and pulled the pillow—with great effort, as if it were unwieldy, heavy, and repugnant—over his body. He lay that way and shook and cried.

The doctor allowed this violent outpouring to go on for about a minute, then he said, "Erlanger! You're all right now, you're out of danger. You're in a hospital, back in the States."

1 4 9

Gradually Erlanger's shivering eased. His huge body became unstrapped by terror and free again. He said, "Don't send me back, I can't go back in there."

"The war's over for you, Erlanger. You're safe now."

"I want to go home." The big man lying on the cot spoke like a little child.

"You're safe now," the colonel said. "You have nothing to fear."

Erlanger seemed to be calmed by these assurances. He shook his head, as if to clear it, and then lay still for some time, looking at the ceiling.

The colonel said, "You can tell me, now, what happened beside the wall."

A brief shiver, repeating in miniature the nightmarish fear Erlanger had just been through, jarred his body.

He turned his face helplessly toward the colonel and said, "Doctor, do I look like a horse, or an ox, to you?"

"What do you mean?"

"Doctor, I'm such a big strong horse of a man, how could I get so weak? What's the matter with my leg? I want to walk, I ought to be strong enough to take care of myself and walk around."

"You will be. Tell me what happened by the wall."

"Don't ask me to talk about that. Let's talk about it tomorrow."

"No, now. Tell me now."

"Doctor, I'll tell you what bothered me even more than beside the wall there. I'll tell you. It was seeing a horse one day, I was going along and I seen a horse lying right out in a field with its legs up in the air and its guts all over the ground, just like that, dead as hell. What could a horse do to the Germans? Just because it couldn't pull them fast enough, it couldn't keep up with the half-tracks and trucks to pull something for them, that was all, so they blew him up in the stomach; it was a yellow, cowardly bastard's trick to do that to a horse. That made me damn sore, seeing that." Erlanger was close to tears again.

"What happened beside the wall?"

Erlanger frowned. "I remember something," he said. "It bothers me. I used to think about it all the time overseas."

"What's that?"

"On my mother's bureau, home, she's got a picture. It's a picture of me when I was three, four years old. I got long curly hair and I got a dress on. I was too old to be like that. How you think that makes a big horse like me feel, to remember that picture?"

The doctor told Erlanger that was nothing to worry about—that in those days mothers often kept dresses on boys a long time.

"Is that true?" Erlanger seemed to be thinking it over. Suddenly he said, "Sometimes I'd like to push Lieutenant Grant's face in."

"Who is he?"

"He was our lieutenant. I remember one time we were walking along—it was a dirt road, I remember that—and I was having some trouble with my foot at that particular time. I had a blister on my heel, it got full of green stuff and my foot swole up, it hurt like hell. So he comes up and he says, 'Erlanger, what's the matter with you? You're the biggest guy in the platoon but you're just like a baby.' I could kill that son of a bitch. He was a second lieutenant, he had gold bars but we used to call them his yellow stripes. I hate the God-damn Army. Nobody is ever a person. You get pushed around because you're just a serial number. I hate the whole God-damn thing. They shout at you and they say you're dumb and you're a baby and you can't take it and get the lead out of your tail and keep going and what's the matter, you afraid of getting killed? I hate it and I don't care who hears me say so. I hate it! I hate it!"

Erlanger had begun this outburst speaking quietly, but his

temper and voice grew. As he shouted the two final protests, he pounded his left fist hard on the wall beside him.

After a few moments Erlanger said, quite quietly, "Horses are okay if they'll do their work, but I don't know, I just don't like cats. My sisters always had cats. I wanted a dog, but they were the baby girls, my mother always favored the baby girls, so they had a black cat with white paws on it, and she said I couldn't have a dog. I don't think my mother ever wanted any boys in the family, anyhow not after Carl—he's older than me. She treated me different. Definitely."

Erlanger paused and then said, "I don't like anyone laughing at me."

The colonel said, "Nobody likes that."

Erlanger said resentfully, "Well, I don't like it. . . . One night, you know how you sit around at night, we were bivouacked in some kind of old college or some monastery, I don't know exactly, and we were all arguing and discussing there; we were talking about automobiles after the war, what we would buy and all that. And I got talking about my first choice, and I pronounced it *coopay*. And all the guys laughed and said any jerk knew it was pronounced *coop*. And when I told 'em my mother was half French and she said it was *coopay*, they all laughed more and called me Frenchie. And also they used to call me Jerry, because I had a German name, like I wasn't a loyal soldier or something, and there was one guy, he was a tech sergeant, he was too wise for his own good, he used to pick on me all the time. He used to call me Moose, because of my size, and whenever I got tired or like that—you know, a big person gets tired just as much as a small one, sometimes more—he always used to chew my tail and say I was soft. . . . They better not pick on me, I can handle any man, I'll beat the crap out of them." Suddenly Erlanger's belligerency broke and he said miserably, "Doctor, it used to make me very nervous, the way they picked on me. I just wanted to be friendly."

In similar words and with rising and falling moods, Erlanger aired his memories of having been fired, at the age of eighteen, from the job of wrestling two-hundred-pound tanks of artificial gas on and off delivery trucks because, his boss said, he was a "big slob but not man enough for a heavy job"; of unwarranted, extravagant abuse received in England from an MP; of being laughed at, the first time he asked a girl for a date; of a dirty trick his friend Ting had played on him—setting Erlanger up as the victim of a practical joke involving an imaginary ammunition-dump detail; of having been recommended for the Bronze Star because, on the way back from the wall that night, he had helped a wounded man in spite of his own already painfully weak leg; of not being able to keep up with smaller men in basketball at school; of being forced to listen to his father's stories of the last war—claims of heroism and loud-laughing histories of debauchery; of having been beaten up, when he first arrived in Syracuse, by the block bully, a boy much smaller than he; of his feeling, often repeated, that he never did anything well; of trying to make love in a brothel, to which he had been taken by friends, and of failing, because he was afraid of catching something; of having been slapped, for a stupidity rather than a misdemeanor, by a teacher in school.

After the interview had lasted in all about fifteen minutes, the colonel broke in and said, "Now, Erlanger, I want you to tell me exactly what happened beside the wall."

Erlanger said weakly, "I don't like to remember that."

The colonel said, "You've got to face it. Now tell me."

"Well," Erlanger said, "I got Ting back there by the wall and the mortars started dropping in, so I thought I better get against the wall, then I thought I ought to go over. So I tried it with Ting—I didn't know was he dead or alive—I tried getting him on my shoulders and over the wall. I couldn't do it, I was too scared and weak. So I fell down and I wanted to take cover, and I didn't have any way. I wanted to get covered over. . . . I didn't have anything else. . . . I took. . . . I had to take. . . ."

Erlanger gave up. "Go on," the colonel said.

"Well," Erlanger said, "I had Ting back to the wall and when the mortars started falling I wanted to get over. . . ." Erlanger had begun the episode all over again.

"You told me that," the colonel said. "Tell me how you took cover."

Erlanger spoke in a tortured voice.

"I killed him and then he saved my life."

"How?"

"I killed him because I let him take the point, and he saved my life because I . . . I had to take cover, I didn't know what I was doing, I was crazy scared. . . . I . . ."

"How did Ting save your life?"

"I used him. He was dead already, but I used him. I got him on top of me for protection, and he kept the mortars off me. He was awful like that; I hated him even when he was alive. So I killed him dead and he turned right around and saved my life."

"Don't you realize that the grenade might have landed anywhere in the dark, that it was just by chance that it didn't hit you?"

"Yeah, but look who it killed."

"But if you'd been up at the point, it might have been thrown a little harder and still hit Ting. That grenade might have had Ting's number on it, no matter what you did. Mightn't it?"

"It could. I suppose it could."

"What does it mean to you to have a big husky body and yet have people tease you for being weak?"

"It means any man who *is* a man doesn't like to be pushed around."

"Exactly. And what does your bad leg mean to you?"

"I guess it means I got hurt by blast, or something. It also means I'm weak."

"You're weak. With a crippled leg, you *can't* be big and strong, so that there's no reason to feel bad if anyone pushes you around?"

"Doctor, I got a lot of blast there by the wall. I figure my leg must've been sticking out from under Ting there."

"But there's absolutely nothing wrong with your leg. The examinations have all shown that."

"Then what's wrong with it?"

"You tell me. Did you ever know anyone with a crippled leg like yours?"

Erlanger lay still a long time. Then he said positively, "No, sir, not like mine."

"Are you sure? Think back."

Erlanger lay quiet.

The colonel said, "Well, what about it?"

Erlanger's upper lip began to tremble. He put his hands over his face and broke out sobbing.

The colonel said, "What's the matter?"

When Erlanger had controlled himself, a confession welled up from layers of his mind which were most secret, and he uttered it calmly, as if it were some commonplace tossed out at random by his conscious mind. "I could kill my old man," he said. "I never told anybody that before. I wish I could kill him."

"Why?"

"He made us work so damn hard. One night I fainted at the churn, and he beat the hell out of me for being a sissy. He used to drive me and threaten me, that I had to be a real man. He wanted me to grow up strong, like he said he was . . . only he was lazy. He was a lazy good-for-nothing no-good bum and a loafer . . . just like Ting was. . . ." Erlanger continued defiantly, as if he had suddenly caught himself red-handed in a

155

tremendous cheat. "Yes," he said, "I knew someone who had a bad leg. It wasn't this bad. It was just a game leg. My father. He caught some shrapnel in it in the last war."

The colonel said, "Was it his right leg, by any chance?"

"Yeah, it was."

"Just like yours."

"Yeah, that's funny, I hadn't thought of that. Every time the harvesting came long, and usually every day about milking time in the evening, and exactly at the time to feed the chickens, and all of that, why, his leg would trouble him. He'd get a spell. He'd say, 'The boys can do it.' He'd limp around and lie down on the porch."

"Did it hurt him?"

"Yeah, he had a big piece in his leg, it used to hurt."

"Was it right here in the thigh, at exactly the place where you say you feel pain?"

Erlanger ignored this question. He said, "He could walk on his leg, though."

"His leg got him out of a lot of work, didn't it?"

"I'll say. And Carl and me, we were the ones that had to do the work."

"And after that patrol you were telling me about, you had some things you wanted to get out of, didn't you?"

"Nobody likes to get killed."

"Of course not. You're no longer bothered by that patrol, are you?"

"I am and I'm not."

"How do you mean?"

"I'm not because I'm away from all that. I am because I seen it."

"But you're no longer afraid of dying, are you?"

"No, sir."

"You don't have to limp around and lie down on the porch any more, do you?"

Erlanger took this as a slur. "I try to do my part, sir. I'm a good patriotic American."

"Nobody's questioning that. I'm just saying that you don't have to be afraid of dying any more, the way you think your father was afraid of working."

Erlanger thought hard about that one, but he said nothing.

"You said you felt guilty about the death of your friend Ting."

"Yeah, I did."

"You did? Does that mean you don't any more?"

"Well, sir, after what you said I figure maybe he would have been killed anyhow, at least I figure there wasn't anything I had to do with it."

"Good. About some of those other things, about being afraid that other people may not think you're quite the man your size indicates, about why you like horses and don't like cats, and all that—you and I are going to have lots of time to talk it all over."

"Gee, doc, maybe that's all kind of silly."

"It's only silly when you try to hide it from yourself." The doctor stood up and pulled his chair back away from the bed. He said, "Now let's try to get up. Let's see if we can walk."

Erlanger looked at the colonel and said, "I can't, sir. You know my leg is no good."

The colonel said, "There's no more pain in it, is there?"

Erlanger squeezed his right thigh with his right hand. Then he put both hands on his leg and prodded and kneaded. Begrudgingly he said, "No, sir, it don't seem to hurt right now."

"I think perhaps it does work. You just told me that your leg did the same thing for you that your father's did for him. Now you're out of danger and away from the thing your leg got you out of, so maybe it will work again."

With a frightened and yet hopeful expression, Erlanger sat

up in bed. He took his right leg, just above the knee, in his hands, and began to lift it to the right, over the edge of the bed.

The colonel said, "You don't have to carry your leg any more. *Use* it. Take your hands off it."

In spite of the colonel's adjuration, Erlanger followed through and lifted his right leg with his hands all the way. He moved his left leg after it and gradually slipped forward, until his feet touched the floor.

The colonel said, "Stand up."

Erlanger looked at the colonel. The patient's face seemed to be appealing to the doctor not to force him to try to walk. It was not easy to abandon his comforting incapacity. The colonel repeated his command to stand up. Erlanger pushed himself upright, but put all his weight on his left leg and kept a hand on the edge of the cot. He put the other hand to his forehead, because the drug had made him dizzy.

"Now walk."

Erlanger let go of the cot. He said, "I'm not sure I know how. I don't know if I can. . . ." He stood still for a long time, studying his feet.

Slowly he shifted his balance. He swung his weight to the right until his legs were bearing him equally, then he eased back on the left leg. With great concentration he turned his body, pushing his right shoulder and hip forward. He dragged his right foot six inches across the floor.

He had begun to tremble and perspire. Again he shifted his weight until he was balanced on both feet. Then, with a look of fear on his face, he continued slowly to move his weight onto his right leg. He took a step with his left foot that was really a quick hop, so that minimum responsibility fell to his pitied leg. He took another, similar eccentric step. Then he took another and looked up at the doctor. He took two more steps. Suddenly, as if a switch had been tripped, confidence seemed to flood through him, and he said, "I can walk."

The doctor said, "Go out in the hall and try it out."

Erlanger stepped forward now with an almost natural pace. He walked along the hallway, and those in the room could hear him say, "I can walk, God, I can walk. Look at me, I can walk. I can walk, look, I can walk, I can walk." Because of the drug he sounded drunk.

He came back down the hall and entered the room. He was weeping; maudlin. "They didn't make me into a cripple or a no-good," he said with a thick tongue.

"Of course not," the doctor said. "Now lie down."

Erlanger sprawled on the bed. He squeezed his forehead with one hand; dizziness had apparently hit him again. Then he raised his head and looked down at his leg, and he lifted his leg off the bed, apparently to show himself that he could do it. His face had a sheepish, bewildered expression.

The doctor said, "In a few minutes, you'll go to sleep, and you'll have a good long sleep. After you wake up, I'm going to have another talk with you, and I want you to remember everything you've told me, and some other things, too." The colonel knew that no more than a beginning had been made in this session, and a precarious one, at that; Erlanger might, in days to come, fight as if for his life against the interpretations that the doctor had put upon his ailment. But a beginning had been made—for if Erlanger remembered nothing else of this morning's ordeal, he would remember one essential fact: that he was not a cripple. He could walk. The colonel now was gentle. He put his hand on Erlanger's shoulder and he said, "You feel better, don't you?"

"Yes, sir, I feel pretty good now. Just I'm shaky. I feel kind of foggy." Erlanger yawned. He put a hand over his mouth and let the yawn have full play, and when it had spent itself, he said, with inappropriate casualness, "Excuse me."

The colonel said, "Go to sleep, son."

SURVIVAL
OF THE FITTEST

Prisoner 339, Klooga

*

Not to Go with the Others

SURVIVAL
OF THE FITTEST

I

W<small>HEN</small> *the Nazis found themselves face to face with defeat,*
not long before the close of the Second World War, they be-
came panicky, confused, vengeful, exterminatory, and Wag-
nerian in a gruesome vein—they visualized a vast heroic funeral
pyre on which all mid-Europe would be immolated; they were
determined that others than themselves would be the first to
meet the flames.

The two stories that follow come from that bad time toward
the end of the drama, when the grandiose scenery collapsed and
the lights flickered. This pair of stories offers, as it happens,
examples of survivals that depended upon almost opposite tal-
ents—one, boldness; the other, caution.

Benjamin Weintraub, the central figure of the first of these accounts, was a natural leader, an easy athlete, one who could not resist probing, an improviser, an irrepressible escapist—not always brilliant in his solutions but always one to try. I met him, still in the enclosure of the Klooga Camp, near Tallin, Estonia, about a week after the culminating events of this story, and he and a couple of his friends laboriously told me about them with the help of a Polish-English dictionary. They could still hardly believe in their having been roused from the nightmare they had endured. I saw all too vivid evidence of the veracity of their wild words, for rains had, in the end, prevented the Nazi flames from doing but a moiety of the intended work of disposal.

Prisoner 339, Klooga

ON THE DARK DAY when the Jews of Wilno were gathered into a ghetto, a tall, athletic, twenty-three-year-old man named Benjamin Weintraub sat down in his room in the presence of his wife and split the heel off his leather knee boot, cut a neat round hole in the inside of the heel, took his wedding ring off his fourth finger, put it in the hollow place in the heel, and nailed the heel back on his boot. The ring was gold and heavy. Inside it were engraved the date of his wedding, 5 IV 41, and the name of his wife, *LIBA*.

Later the same day the young couple were taken to the ghetto, which consisted of two miserable streets and was divided into two parts—one for "specialists," who could claim various skills, the other for "nonspecialists," who had no trade. Weintraub and his wife were put in the "specialists'" ghetto, and, although he was trained as a chemist, he was classified by the Germans, quite arbitrarily, as an electromechanic. There were twenty-three thousand people in the "specialists'" ghetto, and about twelve thousand in the other. The two streets were so crowded that the Weintraubs had to live like sticks of cordwood in a room thirty feet long by twenty wide, with nearly forty people. The ghetto was surrounded by a high wall and was heavily guarded by German and Lithuanian SS and SD men. Every day Weintraub was taken out into the city with a party to do heavy labor—usually having nothing to do with

165

electromechanics. The work was hard, but he found he was lucky to be doing it: five weeks after the ghetto was formed, all twelve thousand of the "nonspecialists" were taken out to a place called Ponary, twelve kilometers from Wilno, and were killed by machine-gun fire. From time to time there were small "clean-outs" of specialists who were considered by the guards unfit or unruly. They would be taken out in small groups and would simply not return. Weintraub's mother, father, and two brothers were killed in these clean-outs.

Weintraub had recently come from a hopeful life, and that made the new squalor even worse. He and his wife reminisced: about the night they had first met at Jack's Sport Club and got on so well because she danced like a professional and he was immodestly willing to admit that he was the best dancer in their students' circle; of the times they went skiing together in the hills and woods near Wilno; their swims together at the swimming club, tennis on the public courts, volleyball at the university—a healthy, noisy life. He recalled the things he had done well: the day he won the eighteen-kilometer race at Neuwilno in 1938, his having graduated second in his class at the secondary school, his skill in basketball at Wilno University. They talked of the futility of all the ambition he had had—his youthful desire to be a great concert pianist and his hard studies at the Wilno Conservatory of Music, then his more sensible decision to make a decent living as a chemical engineer and the years of preparation at the university. He teased her about how hard he had tried to teach her to sing, sitting at the piano in his own bedroom and struggling with her tone deafness, always finally giving up and playing Beethoven sonatas for her. He told her again and again of the wonderful trip to Finland he had taken as a boy of thirteen alone with his father, and of the incredible waterfall there called Immatra. They remembered their wedding party, only five months before they had been taken into the ghetto. She chided him for his stubbornness, for when she had moved into his family's five-room apartment at 2 Teatralna Street, he had not let her change a single thing in his room; he had a "sports corner" there crowded with pictures of athletes, and a "nature corner," with pictures of the Polish countryside in all the seasons.

There had been a time, Weintraub also recalled, when death had been an entertainment, in murder mysteries, his favorite form of reading. . . .

All that life soon faded. Memories of it gave way to a new and absorbing study: how to get away? News had filtered into the ghetto of Jewish partisan groups in the woods near the city, and all in the ghetto dreamed of escaping to them. Weintraub was rather slow to work out a plan, and then it was not a shrewd one.

There were Jewish police in the ghetto, and he thought that if he could obtain a ghetto policeman's uniform, he might somehow bluff his way past the swarm of SS and SD guards at the main gate. He finally managed to steal a uniform, and on September 6, 1943, two years to the day after being taken into the ghetto, Weintraub, disguised as a ghetto policeman, walked with his wife to the gate. They stopped a few minutes, trying to decide what to do, and as they waited, the car of the ghetto's ranking SD man, *Unterscharführer* Kietel, approached the gate to go out. The car stopped for a moment for a guard check and for the gate to open. Weintraub whispered to his wife to jump on the spare tire in the rear. He said he couldn't go out in uniform because he would be spotted outside too easily. Liba jumped on and clung to the spare. The car started up. Weintraub turned quickly away. About fifty yards beyond the gate, the street curved to the right. Looking back, Weintraub saw his wife drop off just before the curve and dart into a side street. That was the last he saw of her.

Weintraub learned two lessons from Liba's escape. Thinking it over, he remembered that the *Unterscharführer* Kietel drove out every day at precisely the same hour, almost to the same minute. The first lesson this taught him was that these Germans were so methodical, so precise, that he might be able to use their precision against them. The other lesson was that an escape had always to be planned from beginning to end. He had not even thought what he would do beyond the gate.

There were at this time less than two thousand Jews left in the ghetto. On September 23, 1943, they were taken to a camp in a pine forest near a town called Klooga in Estonia. Klooga was a labor camp. When the prisoners arrived, there were signs denoting various professions stuck in the sandy soil in front of a barracks. The Jews were told to group themselves around the signs according to their skills. Weintraub had learned from the experience of the "nonspecialists" the importance of declaring a profession. Seeing the pine woods all around the camp, he went to the sign for carpenters.

To inhibit escape a barber ran clippers in a straight, naked line from the middle of each man's forehead to the nape of the neck. The prisoners were given unmistakable striped blue canvas shirts and jackets or coveralls. And they were given numbers. From this time forward Benjamin Weintraub was No. 339, Klooga. A cloth label on his shirt declared his number. On the label, too, was a Star of David.

No. 339 at Klooga and all the other unlucky numbers got up at five a.m., had a single cup of burnt chestnut ersatz coffee, started work at six and had a half-hour rest at noon, during which they were given an unvarying bowl of soup, worked on until dark, and then were given a few slices of bread and twenty-five grams of a margarine which stank so that many were unable to eat it.

The work varied. The prisoners were set to building wooden

sheds and shops. Later they made concrete blocks and tank obstacles. Some made wooden shoes for shipment to Germany. Some cut wood. Some loaded the camp's products into freight cars on a siding about half a mile from the camp.

There was always too much work, there was never enough sleep, and the craving for food was constant and sickening. But the worst thing of all was the mental depression the prisoners felt. Their guards were trained in impersonality and seemed to take pleasure in hurting flesh and bone. The prisoners gradually lost all hope. The urge to survive drove some of them to degradation—they informed against their fellows, some even curried favor with their tormentors.

No. 339 was outstanding among the prisoners. The superiority at skiing, swimming, and basketball of which he had once boasted so immodestly had trained him well for the camp. He kept initiative and even a kind of hope long after the others lost it. Since he was strong and apparently so cheerful, the Germans began to trust him and put him in command of work parties.

He rewarded their trust by planning day and night to escape, not alone but with many others. First he simply observed the daily habits of the Germans—where they walked, their punctual hours of changing guards, of eating, and even of going to the bathroom. Then he began small reconnaissances. He would sneak out of his barracks at night and walk around a while, feeling out the vigilance of the guards. Gradually he began widening his movements.

He began going out through the wire at night at a place where sentries left a gap in their patrol, and he would make his way to the town of Keila, twelve kilometers from the camp. Then he began to have luck. He met some Estonians who were willing to risk their lives by giving him bread, butter, and cheese.

Others, on his instructions, began sneaking out, too. Several were caught and soon disappeared. The Germans said they had "gone to Riga." A terrible whisper went around the camp that there was a gas chamber and crematorium at Riga. "Going to Riga" became the synonym, among the prisoners, for death.

Many lost the will to live and virtually starved themselves to death; when they became too weak to do any kind of work two German doctors, named Bottmann and Krebsbach, put them permanently to sleep with a drug called evipan. Bottmann was not a very good doctor and probably knew it, and very likely it was an inferiority complex which made him, one day, flog a Jewish surgeon named Ovseizalkinson within an inch of what was left of his life. The Germans devised an ingenious whipping cradle whose straps and buckles placed victims in the best possible position to have one man sit on the head while the other whipped the buttocks. For the slightest offenses prisoners were given twenty-five lashes. The number twenty-five, like the word "Riga," came to have an awful significance among the prisoners.

There were a few cases of wanton cruelty. One winter night, when a number of Jews built a bonfire outdoors to warm themselves without having asked permission, the *Unterscharführer* Gendt went berserk with an ax. He killed, among others, a man named Dr. Fingerhut, who had been one of Wilno's outstanding gynecologists. One of the guards had a vicious dog which he occasionally sicked on prisoners. One day some dreadful-looking shadows of people limped into the camp and said they were survivors of a typhus epidemic at another camp near Narva, hundreds of kilometers away, and that the Germans had made them walk all the way along the coast to Klooga. They described how SS guards had disposed of habitual stragglers by drowning them in the sea.

Practically the only thing that kept the prisoners alive now was a sense of common fate and a lingering defiant sense of humanity. They exchanged occasional messages that symbolized these senses. For instance, on his wife Liba's birthday that year Weintraub was handed a note by a guard. It read, "To Prisoner 339 from 359, 329, 563, and 350: We, your comrades, greet you on this day and hope that you may see your wife as soon as possible and that you may then live at her side until her blonde hair turns to gray."

The hopes that 339 had for an escape were jarred one freezing day early that year. He was walking through the camp with a long board on his shoulder when his right foot slipped on a patch of ice and brought him down. His weight fell on the right leg and broke it badly just above the ankle. He was in bed for two and a half months.

When his leg mended, No. 339 was afraid he might have lost his contacts in the village of Keila, but he found that he was able to pick them up again quickly. He was lucky particularly in gaining the trust of a man named Karl Koppel who lived at 58 Hapsal. Koppel was a great help to 339. He managed to get some pistols and some ammunition. He gave the pistols, one by one, to 339. Koppel provided fifty rounds of ammunition per weapon. When he got each pistol back in the camp, 339 went in the dark to the woodpile, only a few feet from the barracks, hauled a log out from low in the pile, took it into the barracks to his bunk, scooped out a hollow with a chisel stolen from the carpentry shop, put the pistol in it, and then took the log back out and returned it to its place in the pile.

Koppel had given 339 only seven revolvers when a miscalculation upset the whole plan. The miscalculation 339 made was not of his adversaries but, ironically enough, of his fellow Jews. He told too many. The word spread. With the help of the whipping cradle the Germans found out a few names. Then, apparently at random, they made a list of almost five hundred Jews. Perhaps they were uncertain who the real leaders were; perhaps the Germans needed manpower too much. At any rate none was executed. Instead all five hundred were taken to another camp at Lagedi, about fifteen kilometers from Tallin.

Here 339 had to start the whole process from scratch. This time he told only his most trusted friends. Ironically, the camp that was intended to punish the escapists turned out to be less severe than Klooga. The SS man in charge was no less harsh personally than the SS man at Klooga. The difference was that he had just been recalled from the Russian front. He knew how the war was going. He had heard about the Moscow declaration on war criminals.

Early in September of that year the Russians launched an attack against the Baltic States. No. 339 and the others were given no war news at all and they did not know what was happening when, on September 18, thirty trucks driven by SD men came to camp. That day most of the men were out constructing anitank bunkers for Tallin. No. 339 was doing some work in the camp with eighteen other men.

The nineteen prisoners in the camp were gathered together near the front gate. The SD men began to argue. No. 339 knew enough German to understand that they were arguing whether to take the nineteen right away or wait for all the prisoners to come back in. He heard the word Riga and the word Klooga. He saw that the guards were taking part in the discussion and that all the Germans were ill at ease and confused.

He was standing near the gate. At a peak in the argument he bolted. He ran straight across the road, where the trucks were waiting, into some woods. Then, banking on the thorough Germans to comb the woods, he doubled back and went into the back door of an Estonian house that stood only a few yards from the camp gate. He persuaded the Estonian who was there to lend him a coat and cap. He took up a piece of material, a needle, and some thread, and told the Estonians to say that he was a tailor who worked there. He thought that if the house were searched the job might be done by one of the visiting SD men, who would not recognize him.

In a few minutes he looked out of the window and saw his eighteen comrades being bundled into a truck. The truck drove off.

The others came back from their work after about two hours. They were not marched into the camp at all but were lined up in groups of about thirty beside the trucks on the road. This time the thorough Germans took no chances. The drivers and guards formed a huge ring around the trucks, the prisoners, the road—and the house in which 339 was trying to hide. Eventually some of the camp guards came in the house, recognized 339, and took him out.

Something made 339 edge his way to the last truck. That instinct saved his life. The last truck left at about nine o'clock in the evening. Along the way it broke down. After it was repaired the driver and guard were at a loss what to do. They inquired of some officers they met along the road. The officers suggested that they take the truckload to Tallin jail.

The truckload of prisoners arrived at the Tallin jail early in the morning and slept there a few hours. In the morning they were bundled back in the truck and driven to Klooga.

When they reached the camp they saw that all of the camp's three thousand prisoners had been gathered in the barbed-wire-enclosed yard behind one of the barracks. The truckload including 339 was put in a group consisting entirely of men brought from Lagedi. No. 339 asked a guard what was going on. The guard said they were being taken to Riga and to Germany. So they were "going to Riga" at last. A few minutes after his truckload arrived, 339 saw, off in the underbrush some distance away, a line of about three hundred men carrying logs. He asked one of his friends who had arrived from Lagedi with the earlier trucks the night before what the logs were being carried for. The friend said he did not know, that early that morning the Germans had picked out the three hundred strongest men in the camp, had given them a huge breakfast, and had taken them out to work.

The breakdown and late arrival of his truck kept 339 out of that working party. That is how the instinct that had made him get in the last truck saved his life, for not one of the strong men carrying wood survived that day.

No. 339 asked the guard where the men were carrying the wood, and why. The guard said that the wood was needed in Germany. It was going along with the prisoners to Riga and Germany. The prisoners, he said, were loading the wood for Riga.

The prisoners were loading the wood for Riga only in the symbolical sense of the word. They were taking it to a clearing in the woods about half a mile from the rear gate of the camp. There they were ordered to construct curious platforms. First they laid four heavy logs in a square. Then they filled in the square with pine boughs. Then they scattered small kindling wood among the pine boughs. Next they put long crosspieces across the square, and across these they laid shorter logs until there was a kind of floor. In the center they put up four poles to form an area about a foot square and kept the space inside that little area free of sticks and boughs. The platforms, of which there were four, were about thirty feet square.

This work took quite a while. In the enclosure, 339 grew suspicious. At noon promptly the methodical Germans fed the prisoners in the enclosure. But the others did not come back for lunch. No. 339 asked the guard what was holding them up. The guard said, "Perhaps they have decided to take them straight to Riga without coming back here."

The men at the platforms must have been terrified at what was happening then. They were being divided into groups of thirty. The first three groups were ordered onto three of the platforms and were told to lie prone. When they were all down, SS men with revolvers stepped onto the platforms and shot those who were lying there, one by one, in the back of the head. Those who tried to run away or tried to resist were shot in the face or stomach.

As soon as all the men on the platforms were shot and before some of them were dead, the others were ordered to build another layer to the platform right on top of the bodies of their companions. Still no boughs or sticks were put in the little square in the center. The Germans had thought of everything: that was to serve as a chimney, to give the fire some draft.

As soon as he heard the first shot in the enclosure, 339 knew that the Germans were determined to kill every Jew, Russian, and Estonian in the camp. He was terrified, but he tried to think clearly. One thing he knew: this would be his last chance to try an escape.

While the men out at the platforms were building the second layer, 339 began to plan. There were just two permanent guards in the enclosure. Others came and went. The two in the enclosure had tommy guns and walked back and forth in front of the two large groups. The guard in front of the women looked across at the smaller Lagedi group really carefully only when he was walking toward it. It took him about twenty seconds to make each lap. The nearest door of the U-shaped barrack was about sixty feet away. It would take perhaps ten seconds to run to the door and disappear to the left up the stairs.

Fortunately he had explored every inch of the barrack many times. He would run upstairs all the way to the double ceiling of the attic. He would go completely around the three sides of the U above the ceiling. At the other end of the building, he would drop down to the top tier of bunks, run around a pile of window frames lying up there, pull them into a crude barricade, crawl through in the dark to the hollow chute down to the next floor. This was large enough for one person to hide in, but it was dark. Beyond that, 339 could not imagine anything.

Out at the platforms the second layer was ready, and three more groups were ordered to climb up. The SS men followed and began putting their pistols to the backs of victims' skulls.

When the noise of the second group of shots was heard in the enclosure, panic broke out. Women began shrieking. There was a commotion among the men. No. 339's friends looked at him to see what he would do. In the excitement over the shooting, he ran.

He made the door all right. As he ran up the stairs he heard the sounds of footsteps behind him, and he tried to run faster. Then he realized that there were many footsteps, and that he was afraid of being followed by only one guard, or at most two. He looked back. Something he had not foreseen had happened. Many other prisoners were following his lead.

Quite correctly the guards out in the yard held their positions with their tommy guns aimed at the bulk of the crowd. But before they could get it under control well over a hundred people had run into both doors of the building. More than forty followed 339 over the course he had planned. By the time they all got behind the barricade of window frames and in and near the chute, the place was a mass of terrified flesh.

All those who had run into the other door of the barracks, on the ground floor three flights down from 339 and his followers, tried to hide on that first floor. They threw themselves under bunks, cringed in corners, and climbed onto upper bunks.

The guards called out for reinforcements. These entered the door on the ground floor under 339's hiding place. One of 339's companions had cut an electric-light wire and caused a short circuit, so the barracks were all dark. Apparently the SS reinforcements were conscious of death themselves that afternoon, because 339 heard two German voices say, in tones that seemed to express fear of the dark, "Are there any guards in there? Come out, you people."

There was a silence. A friend of 339 named Dondes Faiwusz, who had run through the kitchen shed inside the U of the barracks and into a window on the ground floor, saw what happened next. Two SS men entered the main room on the ground floor, where all the runaways were trying so pathetically to hide in exposed places, and they sprayed the room, one to each side, with tommy-gun bullets. Up on the third floor the forty men heard a great deal of firing—enough, they later learned, to have killed eighty-seven of their fellow prisoners. It was hard for 339 and his packed-in companions to restrain themselves from crying out in their panicky conviction that the Germans would come up and find them and spray them with bullets, too.

But after the firing downstairs, and the screaming and groaning that followed it, subsided, 339 and his friends could hear only distant sounds—shouts in the courtyard, more shooting far away.

The shooting came in periodic flurries—as new layers were finished on the platforms. In midafternoon there was an increase in the firing. Apparently the SS men thought they would never get finished, using only the platforms, so they herded seven hundred people into a barracks, shot them there one by one, and set the building afire. No. 339 and his fellows were lucky that the Germans did not choose their barracks. The smell of burning wood and flesh raised their hair on end. They thought their building might be burned.

The shooting and the smell of burning went on until two or three in the morning. Then there were sounds of German voices and trucks and cars driving off. Then there was silence.

No. 339 and the others could not be sure that all the Germans had gone. Nor could they be sure that they would not come back the next morning and hunt them out. The stench of burning flesh and the sound of screaming people were so fresh in their minds that they crouched absolutely still all night without whispering.

The group of forty stayed in their dark hole for five days and nights. On the second night some of them sneaked out, as they often had, and stole bread from the camp commissary. But they did not dare look around much. They went back up to the attic.

On the fifth day one of the men ventured out. The camp was deserted. He saw a Russian airplane overhead. He ran trembling upstairs to tell the others of their deliverance. A few hours later the first Russian soldier came into the camp.

No. 339 thought first about the new life he could now begin. He took a scrap of paper and he wrote a letter he intended to give to a Russian officer:

To the Consul of the American States in Moskau.

Dear Consul!

I stayed from thousands. I have lost my parents and brothers. My wife remained in Wilno and I have no news from her. The only one who remained is my father-in-law, an American citizen who is now living in New York and [with] whom I want to communicate about myself. I had no other chance and I am forced to ask you and I am sure that you will not refuse me. Please send this telegram: Samuel Amdurski, Federal Food Corporation, New York. During a year no news from Liba and Bertha. I am in Estonia. I will do all to find them out.

Benjamin

Then 339 thought about the life he had had. He sat down, pried the heel off his boot, and found his wedding ring there. He tried to put it on his fourth finger. Three years of manual labor for the master race had thickened the fingers that had once played Beethoven and measured chemicals into test tubes. He could not get it on. He put it on his little finger. It just fit.

SURVIVAL
OF THE FITTEST

II

IN THIS TALE *the survivor, Frantizek Zaremski, lived because of his tentative nature. Far from being a leader, he even refused to follow, and in the outcome it was this need to hold back that saved him.*

I met Zaremski and heard his story from him in a dark room in a farmhouse at Rodogoszcz, near Lodz, Poland, a few days after his escape. I had just been shown the detritus of the factory where his ordeal had taken place; many pierced or charred bodies were still strewn about. Zaremski was obviously suffering from shock. As he talked he kept his left hand, which was bandaged, in his trouser pocket; he wore a blue windbreaker with a zippered fly. The skin of his face was drawn tight over the bones and cartilege, and the hair on his head, which had been shaved by the Nazis, was just beginning to grow back in. More than once, as he told his story, he covered his eyes with his free hand, and I thought he might faint.

Not to Go with the Others

In the third year of the war, Frantizek Zaremski was arrested by the invaders on a charge of spreading underground literature —specifically, for carrying about his person a poem a friend from Gdynia had given him, which began:

Sleep, beloved Hitler, planes will come by night . . .

After he had spent six weeks of a three-year sentence for this crime in the Gestapo prison at Inowroczon, Zaremski was sent to Kalice to do carpentry. By bad luck, at the time when his term expired, the Russians had broken through at the Vistula, and his captors, instead of releasing him, took him, in their general panic, to the transfer camp for Polish political prisoners at Rodogoszcz, where he was placed in Hall Number Four with nine hundred men. Altogether there were between two and three thousand men and women—no Jews, only "Aryan" Poles suspected or convicted of political activity—in the prison.

Late in the evening of Wednesday, January 17, 1945, three days before Lodz was to fall to the Russians, all the prisoners were gathered on the third and fourth floors of the main building, even those who were sick, and there they all lay down on wooden bunks and floors to try to sleep. At about two in the morning guards came and ordered the inmates to get up for roll call.

They divided the prisoners into groups of about twenty each and lined up the groups in pairs. Zaremski was in the second group. SS men led it down concrete stairs in a brick-walled stairwell at one end of the building and halted it on a landing of the stairway, near a door opening into a large loft on the second floor. The first group had apparently been led down to the ground floor.

Someone gave an order that the prisoners should run in pairs into the loft as fast as they could. When the first pairs of Zaremski's group ran in, SS men with their backs to the wall inside the room began to shoot at them from behind. Zaremski's turn came. He ran in terror. A bullet burned through his trouser leg. Another grazed his thigh. He fell down and feigned death.

Others, from Zaremski's and later groups, ran into the hall and were shot and fell dead or wounded on top of Zaremski and those who had gone first. At one time Zaremski heard the Polish national anthem being sung somewhere.

Finally the running and shooting ended, and there ensued some shooting on the upper floors, perhaps of people who had refused to run downstairs.

SS men with flashlights waded among the bodies, shining lights in the faces of the prostrate victims. Any wounded who moaned or moved, or any whose eyes reacted when the shafts of light hit their faces, were dispatched with pistol shots. Somehow Zaremski passed the test of pretense.

As dawn began to break, Zaremski heard the iron doors of the main building being locked, and he heard some sort of grenades or bombs being thrown into the lowest hall and exploding there; they seemed to him to make only smoke, but they may have been incendiaries. Later, in any case, the ground floor began to burn. Perhaps benzine or petrol had been poured around. Zaremski was still lying among the bodies of others.

There were several who were still alive, and they began jumping out of the burning building, some from windows on the upper stories. A few broke through a skylight to the roof, tied blankets from the prisoners' bunks into long ropes and let themselves down outside. Zaremski, now scurrying about the building, held back to see what would happen. Those who jumped or climbed down were shot at leisure in the camp enclosure by SS men in the turrets on the walls, and Zaremski decided to try to stay inside.

On the fourth floor, at the top of the reinforced concrete staircase, in the bricked stairwell at the end of the building, Zaremski found the plant's water tank, and for a time he and others poured water over the wounded lying on the wooden floors in the main rooms. Later Zaremski took all his clothes off, soaked them in the tank, and put them back on. He lay down and kept pouring water over himself. He put a soaked blanket around his head.

The tank was a tall one, separated from the main room by the stairwell's brick wall, and when the fire began to eat through the wooden floor of the fourth story and the heat in the stairwell grew unbearable, Zaremski climbed up and got right into the water in the tank. He stayed immersed there all day long. Every few minutes he could hear shots from the wall turrets. He heard floors of the main halls fall and heard the side walls collapse. The staircase shell and the concrete stairs remained standing.

It was evening before the shooting and the fire died down. When he felt sure both had ended, Zaremski pulled himself out of the tank and lay awhile on the cement floor beside it. Then, his strength somewhat restored, he made his way down the stairs, and on the way he found six others who were wounded but could walk.

The seven went outside. Dusk. All quiet. They thought the Germans had left, and they wanted to climb the wall and escape. The first three climbed up and dropped away in apparent safety, but then the lights flashed on in the turrets and bursts of firing broke out. Three of the remaining four decided to take their chances at climbing out after total darkness; they did not know whether the first three had been killed or had escaped. Only Zaremski decided to stay.

The three climbed, but this time the lights came sooner, and the guards killed all three while they were still scaling the wall.

Zaremski crept into the camp's storehouse in a separate building. Finding some damp blankets, he wrapped them around himself and climbed into a big box, where he stayed all night. Once during the night he heard steps outside the building, and in the early morning he heard walking again. This time the footsteps approached the storeroom door. The door opened. The steps entered. Through the cracks of the box Zaremski sensed that the beam of a flashlight was probing the room. Zaremski could hear box tops opening and slamming and a foot kicking barrels. He held the lid of his box from the inside. Steps came near, a hand tried the lid, but Zaremski held tight, and the searcher must have decided the box was locked or nailed down. The footsteps went away.

Later two others came at different times and inspected the room but neither tried Zaremski's box; the third hunter locked the door from the outside.

Much later Zaremski heard a car start and drive away.

Much later still—some time on the nineteenth of January in the year of victory—Zaremski heard the Polish language being spoken, even by the voices of women and children. He jumped out of the box and broke the window of the storehouse and climbed out to his countrymen.

CONSERVATION

Tattoo Number 107,907

CONSERVATION

THIS IS *the story of a man who was able to survive a slow hell invented by the Nazis of Adolf Hitler's Germany. The means of his survival was a hoarding of units of energy. Stirner—his name and others have been changed at his request—realized at the outset of his ordeal that in order to survive he must try to bring into balance the strength, on the one hand, that he was obliged to spend in labor, in terror, in exposure to weathers, and in daily contemplation of the Nazis' appalling barbarities, and the strength, on the other hand, that he could derive from food, from pauses at work, from sleep, and from the society of fellow victims. This he managed for more than two years to do.*

Stirner told me the story later in my home in the United States.

187

Tattoo Number 107,907

Aʟғʀᴇᴅ Sᴛɪʀɴᴇʀ was a young Berlin intellectual, a former student of the law, a would-be social worker, who spent the autumn days of 1941 wearing the mask of a welder; it shielded him from sparks and also warded off, for the time being, by muffling his identity, a fate that was surely in store for him in Hitler's Germany. Twenty-seven years old, he lived with his wife and a small son in a single room in the Halensee section in the western quarter of the city, in a small building crammed with one hundred and twenty working people. The Stirners' little room on the third floor boxed their entire sense of life, for outside the room they had to move on byways, staying clear of Leipzigerstrasse, Unter den Linden, and all main streets, and were barred from bookstores and barber shops, and were not allowed to buy clothes, and had been to no concerts for three years, to no motion pictures, to no plays, and could shop for food only in designated stores, and were not permitted on buses or trams or trains. To reach the factory for work at six-thirty each morning, Stirner had to arise at a quarter to five, for he was obliged to walk more than an hour to the plant. The Stirners wore the Star of David.

The room itself lacked a telephone. A radio was forbidden. The Stirners ate cabbage, black bread, potatoes, scraps of suet, over and over. Since the start of the war, the single window of the room had always been blacked out; Jacob, the child, had never seen a window thrown open to a night of stars and city lights, and one of the first words he had learned to speak was the question that had to be asked when a person entered an unlit room: "Darkened?" Nevertheless the room was home; they were a family in it. There was a couch against one wall, and at night the three Stirners slept on it, together. The spectacle of Jacob growing, with a child's optimism, having no cause to think the world had ever been otherwise, was a source of pleasure and strength to the parents. They had a small gramophone, and some evenings they asked friends in the same building to come in for "home concerts" of Stirner's favorite recordings, the Second Brandenburg Concerto, *Eine Kleine Nachtmusik*, the "Eroica." And whenever they had the energy the Stirners read books: Max Weber's political science, Sombart's economic history, Heinrich Heine, Hermann Hesse, Dubnow's Jewish history, Buber's Jewish philosophy, Franz Werfel, Stefan Zweig, Jakob Wassermann, and Thomas Mann, and translations such as Pearl Buck's *Die Gute Erde*, and Margaret Mitchell's *Vom Winde Verweht*. Besides, the Stirners had many close friends, and conversations in the little room were frequent, large, witty; often peals of laughter came from within.

This was the condition of the Stirner family's life when mass deportations of Jews from the city began.

Alfred had been a nineteen-year-old student when Hitler had come to power in 1933. Among the Jews there had been two groups at that time—those who had decided to emigrate at once and those who, long afloat on German culture, had decided to stay and make fast their anchor lines. Stirner's parents had been among the latter group. As Hitler had consolidated his power, those who held on had felt more and more that they were losing a weird battle, in which they had never been clearly engaged, but even as late as the Munich agreement the Jews in Stirner's circle had felt that all that would be necessary to outlive the nightmare of Hitler would be acquiescence in the loss of certain civil rights. Only in November, 1938, when they learned of the subsequences of the killing of a minor German diplomat in Paris, named Von Rath, had they begun to realize that much worse might be expected, for soon after Von Rath's death, which was advertised as having been brought about by a fanatical Jew, German crowds, displaying an obedient spontaneity, had burned synagogues, looted Jewish shops and apartments, desecrated Jewish cemeteries, and otherwise given notice that henceforth Jews could expect not merely time-honored humiliation and deprivation but also brutality.

At once the Jewish community had organized mass emigration of children to England, Sweden, Belgium, Holland, and France. Stirner, having almost finished his course of law at Berlin University but having come to realize that under Hitler the pursuit of law would be a madman's chase, had quit his studies and joined the welfare office that was setting up the children's "transports"; and soon he had been signalled, by a speech Hitler made in the Reichstag to celebrate the anniversary of his own coming to power, that the work was urgent indeed. "If war comes," Hitler cried, "this war will end not with the extermination of the Aryan race but with the extermination of the Jewish race." Stirner had made several trips to England and Sweden. During Stirner's stays in Berlin, in his spare time, having in the back of his head an idea that he might try to get himself and his own family out of Germany, he had taken training as a welder, so as to have some means of earning a living if his improbable dream of emigration came true. By August, 1939, Stirner's welfare group had shipped out from Germany seven thousand children.

After the outbreak of war, Stirner and his friends had expected to be herded at once into concentration camps like the notorious one for political prisoners at Buchenwald, about which they knew; but at first nothing had happened. Within a couple of months, news had trickled into Berlin of the harsh treatment of Jews in Poland during and after the German campaign there—synagogues burned, ghettos established, non-combatants shot. Early in 1940, the Germans had begun to call more and more Jews for hard labor in their own communities —at street-cleaning, masonry, portage, ditch digging, shelter construction, road laying—but through that year Stirner had managed to continue his welfare work. Emigration no longer being feasible, he had begun supervising a number of small handicraft training schools for Jews, which the authorities had allowed in view of the demand for skilled workers of all kinds. After Hitler had started the Russian campaign, the pressure for manpower had become so great that the schools had been shut down and the pupils put to work. Stirner had resorted to his welder's mask.

October, 1941, was a bad month for the Jews in Berlin. It was then that the first mass deportations to concentration camps began.

On the Day of Atonement that autumn, the heads of the various Jewish centers in the city were called together at Gestapo headquarters and were commanded to deliver to the Gestapo enough apartments to house one thousand people, and those Jews who were to surrender their rooms were peremptorily named on a list. They were not allowed to move in with families or friends but were ordered to gather at a synagogue in Levetzowstrasse. All their property was declared confiscated. They disappeared.

Later those who stayed behind learned through post cards that the evacuees had been shipped by train to the ghetto of

Lodz, Poland. This first deportation was especially vivid to Stirner because his father's sister and her family were among those who were taken away.

Stirner was demoted from his welding job and placed in a heavy-labor gang in a munitions plant. There, in a party of forty-five men of all ages, he had to carry blocks of pig iron and sheets of steel, and occasionally he helped dig new foundations. The strain of this work was complicated not only by his worry about the deportations but also by the fact that R.A.F. raids were then becoming frequent, and his spending entire nights in the Jewish corner of their apartment basement—a shelter consisting merely of the cellar itself, shored with some extra timbers—and then doing this heavy work by day, all on an inadequate diet, drained his strength and untuned his nerves.

Through 1942 one transport of deportees after another left Berlin—to Riga, Lublin, Minsk, Warsaw, Kovno. Stirner and others who were not taken heard only rumors about the fates of the evacuees. They heard that some transports never arrived at their destinations. One camp they did hear about was Theresienstadt, where the Nazis assembled older Jews in a much publicized exhibition camp that was supposed to demonstrate good will and a policy of keeping Jews together. Many Berlin Jews tried to obtain non-Jewish identity papers, but these could only be procured through German friends and at great expense. Even suicide could be dear; Veronal, with which many Jews killed themselves, cost up to two thousand marks a box on the black market.

Six times during the year the Gestapo called on Stirner and questioned him. Each time the papers that marked him a welder made them move on. One evening, when they asked him about his trips to Sweden and England before the war, he felt the edge of the sword at his neck—but once more his welder's certificate saved him.

On December 8, 1942, on his way home from work, Stirner went by his parents' apartment, near his own, to chat with them awhile. When he knocked on their door, a Christian woman, who was a neighbor, opened her door, in great agitation, and said that *SS* troops had come and taken the elder Stirners away on ten minutes' notice. Stirner hurried out and questioned other Jews. He learned at length that his parents were among those quartered in a provisional transit camp in a Jewish elder's house in Grosse Hamburgerstrasse. He arranged to have a little food, some clothing, and some prayer books smuggled in to them. Seven days later he learned that the house was empty. Much later he learned that his parents, whom he never saw again, had been in the first transport to go to a new camp at Oswiecim, Poland. The German name of this camp was Auschwitz.

Every day in the New Year season that winter seemed as if it would be the last. Stirner's sister Rose, who had been ticketed for deportation along with their parents but had been kept in Berlin because she was an experienced stenographer, moved into the Stirners' room. Lena Stirner prepared knapsacks containing work clothing, underclothes, sewing things, a couple of books for the boy Jacob, a chess set, an Old Testament, shoes, handkerchiefs, towels, and toilet articles. Stirner maintained a self-deluding optimism. He had a friend in his factory gang who was married to a Christian and was allowed a radio; at two-thirty every morning this man arose and listened to the BBC and next day whispered the news to Alfred, and the reports of Eisenhower's progress in North Africa and of the Russians' success at Stalingrad gave him heart. "It is a race," he used to say to Lena in those weeks, "between our fate and Hitler's."

A speech Goebbels made on February 25, 1943, in the Berlin Sportspalast, however, depressed him. Goebbels was trying to buck up the Germans and at one point he said, "We have prepared everything to liquidate the enemy in our midst. We declare total war against him."

The very next day Rose Stirner came home from her work with a report that something serious—she had been unable to learn just what—would take place the following day, February 27. Stirner had observed from previous roundups that husbands had been taken from factories and wives from apartments, and often families had been unable to reunite. He determined to stay at home on the twenty-seventh. Rose could not; she had to go to work.

At noon on the twenty-seventh a friend came in and told the Stirners that SS *Leibstandarte* troops had entered all factories in which Jewish gangs worked and had taken them off; other troops seemed to be making the rounds of Jewish apartments and were arresting Jews wholesale. There was nothing to do but wait. Stirner tried to write an objective letter to a friend in Sweden. He gave up and tried to read a novel by Zweig. Soon he gave that up too and just sat with Lena and Jacob.

At four o'clock, two Gestapo men arrived. They told the Stirners to be ready to leave in ten minutes. Jacob—then three years and three months old—was sleeping, and Lena Stirner, who appeared not to be afraid, persuaded the men to give her forty-five minutes to waken the boy, get him dressed, and make arrangements to leave.

During part of the wait Stirner talked with the Germans, and he asked, among other things, how they thought their actions would rest on their consciences.

One of the men said, "What would happen if the Russian

Jews came in here? They wouldn't give us ten minutes' notice. They would give us a bullet in the neck."

When for the last time the Stirners walked out of their little room, one of the Gestapo men fixed on the door, alongside the six-cornered star already there, a seal forbidding entrance in the name of the Gestapo. The Germans first, then the Stirners, trooped downstairs. Outside, Stirner saw an SS truck and six soldiers with rifles. He had a moment of panic, thinking he and his fellows were going to be killed on the spot, but Lena, with the boy in her arms, walked straight up to one of the soldiers, who ordered them into the truck. They got in with a number of other Jews. Soon a soldier closed the door, and they drove about the city, stopping three or four times to take in other Jews, and finally, when the truck was full, they drove some distance. Unable to see out, they did not know where they were going. It was cold. The truck seemed to drive aimlessly, and sometimes it stood still, until altogether some six hours had passed. The boy slept most of the time. Alfred sat holding Lena's hand, and they whispered about their life before the war. They felt consoled in being together, because most of the people on the truck were separated from their families.

Once they heard one of the guards mention Lichterfelde; that meant to Stirner—because of executions there of which he had read—shooting. Later he heard the same man talking about Oranienburg; that meant shooting, too.

At last the truck stopped for good, and the Stirners got out at a place they could not recognize; it was dark. People from several trucks were herded with their luggage into a cavernous shed, where they heard the voices of a crowd. Stirner figured out, eventually, that they were in an immense stable, or armory. Guards' voices barked occasionally. It seemed all the people were to spend the night there. They had no water, no lavatory, no light, no food, and barely room to lie on the ground.

In the morning rumors darted through the frightened crowd. At about noon Rose Stirner, who, as a transit-camp functionary, was permitted to move around Berlin freely, arrived wearing a red brassard—authorized transit-camp organizer. She talked the guards into allowing her to take her brother and his family to her own transit camp, which was more comfortable than the big shed, and later she arranged to have Zinfred and Lena appointed organizers, too, and for nine days, while carrying out duties assigned them, they were able to hunt for friends, provide them with food, carry messages, and reunite a few families. All this time, transport after transport was leaving Berlin for the east.

On the night of March 2–3, the first large-scale night raid of Flying Fortresses took place. After the all-clear, relieved from their terror, the Stirners took vindictive pleasure in looking out and seeing Berlin afire.

"Nero's Rome," Lena said.

Zinfred said, "I hope the railways are destroyed."

But they were not, and five days later, on March 8, the Stirner family was listed for a transport eastward.

The Stirners had three more days in camp before their transport left. On the morning of the ninth, they were handed official decrees which announced to them that in view of their hostile attitude toward the German Reich they were now being deprived of their property and being deported. The three-year-old child, Jacob, was favored with one of these documents. On the eleventh, the passengers of their transport were assembled in a yard with their hand luggage and loaded into trucks, which took them to the Quitzowstrasse freight station, and there SS *Leibstandarte* troops embarked them in cattle cars, sixty people to a car.

Someone locked, from the outside, the door of the car into which the Stirners had been put. The car was bare but for a latrine bucket. There was a small hole in one wall about the size of a man's fist, for ventilation. The sixty people in the car were of all ages—men, women, and about a dozen children. On the whole the Stirners were in fair spirits because they had managed to cling to a group of old friends from the Jewish youth organization to which they had belonged. Lena said, as she had many times before, that she feared only one thing: separation.

Stirner wore a wrist watch, and he noticed that the train pulled out of the Quitzowstrasse station on the dot of four; a schedule was being faithfully followed, it seemed.

The people in the car tried to keep track of their route by reading station signs through the ventilator hole; all they could tell was that they were moving eastward but not on main lines —they could not flatter themselves that they were priority traffic. Rose Stirner wrote post cards to friends ("We are going to the east. We are in a good mood. Keep strong.") and threw them from the hole. Cards from previous transports had been picked up, mailed, and delivered. Jacob behaved well; he was curious about everything. When it became apparent that they were going toward Silesia, Lena and Zinfred talked about their wedding trip, which had been to Silesia, in 1938. They and their youth-movement friends talked of mutual acquaintances who were safely abroad, and they speculated about how long they would have to stay where they were going.

One young man struck up an old song from the movement: *"How good it is when friends sit together. . . ."*

Darkness fell outside. When someone remarked that it was Friday, the Sabbath eve, a woman took a candle from a bundle, and she lit it, weeping, as the whole car watched in silence. An elderly man said prayers, and though the Stirners had not been Orthodox Jews, they were deeply moved.

The next morning a passenger at the ventilator hole saw the station sign at Katowice, and the people in the car concluded that they were destined for Oswiecim—for Auschwitz. About this relatively new camp they had heard little.

On March 12, at exactly four o'clock, the train stopped in Oswiecim station. Everyone in the car was quiet. Lena took her husband's hand. It was obvious to both of them that the next few minutes would be of the utmost importance.

After a short time the door of the cattle car slid back, and the Stirners saw an open field, with a number of SS officers and soldiers in a cluster, a couple of whom stepped to the car door and ordered the Jews out. Most of the passengers were stiff from their long ride in the car, but the soldiers hurried and jostled them, far more abrupt and harsh than the SS troops in Berlin.

Everyone was ordered to put his hand luggage on a big pile. That was the last Stirner ever saw of the family's prudent knapsacks.

Next an officer shouted that they should form into three groups—able-bodied men to the left; women without children to the center; women with children, old people, and the sick to the right.

Lena said, "This is what I have feared the whole time."

She kissed her husband, and he kissed their son.

"Keep strong, Lena," Alfred said. "I'll be with you."

As they separated, Lena and Alfred tried to keep sight of each other, but Stirner soon lost track of his wife in the big crowd.

All the able-bodied men were formed in squads of five, and slowly these squads filed past a gigantic officer. He asked two questions of each man and, depending on the answers, turned his thumb up or down.

199

When Stirner came before him the big officer asked, "How old are you?"

"Twenty-nine."

"What is your profession?"

"Welder."

The thick thumb turned up.

Herded with the Thumb-ups, Stirner looked around, trying to gather impressions. Large trucks were driving up and closing in on the group. Gangs of men in striped uniforms and caps, under guard, were sent in to clean the freight cars. They carried out the slop buckets and, to Stirner's surprise, several corpses. Then Stirner noticed that the trucks were being loaded with evacuees from the far group—women and children, the old and the sick, and men and women, as well, from the flock of Thumb-downs. He craned for a sight of Lena, and as one truck drove off he saw that she had managed to get a place near its rear. She saw him. She waved and beckoned to him in a pleading sort of way, though she seemed to be smiling. She made Jacob wave, but the boy could not see his father in the crowd.

The remaining childless women were marching off in military formation, under the barking of female SS troops—the first Stirner had ever seen—in uniform with revolvers bouncing on their hips.

Later the trucks came back, and the SS men, bristling and snarling in the most astonishing manner, as if they were threatened animals rather than masters, crowded the men in Stirner's group into them. When Stirner's truck seemed to be full, the troopers knocked the passengers forward with rifle butts and mashed in twenty more. The men could scarcely breathe.

The trucks carried the men in a different direction from the one in which the others had taken Lena's category. Stirner tried to talk with two SS guards standing on the running board, but they understood German poorly; some Jews who spoke Slavic languages reported that the guards were Polish *Volksdeutsche*.

The convoy drove through a Polish town, past a tremendous plant that was being built—larger than the Leuna works or any other factory Stirner had ever seen—and then the trucks swung around a sharp curve alongside a huge camp of many wooden barracks in rows, surrounded by double barbed-wire fences strung on porcelain insulators. Along the fences there were several wooden towers, in which Stirner could see soldiers with automatic guns.

As the trucks drove in through a heavily guarded gate, Stirner turned to two of his youth-movement friends, named Kollin and Wertheim, and said in a whisper, "May God help us to get out of here alive!"

The trucks drove into the camp and stopped, the soldiers ordered the men out, and an official came along in a uniform of a style Stirner had never seen—military boots, green riding breeches and jacket, army cap, and a brassard bearing the initials L.A., for *Lager Ältester*, or Camp Elder. It was nearly dark. The *Ältester* and other officials in uniforms like his ordered the men into a barren brick barrack and told them to wait. While they stood around, exchanging speculative whispers, they heard a handbell ring. The officials ordered a group of about twenty to move into an adjacent room. Certain officials circulated among those who remained and offered food in exchange for valuables. Stirner, hungry as he was, kept his watch and ring.

Other squads were moved into the next room, and in time Stirner's turn came. His group filed past a huge trunk, where two SS men ordered the evacuees to drop their watches, rings, money, and all they had of value. When one man protested, Stirner heard a soldier say in a matter-of-fact tone, "Here one needs nothing." Next the evacuees were ordered to remove all their clothing, and guards took from them everything except glasses, belts, and shoes. Barbers went among the two-hundred-odd naked men and with hand clippers cut off head and body hair. Attendants sprayed the captives with a harsh disinfectant solution, and the naked men were herded into large shower rooms, where they had to wait some time in the March cold. There had been vague rumors in Berlin about the concentration camp "showers," that they were gas chambers, and one man made everyone nervous by shouting, "It's all finished now."

While the men were waiting in the shower room, they saw some people moving about on errands in striped uniforms. The group around Stirner stopped one of them, and a man asked, "Where are we?"

"You have arrived," the man said without emotion, "in the concentration camp of Auschwitz. Did you see the big plant as you came in? That's an I. G. Farben factory for metanol and buna where you will work. Now you are *Häftlinge*—inmates. That's your situation."

Someone asked, "What about our women and children?"

The man—Stirner later learned that he was one of the great Nazi-fighters of Hamburg—said in a low voice, "Don't worry about your women and children. They have to make their own way. Here you have your way. And if you think over and over what you cannot change, then you will not find sufficient strength for your own struggle here. If you want to come out, obey my advice. Otherwise you'll never be strong enough. Some of us have been inmates many years already. We've been in Buchenwald, Dachau, Oranienburg, and during this time you have had the luck to live with your families. Think that you have come much later and been very lucky, and keep strong."

Cold water began eventually to spout from the showers. Since the men were cold already, they could stand it, and it even seemed to warm them a bit; afterwards there were no towels. Officials gave them ragged underdrawers and undershirts, and striped pants and jackets such as the Hamburg anti-Nazi had been wearing. Everything took a long time. Finally the men marched far through the cold to various barracks.

Stirner, assigned to Barrack Two, was received there by an official called a *Blockältester*, who took him and his barrack-mates inside a wooden hall about ninety feet long and fifteen feet wide that contained nothing but wooden bunks, in three lengthwise tiers, three deep. Stirner and his youth-movement friends, Kollin and Wertheim and some others, had managed to hang together, and they climbed into the beds, which consisted only of straw paillasses with two thin blankets on plank shelves, but, although it was late at night, no one seemed to be able to sleep. Stirner shivered all night.

Next morning the inmates were rallied from their shelves at four-thirty and were led through sleet to a washroom, a brick shed with eight spigots, in which hundreds of men milled about fighting to get to the faucets. "Keep yourselves clean," the *Blockältester* had said on sending them off. "That's what we want you to do." They had no soap, towels, toothbrushes, or toothpaste, and they were obliged to carry all their so-called clothes all the time, since there were no cupboards or even hooks in the barrack. Those who were too weak simply did not get washed.

Afterwards the inmates went back to the barrack and were told to wait outdoors—in order, the *Blockältester* said, not to dirty their nest—and finally they were marched to a large open field, toward which the whole camp seemed to be moving, and where they were formed into squares, in rows of fives. They stood in their thin jackets and pants in the sleet for an interminable time while SS men went down the squares counting; the troopers reported to a desk set up in the road beside the field and handed in their tallies. At length the camp commander, a *Hauptsturmführer SS* dressed in a fur coat, came to the desk, and the *Rapportführer*, the functionary responsible for the roll call, shouted, *"Häftlinge stillgestanden!"* —calling the inmates to attention. There was a long discussion at the desk; the figures were awry; squares were recounted. At last the roll call was dismissed.

Stirner and his fellow newcomers were led back to their barracks to register, that is to say, to file past an official who, pricking with a needle dipped in tinted solution, tattooed onto each man's forearm a number that would serve from then on in place of his name. Stirner was favored with the number 107907, crudely marked slantwise across his arm. Next, the line went by a couple of officials who asked Stirner, in his turn, for his number and his profession.

"Skilled welder."

The men peered at Stirner's fine glasses, a scholar's spectacles rimmed with artificial gold, and questioned him about his experience. He insisted that he followed that trade and did not mention having been a law student or a social worker, and shaking their heads they put him down as what he said.

Next he received his number stamped upon two swatches of white linen, one to go on his jacket, one on his pants; and, on separate swatches, a pair of stars formed from two triangles, red and yellow. Stirner had already noticed that all the inmates and many of the officials at Auschwitz wore triangles, and he learned now that red stood for political prisoner, yellow for Jew, black for antisocial element, and green for criminal. Apart from the Jews, there were few reds; most were greens.

When the registration of the newcomers was completed, it was time for another roll call. Stirner was informed by an old inmate that there were two roll calls every day; this being Sunday, the second came before the midday meal, and it was as tedious, as cold, as confused as the first.

Now Stirner was treated to his first meal, apart from the snacks Lena had packed in the knapsacks, since Berlin. He formed in line and filed through the day room of Barrack Two —the room at the end in which the *Blockältester* and his assistant, together with two or three other privileged senior inmates, lived. The second-in-command of the barrack, the *Stubendienst*, served the meal from big kettles, and he gave Stirner a rusty basin in which lay a shallow swamp of pasty gray gravy. He was told to hold out his cap, and several boiled potatoes were put into it. He was handed a spoon with which to eat. The line moved into the main hall of the barrack, and the inmates ate sitting on the edges of the bunks.

Sunday afternoon was free, and Stirner moved about seeking out acquaintances from other barracks. Some inmates, who had been around awhile, telling of their days, said the work was frightfully hard, but—with a shrug—they were alive. There were no papers, no books, no radios, no stationery; there was nothing to do but talk and talk. Stirner quickly learned not to approach the German green triangles, the criminals, who were haughty as noblemen. There was even an attitude of superiority on the part of some of the senior Jewish inmates, who were known as "prominents," and who could be identified by the cleanliness of their uniforms. Stirner kept thinking about Lena and Jacob, and he tried to visualize their going through the same trials as he. At one point he asked a prominent about the women and children, and the man brusquely said, "We've been in this business for years, and we've never asked about our relatives."

The *Häftlinge* had been told they could not go to bed before the official hour. Late in the day the newcomers heard the handbell they had heard the day before—it was the curfew bell, knelling their retirement to barracks. No more food was to be served that day. On his bunk Stirner drifted in shallow naps.

The ground was frozen next morning. It was still dark when the inmates huddled into the washrooms, and Stirner had a cold, as had most of his fellow newcomers. This morning, after the washing period, the *Stubendienst* served breakfast outside the barrack: a chunk of bread, a dab of margarine, a thin wafer of *Wurst*, and a cup of ersatz coffee; and as each man received his meal his number was checked off, to prevent his going around twice. While they ate, the inmates stood in tight clumps, like sheep, for warmth.

At dawn the inmates were marched off for roll call on the frozen parade ground, where the wind sifted through their thin uniforms, and the counting seemed to last forever. At the end the inmates were ordered to form into labor gangs, known as *Arbeitskommandos,* and all the newcomers—Stirner did not realize this until later—were dragooned into the hardest *Kommando,* which was Number Four, evidently according to a definite policy of weeding out the weaklings through exhaustion and death. Each *Kommando* was divided into squads, and each squad was under a *Kapo*—the etymology of which term Stirner never figured out—who held the fates of his workers in his hands. Most *Kapos* at that time were German or Polish green triangles, the criminal inmates.

Kommando Number Four consisted of more than three hundred inmates, as was ascertained by three successive counts, and it was marched to a gate, where its members, after removing their hats at an order, were counted yet again. Then they filed across the perimeter roadway into a huge area where several buildings were under construction. Railway tracks led into the area from one side. There were no proper paths or roads; it was a great yard of mud. *Kommando* Number Four trudged half an hour, so large was the enclosure, to its far side, hemmed in all the way by a cordon of SS troops who tried to enforce military regularity on the sloshing men.

The inmates were told to strip off their striped jackets, and in undershirts they were ordered to unload bags of cement from a long line of railway cars and to carry them by hand to a large dump. The *Kapos* and the SS men kept shouting that the whole train must be cleared by noon, and the *Kapos* had sticks with which they belabored men who seemed not to be overreaching themselves. Stirner's clothes grew heavy with cement powder, the dust worked into his skin, and he became fatigued, but his work in the labor gang in Berlin had put him in better condition than many others. During the morning he saw his first death in Auschwitz: a Dutch Jew who threw himself under the wheels of a shunting engine on a siding near the cement train.

By noon the train was still not wholly unloaded. Kitchen trucks drove into the plant area and each *Häftling* received a bowl of soup, which he ate as he stood. After half an hour work commenced again. When the train was empty the *Kapos* shouted that the inmates should push it out of the siding, whereupon three hundred men put their shoulders to the cars, but they could not move the train. The *Kapos* grew furious and beat several inmates, and only then was it discovered that the brakes were fastened; upon their release, the inmates moved the train with ease.

Another train, loaded with steel I-beams, rolled into the same spur of track, and *Kommando* Number Four was put to work unloading it. Stirner had done this kind of work in Berlin; there he had had a pad to put on his shoulder to cushion the load. He picked up a piece of cement bag and folded it and put it on his shoulder, but an SS man took it away. Still, he knew how to time his steps with those of his partners and ease the jolting of steel on bone.

The first day's work—and each day's thereafter for those who survived—lasted from seven in the morning until six at night. When work was over, *Kommando* Number Four was counted;

all the *Kommandos* formed in parade ranks in the factory area and were counted; they marched, singing at the *Kapos'* demand a German marching song, to the gate, where they took their hats off and were counted; and inside the camp they reported for roll call and were counted.

After roll call, Stirner and his companions repaired to their own barrack, went to the washroom and fought with hundreds of inmates over the eight faucets, to try to clean off the cement dust. Back at the barrack they wanted only to fall into bed, but they had to submit to a lice search, a check of their numbers, and bunk inspection. Each was served a liter of soup in a rusty bowl, and some beets and sauerkraut. Then they went to bed in their cement-caked clothes.

Several newcomers fell dead at the roll call the next morning, their third at Auschwitz, and from then on, for three weeks, death was commonplace on the chilly parade ground. Stirner had heard an old hand say that if one lived through his first month at a concentration camp, one might live forever.

When a man collapsed at roll call, an SS trooper would prod him with his foot to see whether he was dead, and only after roll call could friends remove the sick man, if he was still living. There were several hospital barracks, but even inmates with pneumonia were granted no more than three or four days in bed, without medication, before they were sent back to work.

On the fourth day Stirner witnessed the death of an acquaintance—a famous cantor he knew from Berlin named Winter, who had swiftly lost his resistance; he fell at roll call, and when an SS man kicked him, he moved but could not rise. After dismissal, Stirner and two friends picked Winter up and started for the hospital barracks. Winter was delirious. It was a long way to the infirmary area, and on the way the cantor died. The men put the body down at once, for they knew they must save their own energies, and one of them said, "Think how many people have taken pleasure from that man's voice."

Stirner found the first days shocking, but he withstood them. His cold even improved; he felt he must have been stronger than he had known in Berlin. The mornings at Auschwitz were frigid, but the days were sunny, and at every hour his friends Kollin and Wertheim were near him.

On the eleventh day a worsening came. The weather turned to water; the rain pounded. There was mud everywhere, and shoes dragged, and Stirner's *Kommando* still worked outdoors, and he was soaked all the time, and the paper of the cement bags grew wet, and the bags broke, and the *Kapos* were insanely furious, but there was no way to prevent any of it. In the evenings Stirner staggered home covered with water, mud, and wet cement. No way could be found to get dry or clean; he started each new day wet and filthy, ended it so, slept so, and ran so in his nightmares. He developed an infection in his right foot.

Now marching out and back was painful. The morning march was known as suicide time, for the inmates had been warned that attempts to escape would earn death, and thus an easy way to put an end to things was to break out from the SS cordon while parading across the plant area; the guards, who received twenty marks and three days' holiday for preventing an escape, always shot a breakaway down within a few feet. In the evenings the inmates were too weary even to bother to get themselves killed. They walked by twos and threes, leaning against each other, supporting weak friends, all the while singing marching songs under duress from the *Kapos*. The Jews were forced to carry back their dead, and the bodies were placed in their regular places at roll call and were counted one last time along with the living.

It seemed as if every official had the right to beat an inmate. The SS men in the plant, who were especially cruel, would often strike a man for asking permission to go to the open hole in the ground that served as a latrine. These guards, needing constant nourishment of their belief in tales they had been told of their own supermanhood, were insistent upon subservience —Jews' humbly taking hats off, keeping three paces away—and they were driven to fury by lassitude and faintness. Stirner saw several feeble men killed by impulsive slaps.

In those wet days Stirner felt himself losing strength. He became obsessed with hunger. If only he could be sated just once! He talked with his friends about food; they devised rich menus. Stirner was always damp, and he was finding it harder and harder to march on his infected foot, and each death he saw made him wonder how long he could carry his load of life.

Then he chanced on a revivification. One day he went to the latrine and he saw, at the edge of the pit, a small square of newspaper that one of the SS guards had evidently intended to use as toilet paper but had left on the ground. Stirner looked around and waited for his chance, and when no guards were watching he stuffed the paper into his underwear pants. He carried it back into camp, and in a corner of his barrack, just before the lights went out, with his friend Kollin standing sentry, he avidly read the few words of print on the square. One of the fragments in a torn column was on military affairs. It seemed the Germans had been pushed back from Stalingrad; they were still at Kharkov.

Stirner trembled with hope when he went to bed that night. He felt it was not so much the scrap of news of German reverses as the glorious act of reading itself that had given him this astonishing sense of flickering vitality. He made wildly optimistic calculations for Russian operations, however, and he thought

to himself, "I must try to live for six weeks," for it was then the
end of March, and six weeks would tide him to the warmth of
May.

Terrible days followed, however, in which Stirner doubted his
capacity to survive. Along with Kollin and Wertheim he was
shifted to a digging squad under a German *Kapo*, whose nick-
name, "Judenfranz," had been jokingly given him by SS troops
because he was such a grinder of Jews; he was a green triangle
who had committed a murder in his home town in Upper
Silesia, and he was in charge of ditching for a foundation. Digging in mud with heavy shovels was worse than carrying cement
and steel, and Judenfranz would not let his workers sit down
during the noon interval; he made them carry their own field
kettles; he forced many to surrender their shoes to him in exchange for worse ones from dead men so he might barter the
good shoes outside camp. One day he decided to make his men
shove small iron dump trucks through mud, rather than along
tracks. He had a brute's fist, which Stirner saw kill several weak
men, and Stirner felt he was getting weak.

On the second day of April, in the evening, one of Stirner's
old friends from the Jewish youth movement, a man named
Schoenfeld, came to him in despair. Schoenfeld, who had
been employed by the Jewish community in Berlin, was a
sensitive man once full of music; he had had a warm tenor voice.
Now pale and meager, he had been in the hospital for four days
with pneumonia and was obviously still sick, and he told Stirner
he wanted to kill himself, and he said, "I don't want to die being
kicked." Stirner dredged up a little strength to argue with him,
although he himself had, from time to tired time, given a mo‹
ment's thought to a breakaway death. Schoenfeld quieted down.

The next morning, before the bell, there was shooting outside—no great rarity, for in the night and near the dawn it

sometimes happened that an inmate would run toward the barbed wire in order to be shot—and Stirner scarcely noticed it. The morning was rainy and cold, and during the march out to the plant Judenfranz began tormenting an elderly Jew who could not march properly, chasing him, pushing him, thrusting him outside the cordon, where he might be shot. The old man got back in and tried to march, but he was feeble; two inmates supported him, and the whole troop sang a marching song gaily in an effort to encourage him. Finally he collapsed. In triumph, disguised as anger, Judenfranz halted his squad.

While the formation was at ease, a man said to Stirner, "Did you hear the shooting this morning?"

Stirner answered, "Yes—anything special?"

"Your friend Schoenfeld," the inmate said. And he told how Schoenfeld had tried to gain readmittance to the hospital the night before but had been turned away, and how, early in the morning, he had run for the wire and been shot.

Stirner felt a sinking rush of fear, for he realized that his arguments in favor of life had failed. He had a bad day and night. He wondered how long he could resist. At breakfast next morning he fainted. Kollin and Wertheim roused him and supported him to the dawn counting and along the morning march, but he felt shaky all day, and he thought he was near the breaking point.

Three encouragements came in the next few days which, in sum, helped Stirner to keep a grasp on his spirits.

In the first place, the Germans, suffering their first strategic reverses in Russia and North Africa and evidently pressed as never before for manpower, removed part of the SS contingent from Auschwitz, and this meant that during the daytime the camp authorities, instead of keeping a cordon of soldiers around each *Kommando* and each working squad, were reduced to throwing a peripheral ring around the whole plant area. Since this was immense, embracing more than a hundred buildings, the ring seemed far away; one element of brutality receded from the foreground. Now only the *Kapos* were on their shoulders—and they were inmates themselves. The withdrawal of the SS gave a special lift to Stirner and his companions under Judenfranz, because the big German had seemed most anxious to please the German soldiers by his prankish persecutions, and now his audience was removed.

Then, one evening, just after mealtime, under a darkling sky, at a time when Stirner, bone-racked and downhearted, was brooding about putting an end to his sufferings, an unexpected bell rang and an extra roll call was ordered. At the desk in the road before the assembled inmates on the parade ground, a civilian alongside the *Arbeitsdienstführer*, or work commander, announced that each camper was to be registered by profession, especially according to craft skills, if any—as mechanics, locksmiths, tinsmiths, carpenters, and so on—and at Stirner's turn before the registration desk he announced that he was a welder. This turned out to be simply a registration; nothing came of it. Yet it gave Stirner great hope that he might be excused from the exhausting *Kommando* Number Four and be put to skilled work, which would be far less exacting.

And, finally, one afternoon, a new batch of Jews arrived in what was described as a transport from Neuendorf; and the following day another transport came from Belgium. Stirner and his companions, who in less than a month had been struck down from two hundred forty to one hundred fifty souls, were suddenly no longer the freshman group. As it was the policy of the camp to visit special hardships on newcomers, so now did the brutalities to the preceding group somewhat abate. Psychologically, also, the arrivals helped Stirner's crowd, who could now consider themselves experienced *Häftlinge*, and who could give the advice of iron men to frightened neophytes. Besides, Stirner found several former friends in the Neuendorf transport, most of the members of which were Jews from agricultural projects who had been preparing themselves for Palestine—hard young men with a strong Jewish national feeling. The Belgians meant a lot to Stirner because they brought news from outside Germany, and he spent hours on end questioning them on the strategic positions of the great enemies.

Inspirited by these events, Stirner now began to work at growing stronger. He had learned that men in a concentration camp survived on a margin of a very few calories of surplus energy each day, and that there were certain tricks for hoarding one's inner warmth.

He had learned, above all, to be watchful, to send his eyes always ranging—on Judenfranz, on other *Kapos*, on the camp officials—so as to grasp every chance to relax. Five seconds' rest in every minute meant five minutes' rest in every hour. He had learned to ask permission to go to the latrine as often as possible without actually rousing suspicion, and to spend the maximum time there; to excuse himself, furthermore, when several others had already gone, because then he would have to wait, at ease, for a free pit.

Even such an act as tearing bread at breakfast was a dangerous waste of energy, and Stirner sharpened one edge of his spoon—his only personal possession, which he kept always in the single pocket on the front of his trouser leg—by rubbing it against a stone in his bunk at night, so that he could easily cut the chunks of bread. (He did this after weighing carefully in his mind the labors needed, on the one hand, for tearing bread and, on the other, for sharpening his alloy spoon and cutting the bread; he concluded that one sharpening would serve many cuttings.) He did not eat all his bread in the morning, as most did, but put some in his pocket, that starch at noon might give him a boost of strength for the afternoon.

Other men's strength, he observed, was sapped by infection, so he took finicky care of the sore on his foot, keeping it as clean as he could. The cement bags were made of three layers of paper, the middle one of which was quite clean, and he used some of this to bandage his foot, and also as wrapping for his bread, as toilet paper, and to wipe his face clean on rainy days. He felt more and more the psychological importance of cleanliness, and he devised ways of penetrating to the washroom faucets, and once a week, when inmates were allowed to be shaved—by camp barbers, with cold water and dull blades—he always did so, no matter how tired he was.

In the *Kommando* he now recognized the importance of humoring Judenfranz, for conflict with that loathsome man was a worse drain on an inmate's strength than the actual labor under the *Kapo*'s eyes.

Easter Day of that year, April 25, 1943, was also Alfred Stirner's thirtieth birthday. The *Kommandos* were sent out to work as usual in the morning. The sky was pure as a freshwater wellspring, and at one point Stirner had his breath taken away as he saw, in the far distance, blue against dazzling blue, the Beskid Mountains. But the afternoon was free, idle, empty, and appalling. He was thirty. He felt twice that. He thought about Lena and Jacob more than he had for a long time. He was thoroughly daunted.

Then—perhaps because it was Easter—the inmates were given bread for supper, and on each chunk of bread was a glaze of marmalade. "It's your birthday cake," Kollin said, and suddenly Stirner felt quite cheerful.

One day in May, Judenfranz abruptly stopped beating the workers in Stirner's squad. He was as usual surly, and his tongue was abusive, but he kept his hands at his sides. That evening all the camp buzzed with speculation, for all the *Kapos* at once had abstained from physical violence. This must have been by general order. The inmates could make only one guess—that Germany was now so pressed for manpower that even Jews had a kind of potential value.

This order did not, however, make life suddenly easy. Scores of men from the Neuendorf and Belgian transports wasted and collapsed and died, just as had happened—and, for that matter, was still happening to a lesser extent—among Stirner's contemporaries. The SS, sensing a reaction of hope among the inmates in response to the *Kapos'* restraint, set out to show the camp that cruelty was still the law. A man who was caught with a pencil was given twenty-five lashes with a whip in front of the roll call one morning. Another who refused to serve as an informer for the camp political department had his hands tied behind his back and was hung up for two hours by the knot.

At this time a transport of six hundred German criminals from the concentration camp at Mauthausen arrived. It appeared that the authorities felt Jews were becoming proportionately too numerous in Auschwitz; for want of Germans and Poles, some of the Jewish prominents had been given administrative jobs. All the Mauthausen green triangles were at once made functionaries. Bad as these men were, they were newcomers themselves, and Stirner, who was beginning to feel like an old survivor in Auschwitz, was not afraid of them.

As summer came on, Stirner began to recover a sense of humanness. He had seen such misery and degradation that for a time he had lost all sympathy, except an animal self-sympathy, but now friendships began to be important again. Kollin, who was quiet and temperamental, and Wertheim, an idealist, had been close to him all through the worst times; now he began to widen his circle.

One day Stirner struck up a conversation with a savant of survival, an old hand in Auschwitz, a graduate besides of Buchenwald, and he asked the man's name. Bernhardt. Stirner recalled that he had met Bernhardt once in the youth movement many years before. Bernhardt, who was from Halle, had been a dentist until he was arrested as a political prisoner in 1938. He was a powerful and energetic man, and, besides having fairly easy work in the plant, he was doing some dental work and had acquired some minor functions in his barrack that earned him extra bread. Dr. Bernhardt undertook a kind of patronage of Stirner, inviting him often to visit his quarters in the evenings and occasionally giving him chunks of bread from his surplus, on which Stirner rapidly began to build a reserve of strength.

Stirner also met an Orthodox Jew from Vienna, another transfer from Buchenwald, who had organized daily rites, morning and evening, for about ten men at a time. Stirner, though not Orthodox in the past, joined them quite often. They gathered unobtrusively, as if for casual talk, in a corner of their barrack, and, while the rest feigned conversation, the man from Vienna murmured prayers that were, in their conspiratorial tone and the sense they gave of common cause, as nourishing as calories.

Among the young Zionists of the Neuendorf Transport Stirner found several new friends, a sturdy lot, youths with a strong sense of comradeship and mutual responsibility, who helped each other and their new friends in every way they could. They influenced many inmates to think of Palestine as their future home—and to think in terms of a future home was itself a sustaining act. Some inmates who had been anti-Zionist began to say regretfully that they could have left for Palestine in plenty of time to escape Hitler's repressions. The inmates all felt rootless. Germany was no longer a home, and it was easy to look to Palestine as a center for their future lives. When news filtered into Auschwitz that the Palestinian Jewish Brigade had been formed, and that young Jews were now engaged as a unit in this war that was palpably against Jews, the Neuendorf boys became excited, and Stirner caught some of their infectious enthusiasm.

Quite often Stirner joined with a circle of friends, several of whom worked in the camp *Krankenbau*, the infirmary, and talked about politics, strategy, and even literature and philosophy. Dr. Bernhardt was in this group, and it often met in his dentist's quarters in one of the hospital barracks. Whenever these men discussed survival, they pictured a Europe, with Nazism prostrate, in which Jews would be able to move about freely like everyone else. They would be able, they imagined, to go back to their old homes; or, if they wished, they might go to Palestine or to America, without hindrance. It was good to have friends like this to talk over such things. All day long Stirner looked forward to seeing them, so he could tell them what he had observed and what he thought.

Marching to and from the plant, the *Häftlinge* were still obliged to sing marching songs, but beginning early that summer Stirner could hear men singing, ever so softly, in the barracks at night, certain Jewish songs. There was a tremendous song from the Warsaw ghetto, *Es brennt*. There was:

> *Never, never say,*
> *You're going the last way.* . . .

One night early in June, after work, Stirner was called to the *Arbeitsdienst*. An official there said, "You are registered as a welder. Are you really a welder?"

2 1 8

Stirner gave what evidence he could; he was able to persuade the man he knew the terms and motions of the trade.

The official ordered him to report next morning to a *Kommando* of skilled metal workers. He was wildly happy that night, for he felt sure he would survive.

A new chapter in his life opened at dawn—there was a difference even in the marches to roll call and to the plant, because Stirner's new *Kapo* was a German red triangle, a political prisoner from Dresden, and since he was an anti-Nazi, he had his own ideas of his function. He was not a pleasant man, but neither was he a Judenfranz.

It turned out that Stirner's work was not to be welding, after all, for he was assigned to clean tremendous metal plates from Leuna, which were to be used in gasoline distillation columns. He worked with a hand file all day long, but the exertion was far less than on his previous jobs. Sometimes he could sit down on a plate as he worked, and he could almost feel the health trickling back into his body. He was by no means well—both his feet were swollen all the time—but now he sensed that he was gaining, rather than losing, strength.

His transfer to the new job brought in its train one misfortune. He had to move from Barrack Two to Barrack Six, away from Kollin and Wertheim, and he worried about them, still on the digging-and-carrying *Kommando* under Judenfranz. Neither of them was registered as a craftsman, so neither had much chance of being transferred.

Before the war Stirner had had poor teeth, and he had in his mouth several crowns and some bridgework. One morning as he bit into his bread he felt something give way, and taking the bread from his mouth he found a gold crown in it. He put the crown in his pocket. That evening he went to Dr. Bernhardt and asked what he should do.

The dentist told him to forget the cavity and barter the crown to one of the camp's corruptibles for extra food.

Stirner negotiated with the *Stubendienst* in Barrack Six, and the man agreed to give him three extra loaves of bread and extra soup for a fortnight. That evening, for the first time since he had arrived in Auschwitz, Stirner ate to satiety.

Each advantage, once gained, produced a new one. Each ounce of energy Stirner saved over from his regular work he could spend on extra work for extra food, which in turn gave him a bonus of strength.

Warm weather, which now arrived, helped in this hoarding. The days became so bland that the *Häftlinge* were issued light summer clothing that caused the French Jews to refer to their fellow inmates as *pyjamas*. "*J'ai vu un pyjama qui . . . L'autre pyjama m'a dit que . . .*"

After Stirner had been in the skilled metal workers' *Kommando* for a few weeks, he put in some time, in the evenings, practicing bedmaking, and at length he persuaded his *Blockältester* to appoint him as *Bettenbauer*, official bedmaker for the barrack. This meant he could have his breakfast indoors in the mornings and could stay inside until roll call; on rainy mornings this made a difference. The job also earned him a supplementary ration.

As Stirner grew stronger, his efforts in the plate-cleaning squad improved so much that his name was tacked onto a list of good workers, and one evening late in the summer he was called to the *Arbeitsdienst* again, along with three others. The *Arbeitsdienstführer* and a civilian employee of I. G. Farben interviewed the quartet, and again the officials doubted Stirner's qualifications as a welder, because of his glasses and his intellectual look.

The civilian asked, "Do you know anything about plumbing?"

Stirner said, "Yes." If the man had asked him if he knew how to fly a Focke-Wulf, he would have said, "Yes."

"How do you bend a pipe?"

By good fortune Stirner had seen a pipe bent in the Berlin factory where he had worked in the labor gang. "You ram some sand into the pipe to the place where you want to bend it," he said, "and then you heat the place, bend the hot metal slowly around a form, cool it, and get the sand out."

When all four men had been interviewed, Stirner and a strong youth were selected to work on a plumbing project, and the next morning, having marched out with the skilled workers' *Kommando*, they were met at the plant by a German civilian, who turned them over to a plumber in one of the buildings.

This man was a Saxon, a careful craftsman who did not like the war or Hitler but submitted to both. Work was his religion. He was reckless with himself in his labors and expected his subordinates to be, too. He treated Stirner and the boy as skilled workmen, not as *Häftlinge*, and he made them feel that he needed their help, and this gave Stirner a sense he had long missed, of having some value.

At first the plumber would not discuss politics at all, saying he wanted no controversy. Later Stirner began to explain the Jews' predicament and to try to persuade the plumber that acquiescence in Hitler was tantamount to full support of his methods of extermination, but the plumber said he did not understand any of that; he understood only plumbing.

Never had Stirner met such a dedicated and skillful technician, and he quickly mastered the apprentice skills, and as his work improved the plumber seemed to begin to respect him. The boy fell sick, and Stirner was then alone with the Saxon. The work was under a roof, out of the weather, and Stirner no longer had to submit to a *Kapo's* whims, and he grew ever stronger. The Saxon began to give him two or three cigarettes a day, which he bartered for bread in camp, and thus he gained more atop the earlier more. The plumber allowed Stirner to do some welding, so his claim of being a skilled welder was gradually consolidated. Best of all, his boss undertook to tell him the daily news. The plumber understood only plumbing; he did not seem to realize that Germany was being beaten, day by day. But Stirner did, and that knowledge was as good for him as bread.

Late in the summer, following a controversy between I. G. Farben and the camp authorities over whether the company should pay the camp a full salary for Stirner's—an inmate's—labors, he was taken from the Saxon and assigned to a new *Kommando* of welders, which actually had a Jewish *Kapo*. Stirner was moved into Barrack Five, where he again wheedled the job of *Bettenbauer*. He received extra rations for welding, and extras for bedmaking. In the plant he was under the supervision of a young Polish civilian named Smuda, one of a number of Polish employees of I. G. Farben who lived near the plant, a Polish nationalist, a German-hater, a rare Pole in that he was on an easy footing with Jews. Smuda was capable of beautiful work, but his delight was the opposite—sabotage; he accomplished as little as possible and carefully and joyfully wrought hidden faults in metal seams. In these enterprises Stirner became a fanatic pupil.

Smuda soon was bringing Stirner a couple of slices of bread and some sausage every day. Better than that, he began to bring a newspaper, which he handed to Stirner; Stirner put it under his drawers in the small of his back and smuggled it into camp each evening. For the first time he became a person of importance in the barracks—not quite a prominent, but one who was sought and consulted.

Wertheim died in August. Stirner's dear friend Benjamin Wertheim had been in the youth movement and had always been a social worker, in charge of a Jewish children's home in Berlin, a gentle and rather childish person himself. He had an active temperament, but he had an idea that everyone ought to be a good human being, and the sight of so much brutality and degradation, an awareness of corruption and meanness even among those who were being brutalized, and above all an understanding of what the Hitler system really meant, that the ideality of man was a putrid lie—these things broke his desire to survive, and he welcomed typhus from a louse and died.

The inmates could see that Auschwitz was being expanded. The barbed wire was moved back. Many new barracks were built. It seemed that transports must be coming to this haven from every corner of Europe.

One Sunday morning all the welders were called to the *Arbeitsdienst*, where a *Kapo* of plumbing received them and said, "Boys, we need two welders to put central heating into the new SS barracks. We're going to give you an examination in welding. Do your best, because this is a big chance for you."

What the *Kapo* had said was true; it was a big chance, for those who worked within the camp were spared an hour of marching to and from the plant; this would be a special boon for Stirner, whose feet remained swollen.

The test was a hard one—in overhead welding. Stirner

thought he did his first join badly but knew the second was good.

Stirner was chosen, and now another new phase began for him. He did not have to march. He worked on plumbing in SS buildings, in one of which, later, female inmates lived; the *Häftlinge* always called that barrack "the brothel." Stirner's shop was near the kitchens, and he was able, from time to time, simply to tease extra food from the kitchen staff. When anybody had trouble with plumbing, he brashly demanded food as payment for repairs—and collected it, too. He was on the team that prepared heating and plumbing for an operating room in one of the hospital barracks, and he made new friends among the Jewish doctors, one of whom, having examined Stirner's feet, gave him a second-hand pair of shoes in place of his own, which were falling apart, and the sores on his feet soon mended. He even acquired spare clothing—one suiting for work and one for free time. He could at last keep clean.

One evening early in the autumn of 1943, Stirner heard some electrifying news from friends who had come back from the plant: British prisoners of war had arrived at Auschwitz.

These prisoners were housed in a separate camp, but they were to work in the factory. They were mostly from the African theater, from Tobruk and the desert, and they had been held in Italy until the landings there, then had been taken to Lambsdorff, in Silesia; twelve hundred of them had now been brought to Auschwitz to work—in violation of the Geneva convention.

From the moment of the prisoners' arrival the whole psychology of the *Häftlinge* changed. These men had fought Hitler. They despised the Germans and were cheerful to the Jews. The tide of war had changed, and the Britishers were cocky. The German guards shouted at them; the prisoners answered by laughing, thumbing their noses, spewing English oaths. They were ostentatiously lazy, and they seemed to be enjoying themselves like bad schoolboys. All this was wine to the Jews.

Stirner was so excited by what he heard of the P.W.'s that he asked to be shifted back into Barrack Five and the welders' *Kommando*, even though that meant marching again. He wanted to see for himself. His transfer was granted, and the first day he marched out and saw Tommies parading across the plant area in uniform, arms swinging stiffly in the British way, roaring, "Roll out the barrel . . . ," he almost wept. He was assigned to a welding shack adjacent to one where a trio of British noncoms worked under his old friend Smuda. After so many emaciated Jews trying to stand up to the Germans, these men seemed to be energy, power, the force of life itself; they were bears. "We'll be home by Christmas!" one of them shouted to Stirner that first morning. How devoutly Stirner hoped so!—though in truth he had no idea where his future home might be.

During the autumn Stirner undertook all sorts of new enterprises. He talked his *Blockältester* into letting him use spare time to make small metal hooks for clothes, which he sold first to the German functionaries around the camp for food, and later even to Jewish prominents; using thin pipes, he fabricated curtain rods, which the Germans bought for their rooms; he made and sold frames for lamp shades. The material for all these things he scrounged from scraps at the plant, and for his work he earned not only food but also extra clothing and even some soap.

Cold weather came, and with it new transports of Jews from France, Italy, Belgium, North Africa, and Greece. Those from sunbaked lands could not stand the damp cold and died in droves. The camp became crowded, nevertheless, and in the late autumn the Germans gave everyone physical examinations, and those who were weak were taken away—presumably to the gas chambers; the use of them by the Nazis for purposes of extermination was now common knowledge in the camp.

When the Jewish holidays came, the camp authorities of course ignored them, and, indeed, on the Day of Atonement, morning roll call took nearly three hours. A Polish red triangle had escaped. Poles quite often got away, because Polish civilians living outside the camp smuggled in clothes and documents. Finally the search ended, and the *Kommandos* were sent off to work. In the evening the Orthodox Jew from Vienna who had organized services gathered ten men in one of the barracks, and as the other nine murmured, pretending to converse, he said the prayers of the day, in an unusually loud and bitter voice.

In the autumn months Stirner was assigned to a German *Meister* from Breslau, named Paul Brandt, who seemed to him a wonderful man. The first day Stirner joined Brandt, the *Meister* said, "I am an old Social Democrat. I am not interested in your stripes. To me you are a worker, no more, no less." Brandt was the first boss in Auschwitz with whom Stirner got on a *Du* basis. Brandt hated Hitler. He was perfectly willing to have Stirner associate with the British P.W.'s "Do anything you want," he said, "but don't get me in trouble." Once, when Stirner suffered a stomach disorder, Brandt brought him white bread for several days.

One evening at the showers Stirner conversed with the Jewish supervisor of the clothing supplies, a man with prematurely white hair, whose name, Stirner had heard, was David, and Stirner asked if he was related to some Davids he had known in

Berlin. The man said he was not and in turn asked Stirner his name. Upon hearing it, David asked, "Are you related to Maria Stirner who was a Herrmann?"

"Good God," Stirner said, "she was my mother."

"Then you are some kind of nephew of mine. She was my cousin."

David was a prominent, and had a formidable reputation and influence in the camp; he was in charge of the precious linen in the hospital. "Listen," he said, "if there is anything you need, come to me. You are the only relative I have left in the world, so far as I know."

On snowy days that winter, when the SS men strode out in fur coats and inmates collapsed by the score, Stirner could wear warm underwear under his uniform, thanks to his Some-Kind-of-Uncle David.

On Christmas Day, 1943, Stirner was given a wonderful present. His *Blockältester* invited him to move into the day room at the end of the barrack and promoted him from *Bettenbauer* to *Schreiber*, or secretary, with duties that took little energy— he checked off men's numbers as they passed through the line for food; assigned beds; handled complaints. He now had a quiet bed and a small cupboard for his property.

Before New Year's Day, when a fresh transport arrived, he managed to obtain, by barter of food, a razor and some shaving cream.

Alfred Stirner had become an old-timer. He was near the pinnacle of Auschwitz society, and if even that was a position of utter debasement for a human being to occupy—well, that hardly mattered. There was something worse: not to exist.

Stirner's friend Kollin contracted jaundice in the first days of 1944, and he was selected for the gas chambers. Besides feeling melancholy—and a survivor's guilt—over losing his old friend, Stirner thought: *The Germans are giving ground on both fronts. When things get really bad, what will they do with us? They'll surely send us all where they've sent Kollin.*

A transport came in from Birkenau, and among its passengers Stirner found a man who had worked in the vicinity of the gas chambers at that camp. He asked the new arrival, "What do they do with the women who have children?"

"What do you expect?" the man said.

"We've had no details, only rumors," Stirner said. "Tell me."

"You are wondering about your own wife and children?"

"Yes. One son only."

"How did they leave the transport? In a truck, at once, with the old and sick?"

"Yes."

"Well, I have to tell you that I can't give you any hope."

Stirner asked, "Even healthy women?"

The man from Birkenau grew angry. "I've been near the gas chambers day and night," he said. "I tell you women with children simply don't exist."

Early in the spring of 1944, Stirner found a new friend, a young Czech Jew named Edouard Kohn, who had a gentile wife at home in Prague. He had gone to Poland early in the war, in an effort to make his way to Sweden, but he had been caught, extradited, and put into a concentration camp; he had escaped, been found, escaped again, been found again, and at last had been sent to Auschwitz. He had a buoyant spirit, and he and Stirner became *Pauker*—buddies. Edouard's wife sent him parcels, which he shared with Stirner. So many Germans were being withdrawn from the camp that Jews were moving, by default, into many of the administrative posts, and Kohn was given charge of a storehouse for chemical instruments in the plant, which by this time was in partial operation. He was able to smuggle pots, thermometers, water glasses, and even, sometimes, pure grain alcohol into camp, and when the news was good, he and Stirner had a few surreptitious drinks together. That was something new indeed for Auschwitz.

The three British P.W.'s in Smuda's welding shack had grown friendly with Stirner. One was George Watson, who had grown up in India and had never seen England; Stirner enjoyed telling him about his own country. The second was Dennis Deerfield, a Yorkshire boy, and tough. The third was James Simpkins, who had been in France in 1939 and 1940 and had gone through Dunkirk, only to be captured later in North Africa. These three shared with their Jewish friends chocolates, which Stirner had not seen for years, and soap and other treasures from their Red Cross parcels. Stirner told them everything he had seen in the camp; they found it hard to believe his stories. "How is it possible," Walton asked once, "that there are ordinary Jerries living outside here, and that these frightful things could have been happening only a few hundred yards away?" Somehow the British had acquired a radio, and they relayed the BBC news each day; Stirner translated the German communiqués from Smuda's paper; and then they discussed operations and strategy. All through the spring, they wondered when the second front would come.

Just for fun, Stirner also wrote love letters for them, to German, Czech, and Polish girls who lived near the camp, whom they had of course never met, but whose addresses they wheedled from Smuda. "I'll marry you," one of them dictated one day. "I give you the word of a British soldier that I'll marry you."

In order to improve his English, Stirner asked the men for reading matter, and when Simpkins gave him a pamphlet from an evangelical society in Boston, Stirner asked if he had connections in America, and he said he had. Stirner asked Simpkins to write his American friends, requesting them to forward a message to some friends of his own in Decatur, Illinois. At once they drew up a letter: "I have been in touch with Alfred Stirner. He is in good health. He knows nothing about any of his relatives in Europe. He says he would like to hear from you, and if you have time. . . ."

That spring the *Häftlinge* were permitted to form a marching band, under the leadership of a Polish Jew who had played in orchestras on the French liner *Normandie* and on several ships on the Mediterranean; the bandsmen used instruments that had been brought to the camp by musicians, been taken away from them, and been stored in the camp warehouses. At first this was pleasant. The band played every morning and evening, as the *Kommandos* marched to and from the plant. There were concerts on Sunday afternoons.

Then one day a Pole who had escaped was caught and brought back into camp. He was marched around the camp wearing a placard that said, "I am glad to be back." The next morning at roll call he was given twenty-five lashes, and while he was being whipped the band was ordered to play patriotic German music. After that it played for all whippings, and from then on band music gave no joy.

Stirner wagered Dr. Bernhardt two loaves of bread one day, a tremendous stake that might have meant life or death for some inmates, that the Allies would land in France before April twentieth. He lost. Late in May—by that time there were only a handful of men alive from the two hundred forty who had been in Stirner's transport—everyone was aroused by a rumor that the second front had begun. This was the false D-day rumor started by an Associated Press girl in London practicing on the office transmitter, and somehow it made its way to Auschwitz.

The wealthy men and the riches of European Jewry were finding their way to camps like Auschwitz. Some men had managed to keep a few gems as they entered camp, and a lively trade grew up between the camp and the civilian populace living around it. In this trade the prominents, who had longstanding contacts with civilians, acted as middlemen. Of course the jewels were bartered for a tiny fraction of their true value, but nevertheless they often saved lives. Prominents could use their influence in other ways. Stirner tried to do what he could for a rich man named Emil Buenos, who had been born in Egypt and had been an art dealer in France and America, and who really tried to adjust himself to conditions in camp. Stirner managed to have him transferred from *Kommando* Number Four, the hard-labor gang, to lighter work; but the life was too hard, and Buenos died. Some men could not accept the camp's ruthless levelling. The Frenchman Jules Mossé, who had served as a high official in the French government, never could understand that to be a *Häftling* really meant being a non-person; he tried to keep his dignity and his sense of position, and no matter how much Stirner and other prominents attempted to ease

231

his fall into the anonymous mass, it crushed him, and he, too, died.

At four o'clock in the afternoon of June 7, Stirner looked out of a window in his welding shack and saw one of the foremen, a young Jew, running wildly across the factory enclosure toward the shack. Stirner hurried outside and met the foreman.

The youth said breathlessly, "They've landed! They've landed!"

"It's another rumor," Stirner said.

"I tell you it's true, since yesterday morning."

Stirner ran in to Watson, Deerfield, and Simpkins, and asked them if the news was true. They said they didn't know; they would have to wait for that night's BBC.

When the *Kommandos* marched back to the barracks that evening, all had heard—and by this time believed—the report. It was as if all the inmates were drunk. There was dancing in the barracks. The older men wept. Each person sought out his friends and congratulated them. Stirner hurried to see Dr. Bernhardt, who had not heard the news and said flatly, "It's a lie."

Stirner was convinced that the invasion had begun, and he tried to persuade the dentist. Dr. Bernhardt's hands started to tremble, and he said, "If we knew this were true, and if we knew our women and children were alive, we would be like newborn children—we could begin our lives all over again."

At the plant, first thing next morning, Stirner hurried in to Smuda's shack to see his British friends. They were raucous and jubilant, and Stirner knew at once that the news was irreversibly true.

That afternoon the German communiqué said that most of the Allied forces attempting to land in Normandy had been thrown into the sea. The Germans in the camp, who had been visibly nervous for twenty-four hours, seemed more confident. For the *Häftlinge* there were several days of anxious waiting. Then it was certain that a permanent bridgehead had been established, and they knew that it could only be a matter of time till they re-entered the world.

During the next days a strange figure entered Auschwitz. He was a Czech Jew, a gynecologist who before the war had gone from Czechoslovakia to Poland to Sweden to England. There he had enlisted as a naval doctor, and he had been put aboard a former Blue Funnel liner that had been converted to a transport. On the ship's second voyage to Singapore, the vessel had been waylaid in the Straits of Malacca by a German raider, the *Atlantis,* and during the gunfight the captain of the British ship had been killed, and the *Atlantis* had taken the vessel into its convoy as a prize. The raider and its half-dozen victims had then crossed the Indian Ocean, had rounded the Cape of Good Hope, and had put in at last at Bordeaux, then in German hands. On the British transport's manifest, in the ship's safe, the doctor was found to have been registered as a Czech, not a Briton, and after the ship's crew had been lodged in a P.W. camp at Bremen, the Gestapo had made inquiries in Czechoslovakia and had discovered that the doctor was Jewish. A few days later the doctor had been honored with a warrant of arrest personally signed by Heydrich, the SS chief, and had been taken to Auschwitz. He made a sensational stir among the inmates of the camp, trembling with hope over the Allied landings in the west, when he arrived there in a British naval officer's uniform.

Stirner befriended this hero and tried to get messages about him to Czech authorities in London, through his British friends, but no answer ever came.

There was nothing to do but wait. Caen. Bayeux. Papers, maps, more waiting. June, July, August—then, suddenly, Avranches, Paris, and the French border; the Russians near Krakow.

The atmosphere in camp grew tense. Some kind of decision was approaching, and no one could tell what the Germans would do in the last death struggle.

Then the Allies were stopped. The Russians paused at the Vistula; the Americans stalled at Aachen.

Early in August inmates of Auschwitz saw their first Flying Fortresses by day, when the Americans raided an oil refinery at Trzebinia, near Oswiecim. The German and Polish civilians who worked in the Auschwitz plant had concrete bunkers for shelters; the *Häftlinge* had only ditches—but this meant that they could watch the planes, and cheer. Bombs hit the refinery, and for days Trzebinia's black smoke gave the inmates a grim pleasure.

On August 20, at eleven o'clock in the morning, Fortresses attacked Auschwitz itself. It was a Sunday, and when the attack came, Stirner was fortunately doing some paper work inside the camp. The plant was the target. The barracks shook. A bomb that landed in the British P.W. camp killed forty; nearly eighty Jews were killed in the factory. The bombing was over in a few seconds. The plant, so painfully built, was a shambles: buildings had fallen, railroad tracks were overturned, big craters had been formed. The Germans set the *Häftlinge* to work cleaning up.

From that day morale broke. There was an alarm nearly every morning for a few days, and a second attack came soon, and the inmates panicked and ran in every direction. There were a couple of attacks early in September, and the plant was again damaged, and again the Germans gave the inmates the task of making repairs.

After the rebellion in Budapest that summer, when the dictator Admiral Horthy was pushed out by Szálazi, a whole string of transports began arriving at Auschwitz from Hungary, full of Jewish prisoners destined for the gas chambers. Upon their execution, the crematories were so overloaded that many bodies had to be burned in the open fields. The prevailing winds blew across the camp. At the plant there were already foul smells from the manufacture of metanol and buna—a nauseous odor above all of sulphur. When the new smell came, Stirner made a business of going around among the German civilians holding his nose.

One German shook his head and said, "It's bad."

Another shrugged his shoulders and said, "These things happen."

One morning in October, Stirner noticed that all the German civilians showed up at work in their *Alarmkompanie* uniforms, and he asked some of them what the reason was, and they said they were mobilized to assist the SS in case of riots. Later Stirner found out the real reason. A few days before, when a number of transports had come from Theresienstadt, the Auschwitz authorities had decided to exterminate the *Kommando* that had been working in the crematories and to set up a new one. Somehow the intended victims heard about the plan, organized a contact with another *Kommando* working in a munitions plant, obtained some dynamite, shoved their green-triangle *Kapo* into the crematories, and blew them and him up.

If Stirner and the others in the men's camp had heard the explosion, they had not paid much attention to it.

The *Kommando* had done a good job on the crematories. There were no more gassings at Auschwitz.

Winter came on, and the inmates' mood was bitter. The Allies seemed to be mired. The air raids were frightening. Winter itself was unbearable. Death was a daily collector at the roll calls on the parade ground. The British P.W.'s no longer received parcels, and the Jews, remembering the generosity of their British friends, began sharing their own meager food with them.

Lena's birthday had been in December. On the day after her birthday, a snowy day, Simpkins took Stirner aside and handed him a miraculous piece of paper. It was a note from Stirner's friends in Decatur, Illinois. He hurried to one of the plant lavatories, where the guard was a *Häftling*. "Close the door," Stirner whispered. "I have to read a letter." Inside he unfolded the sheet and read the wonderful words:

"As soon as the war is over, come to see us. We are still the same friends, Alfred, no matter what you have been through. . . ."

Stirner took great courage from that scrap of paper. He recklessly carried it into camp and showed it to all his friends.

Just after Christmas there was a severe air raid in which the plant was almost totally destroyed, and after that the Germans made only halfhearted efforts to clean up the area.

On January 13, the Russians broke through on the Vistula. Two days later there was a long night air raid. In the morning it was freezing cold. The guards were tired, and the authorities announced that there would be no work that day. A rumor went around during the day that the whole camp would be evacuated. Five days later, in the evening, the order was given to prepare for evacuation. Stirner put on some long woolen underwear that his prominent friends had procured for him, and he wrapped up some reserve bread and margarine that he had been hoarding since the first evacuation rumor.

One last roll call was held, and then, escorted by the entire SS force, the inmates of Auschwitz, and even the women from the "brothel," marched out to the west. The temperature was eighteen degrees below zero, Centigrade. The march lasted for thirty-six hours. Any who lagged were shot. All the way the SS men were in terror of being cut off by the Russians.

Those who could make it reached the town of Gleiwitz, where all were embarked on a freight train. In Stirner's transport from Berlin, he had had sixty people in his car; now he had nearly two hundred. There were five thousand five hundred on the train altogether.

First the train went to the concentration camp at Mauthausen, in Austria, where the authorities declared they would not accept the Auschwitz inmates; their place was already overcrowded. So the train moved by slow stages toward Berlin. The inmates were inside the freight cars seven days and nights. Those who lived, lived on snow. More than a thousand died along the way. Many jumped out. Stirner's Czech friend Edouard Kohn jumped out and ran away, and Stirner kept thinking that after all that he had survived he could not die on the way to freedom.

The survivors were taken to an airplane factory in Berlin, where, at last, they were fed bread and soup. For a week they slept on a cement floor, and then they were moved into barracks and were put to work in the plant. They labored there for three months, through many air raids. Stirner maneuvered himself into a clerical job in the *Schreibstube*, and he obtained civilian clothes by barter.

By April 21, the Russians had approached very near to Berlin so the authorities decided to march the Auschwitz *Häftlinge* westward again. The inmates walked day and night through Mecklenburg. Near Schwerin, one night early in May, Stirner and a few friends, having heard rumors that they had walked into a pocket between the Americans and the Russians, decided to make a break. They slipped off into the night, and though they were challenged once, they got away.

On May 3, 1945, Alfred Stirner and six companions walked out of some woods into a clearing at one side of which an American flag was draped across a bush. For several minutes the seven men stood at the edge of the clearing and wept. When Stirner felt able to speak, he walked out and approached an officer.

"We are political prisoners who have escaped," he said. "We are Jews."

Stirner was to remember for a long time the exact words the American spoke. "You're welcome here," he said. He turned to an enlisted man with him and said, "Break out some C rations for these people."

The meal was delicious, but afterwards the officer didn't seem to know what to do with his guests. There did not seem to be a plan for handling Jews. Stirner was ecstatic over the idea of freedom, but after the horrors he had seen, he thought it strange that there was no plan at all.

Later in the day, in the continuing confusion, Stirner saw a young American soldier descending from a jeep, who, Stirner thought, might be Jewish. He asked the American if he was. The American asked the stranger why he wanted to know. Stirner said that he himself was Jewish, and with deep emotion acknowledged that to shake hands with a Jew who had borne arms against Hitler would give him a sense of returning, at last, to a sane world. The young American, overcome with understanding, embraced Stirner and said, over and over, *"Sholom aleichem,"* which means, Peace be with you.

THE BIG IF

Hiroshima

THE BIG IF

MAN *is here to stay—IF . . .*

No one needs to be told the nature of the big if in human survival on this earth, but perhaps a reader of the remainder of this book will be willing to look this conditional, which underlies so many of our anxieties, squarely in the face. This he can do by bearing in mind, as he reads, three figures.

First, President Truman, announcing the Hiroshima bombing, told the world that the force of the atomic explosion that day was equivalent to that of some twenty thousand tons of TNT.

Second, one of the atomic powers had detonated, some months before this book went to press, a nuclear explosion that was said to have had the equivalence of fifty-eight million tons of TNT. It was, in other words, two thousand nine hundred

*times as powerful as the bomb that did to a city what the fol-
lowing pages describe.*

Third, it has been said on good authority that there is no
theoretical reason why a nuclear weapon should not be developed with a capacity of one thousand megatons, the equivalent of one billion tons of TNT, which would, after all, be only
twenty times as large as the test explosion of the last paragraph,
and that if such a weapon could be suspended and exploded
high above the western United States, it would create a fire
storm that would render six entire states—Idaho, Montana,
Wyoming, Nevada, Utah, and Colorado—incapable of supporting life of any kind.

HIROSHIMA

I · A Noiseless Flash

At exactly fifteen minutes past eight in the morning, on August 6, 1945, Japanese time, at the moment when the atomic bomb flashed above Hiroshima, Miss Toshiko Sasaki, a clerk in the personnel department of the East Asia Tin Works, had just sat down at her place in the plant office and was turning her head to speak to the girl at the next desk. At that same moment, Dr. Masakazu Fujii was settling down cross-legged to read the Osaka *Asahi* on the porch of his private hospital, overhanging one of the seven deltaic rivers which divide Hiroshima; Mrs. Hatsuyo Nakamura, a tailor's widow, stood by the window of her kitchen, watching a neighbor tearing down his house because it lay in the path of an air-raid-defense fire lane; Father Wilhelm Kleinsorge, a German priest of the Society of Jesus, reclined in his underwear on a cot on the top floor of his order's three-story mission house, reading a Jesuit magazine, *Stimmen der Zeit*; Dr. Terufumi Sasaki, a young member of the surgical staff of the city's large, modern Red Cross Hospital, walked along one of the hospital corridors with a blood specimen for a Wassermann test in his hand; and the Reverend Mr. Kiyoshi Tanimoto, pastor of the Hiroshima Methodist Church, paused at the door of a rich man's house in Koi, the city's western suburb, and prepared to unload a handcart full of things he had evacuated from town in fear of the massive B-29 raid which everyone expected Hiroshima to suffer. A hundred thousand people were killed by the atomic bomb, and these six were among the survivors. They still wonder why they lived when so many others died. Each of them counts many small items of chance or volition—a step taken in time, a decision to go indoors, catching one streetcar instead of the next—that spared him. And now each knows that in the act of survival he lived a dozen lives and saw more death than he ever thought he would see. At the time, none of them knew anything.

The Reverend Mr. Tanimoto got up at five o'clock that morning. He was alone in the parsonage, because for some time his wife had been commuting with their year-old baby to spend nights with a friend in Ushida, a suburb to the north. Of all the important cities of Japan, only two, Kyoto and Hiroshima, had not been visited in strength by *B-san*, or Mr. B, as the Japanese, with a mixture of respect and unhappy familiarity, called the B-29; and Mr. Tanimoto, like all his neighbors and friends, was almost sick with anxiety. He had heard uncomfortably detailed accounts of mass raids on Kure, Iwakuni, Tokuyama, and other nearby towns; he was sure Hiroshima's turn would come soon. He had slept badly the night before, because there had been several air-raid warnings. Hiroshima had been getting such warnings almost every night for weeks, for at that time the B-29s were using Lake Biwa, northeast of Hiroshima, as a rendezvous point, and no matter what city the Americans planned to hit, the Superfortresses streamed in over the coast near Hiroshima. The frequency of the warnings and the continued abstinence of Mr. B with respect to Hiroshima had made its citizens jittery; a rumor was going around that the Americans were saving something special for the city.

Mr. Tanimoto is a small man, quick to talk, laugh, and cry.

He wears his black hair parted in the middle and rather long; the prominence of the frontal bones just above his eyebrows and the smallness of his mustache, mouth, and chin give him a strange, old-young look, boyish and yet wise, weak and yet fiery. He moves nervously and fast, but with a restraint which suggests that he is a cautious, thoughtful man. He showed, indeed, just those qualities in the uneasy days before the bomb fell. Besides having his wife spend the nights in Ushida, Mr. Tanimoto had been carrying all the portable things from his church, in the close-packed residential district called Nagaragawa, to a house that belonged to a rayon manufacturer in Koi, two miles from the center of town. The rayon man, a Mr. Matsui, had opened his then unoccupied estate to a large number of his friends and acquaintances, so that they might evacuate whatever they wished to a safe distance from the probable target area. Mr. Tanimoto had had no difficulty in moving chairs, hymnals, Bibles, altar gear, and church records by pushcart himself, but the organ console and an upright piano required some aid. A friend of his named Matsuo had, the day before, helped him get the piano out to Koi; in return, he had promised this day to assist Mr. Matsuo in hauling out a daughter's belongings. That is why he had risen so early.

Mr. Tanimoto cooked his own breakfast. He felt awfully tired. The effort of moving the piano the day before, a sleepless night, weeks of worry and unbalanced diet, the cares of his parish—all combined to make him feel hardly adequate to the new day's work. There was another thing, too: Mr. Tanimoto had studied theology at Emory University, in Atlanta, Georgia; he had graduated in 1940; he spoke excellent English; he dressed in American clothes; he had corresponded with many American friends right up to the time the war began; and among a people obsessed with a fear of being spied upon—perhaps almost obsessed himself—he found himself growing increasingly uneasy. The police had questioned him several times, and just a few days before, he had heard that an influential acquaintance, a Mr. Tanaka, a retired officer of the Toyo Kisen Kaisha steamship line, an anti-Christian, a man famous in Hiroshima for his showy philanthropies and notorious for his personal tyrannies, had been telling people that Tanimoto should not be trusted. In compensation, to show himself publicly a good Japanese, Mr. Tanimoto had taken on the chairmanship of his local *tonarigumi*, or Neighborhood Association, and to his other duties and concerns this position had added the business of organizing air-raid defense for about twenty families.

Before six o'clock that morning, Mr. Tanimoto started for Mr. Matsuo's house. There he found that their burden was to be a *tansu*, a large Japanese cabinet, full of clothing and household goods. The two men set out. The morning was perfectly clear and so warm that the day promised to be uncomfortable. A few minutes after they started, the air-raid siren went off—a minute-long blast that warned of approaching planes but indicated to the people of Hiroshima only a slight degree of danger, since it sounded every morning at this time, when an American weather plane came over. The two men pulled and pushed the handcart through the city streets. Hiroshima was a fan-shaped city, lying mostly on the six islands formed by the seven estuarial rivers that branch out from the Ota River; its main commercial and residential districts, covering about four square miles in the center of the city, contained three-quarters of its population, which had been reduced by several evacuation programs from a wartime peak of 380,000 to about 245,000. Factories and other residential districts, or suburbs, lay compactly around the edges of the city. To the south were the docks, an airport, and the island-studded Inland Sea. A rim of mountains runs around the other three sides of the delta. Mr. Tanimoto and Mr. Matsuo took their way through the shopping center, already full of people, and across two of the rivers to the sloping streets of Koi, and up them to the outskirts and foothills. As they started up a valley away from the tight-ranked houses, the all-clear sounded. (The Japanese radar operators, detecting only three planes, supposed that they comprised a reconnaissance.) Pushing the handcart up to the rayon man's house was tiring, and the men, after they had maneuvered their load into the driveway and to the front steps, paused to rest awhile. They stood with a wing of the house between them and the city. Like most homes in this part of Japan, the house consisted of a wooden frame and wooden walls supporting a heavy tile roof. Its front hall, packed with rolls of bedding and clothing, looked like a cool cave full of fat cushions. Opposite the house, to the right of the front door, there was a large, finicky rock garden. There was no sound of planes. The morning was still; the place was cool and pleasant.

Then a tremendous flash of light cut across the sky. Mr. Tanimoto has a distinct recollection that it travelled from east to west, from the city toward the hills. It seemed a sheet of sun. Both he and Mr. Matsuo reacted in terror—and both had time to react (for they were 3,500 yards, or two miles, from the center of the explosion). Mr. Matsuo dashed up the front steps into the house and dived among the bedrolls and buried himself there. Mr. Tanimoto took four or five steps and threw himself between two big rocks in the garden. He bellied up very hard against one of them. As his face was against the stone, he did not see what happened. He felt a sudden pressure, and then splinters and pieces of board and fragments of tile fell on him. He heard no roar. (Almost no one in Hiroshima recalls hearing any noise of the bomb. But a fisherman in his sampan on the Inland Sea near Tsuzu, the man with whom Mr. Tanimoto's mother-in-law and sister-in-law were living, saw the flash and heard a tremendous explosion; he was nearly twenty miles from Hiroshima, but the thunder was greater than when the B-29s hit Iwakuni, only five miles away.)

When he dared, Mr. Tanimoto raised his head and saw that

the rayon man's house had collapsed. He thought a bomb had
fallen directly on it. Such clouds of dust had risen that there
was a sort of twilight around. In panic, not thinking for the moment of Mr. Matsuo under the ruins, he dashed out into the
street. He noticed as he ran that the concrete wall of the estate
had fallen over—toward the house rather than away from it. In
the street, the first thing he saw was a squad of soldiers who had
been burrowing into the hillside opposite, making one of the
thousands of dugouts in which the Japanese apparently intended to resist invasion, hill by hill, life for life; the soldiers
were coming out of the hole, where they should have been safe,
and blood was running from their heads, chests, and backs.
They were silent and dazed.

Under what seemed to be a local dust cloud, the day grew
darker and darker.

At nearly midnight, the night before the bomb was dropped,
an announcer on the city's radio station said that about two
hundred B-29s were approaching southern Honshu and advised the population of Hiroshima to evacuate to their designated "safe areas." Mrs. Hatsuyo Nakamura, the tailor's widow,
who lived in the section called Nobori-cho and who had long
had a habit of doing as she was told, got her three children—a
ten-year-old boy, Toshio, an eight-year-old girl, Yaeko, and a
five-year-old girl, Myeko—out of bed and dressed them and
walked with them to the military area known as the East Parade
Ground, on the northeast edge of the city. There she unrolled
some mats and the children lay down on them. They slept until
about two, when they were awakened by the roar of the planes
going over Hiroshima.

As soon as the planes had passed, Mrs. Nakamura started
back with her children. They reached home a little after two-
thirty and she immediately turned on the radio, which, to her

distress, was just then broadcasting a fresh warning. When she looked at the children and saw how tired they were, and when she thought of the number of trips they had made in past weeks, all to no purpose, to the East Parade Ground, she decided that in spite of the instructions on the radio, she simply could not face starting out all over again. She put the children in their bedrolls on the floor, lay down herself at three o'clock, and fell asleep at once, so soundly that when planes passed over later, she did not waken to their sound.

The siren jarred her awake at about seven. She arose, dressed quickly, and hurried to the house of Mr. Nakamoto, the head of her Neighborhood Association, and asked him what she should do. He said that she should remain at home unless an urgent warning—a series of intermittent blasts of the siren—was sounded. She returned home, lit the stove in the kitchen, set some rice to cook, and sat down to read that morning's Hiroshima *Chugoku*. To her relief, the all-clear sounded at eight o'clock. She heard the children stirring, so she went and gave each of them a handful of peanuts and told them to stay on their bedrolls, because they were tired from the night's walk. She had hoped that they would go back to sleep, but the man in the house directly to the south began to make a terrible hullaba-loo of hammering, wedging, ripping, and splitting. The prefec-tural government, convinced, as everyone in Hiroshima was, that the city would be attacked soon, had begun to press with threats and warnings for the completion of wide fire lanes, which, it was hoped, might act in conjunction with the rivers to localize any fires started by an incendiary raid; and the neigh-bor was reluctantly sacrificing his home to the city's safety. Just the day before, the prefecture had ordered all able-bodied girls from the secondary schools to spend a few days helping to clear these lanes, and they started work soon after the all-clear sounded.

Mrs. Nakamura went back to the kitchen, looked at the rice,

and began watching the man next door. At first, she was annoyed with him for making so much noise, but then she was moved almost to tears by pity. Her emotion was specifically directed toward her neighbor, tearing down his home, board by board, at a time when there was so much unavoidable destruction, but undoubtedly she also felt a generalized, community pity, to say nothing of self-pity. She had not had an easy time. Her husband, Isawa, had gone into the Army just after Myeko was born, and she had heard nothing from or of him for a long time, until, on March 5, 1942, she received a seven-word telegram: "Isawa died an honorable death at Singapore." She learned later that he had died on February 15th, the day Singapore fell, and that he had been a corporal. Isawa had been a not particularly prosperous tailor, and his only capital was a Sankoku sewing machine. After his death, when his allotments stopped coming, Mrs. Nakamura got out the machine and began to take in piecework herself, and since then had supported the children, but poorly, by sewing.

As Mrs. Nakamura stood watching her neighbor, everything flashed whiter than any white she had ever seen. She did not notice what happened to the man next door; the reflex of a mother set her in motion toward her children. She had taken a single step (the house was 1,350 yards, or three-quarters of a mile, from the center of the explosion) when something picked her up and she seemed to fly into the next room over the raised sleeping platform, pursued by parts of her house.

Timbers fell around her as she landed, and a shower of tiles pommelled her; everything became dark, for she was buried. The debris did not cover her deeply. She rose up and freed herself. She heard a child cry, "Mother, help me!," and saw her youngest—Myeko, the five-year-old—buried up to her breast and unable to move. As Mrs. Nakamura started frantically to claw her way toward the baby, she could see or hear nothing of her other children.

In the days right before the bombing, Dr. Masakazu Fujii, being prosperous, hedonistic, and at the time not too busy, had been allowing himself the luxury of sleeping until nine or nine-thirty, but fortunately he had to get up early the morning the bomb was dropped to see a house guest off on a train. He rose at six, and half an hour later walked with his friend to the station, not far away, across two of the rivers. He was back home by seven, just as the siren sounded its sustained warning. He ate breakfast and then, because the morning was already hot, undressed down to his underwear and went out on the porch to read the paper. This porch—in fact, the whole building—was curiously constructed. Dr. Fujii was the proprietor of a peculiarly Japanese institution: a private, single-doctor hospital. This building, perched beside and over the water of the Kyo River, and next to the bridge of the same name, contained thirty rooms for thirty patients and their kinfolk—for, according to Japanese custom, when a person falls sick and goes to a hospital, one or more members of his family go and live there with him, to cook for him, bathe, massage, and read to him, and to offer incessant familial sympathy, without which a Japanese patient would be miserable indeed. Dr. Fujii had no beds—only straw mats—for his patients. He did, however, have all sorts of modern equipment: an X-ray machine, diathermy apparatus, and a fine tiled laboratory. The structure rested two-thirds on the land, one-third on piles over the tidal waters of the Kyo. This overhang, the part of the building where Dr. Fujii lived, was queer-looking, but it was cool in summer and from the porch, which faced away from the center of the city, the prospect of the river, with pleasure boats drifting up and down it, was always refreshing. Dr. Fujii had occasionally had anxious moments when the Ota and its mouth branches rose to flood, but the piling was apparently firm enough and the house had always held.

Dr. Fujii had been relatively idle for about a month because in July, as the number of untouched cities in Japan dwindled and as Hiroshima seemed more and more inevitably a target, he began turning patients away, on the ground that in case of a fire raid he would not be able to evacuate them. Now he had only two patients left—a woman from Yano, injured in the shoulder, and a young man of twenty-five recovering from burns he had suffered when the steel factory near Hiroshima in which he worked had been hit. Dr. Fujii had six nurses to tend his patients. His wife and children were safe; his wife and one son were living outside Osaka, and another son and two daughters were in the country on Kyushu. A niece was living with him, and a maid and a manservant. He had little to do and did not mind, for he had saved some money. At fifty, he was healthy, convivial, and calm, and he was pleased to pass the evenings drinking whiskey with friends, always sensibly and for the sake of conversation. Before the war, he had affected brands imported from Scotland and America; now he was perfectly satisfied with the best Japanese brand, Suntory.

Dr. Fujii sat down cross-legged in his underwear on the spotless matting of the porch, put on his glasses, and started reading the Osaka *Asahi*. He liked to read the Osaka news because his wife was there. He saw the flash. To him—faced away from the center and looking at his paper—it seemed a brilliant yellow. Startled, he began to rise to his feet. In that moment (he was 1,550 yards from the center), the hospital leaned behind his rising and, with a terrible ripping noise, toppled into the river. The Doctor, still in the act of getting to his feet, was thrown forward and around and over; he was buffeted and gripped; he lost track of everything, because things were so speeded up; he felt the water.

Dr. Fujii hardly had time to think that he was dying before he realized that he was alive, squeezed tightly by two long timbers in a V across his chest, like a morsel suspended between two huge chopsticks—held upright, so that he could not move, with his head miraculously above water and his torso and legs in it. The remains of his hospital were all around him in a mad assortment of splintered lumber and materials for the relief of pain. His left shoulder hurt terribly. His glasses were gone.

Father Wilhelm Kleinsorge, of the Society of Jesus, was, on the morning of the explosion, in rather frail condition. The Japanese wartime diet had not sustained him, and he felt the strain of being a foreigner in an increasingly xenophobic Japan; even a German, since the defeat of the Fatherland, was unpopular. Father Kleinsorge had, at thirty-eight, the look of a boy growing too fast—thin in the face, with a prominent Adam's apple, a hollow chest, dangling hands, big feet. He walked clumsily, leaning forward a little. He was tired all the time. To make matters worse, he had suffered for two days, along with Father Cieslik, a fellow-priest, from a rather painful and urgent diarrhea, which they blamed on the beans and black ration bread they were obliged to eat. Two other priests then living in the mission compound, which was in the Nobori-cho section— Father Superior LaSalle and Father Schiffer—had happily escaped this affliction.

Father Kleinsorge woke up about six the morning the bomb was dropped, and half an hour later—he was a bit tardy because of his sickness—he began to read Mass in the mission chapel, a small Japanese-style wooden building which was without pews, since its worshippers knelt on the usual Japanese matted floor, facing an altar graced with splendid silks, brass, silver, and heavy embroideries. This morning, a Monday, the only worshippers were Mr. Takemoto, a theological student living in the mission house; Mr. Fukai, the secretary of the diocese; Mrs. Murata, the mission's devoutly Christian housekeeper; and his fellow-priests. After Mass, while Father Kleinsorge was reading the Prayers of Thanksgiving, the siren sounded. He stopped the service and the missionaries retired across the compound to the bigger building. There, in his room on the ground floor, to the right of the front door, Father Kleinsorge changed into a military uniform which he had acquired when he was teaching at the Rokko Middle School in Kobe and which he wore during air-raid alerts.

After an alarm, Father Kleinsorge always went out and scanned the sky, and in this instance, when he stepped outside, he was glad to see only the single weather plane that flew over Hiroshima each day about this time. Satisfied that nothing would happen, he went in and breakfasted with the other Fathers on substitute coffee and ration bread, which, under the circumstances, was especially repugnant to him. The Fathers sat and talked awhile, until, at eight, they heard the all-clear. They went then to various parts of the building. Father Schiffer retired to his room to do some writing. Father Cieslik sat in his room in a straight chair with a pillow over his stomach to ease his pain, and read. Father Superior LaSalle stood at the window of his room, thinking. Father Kleinsorge went up to a room on the third floor, took off all his clothes except his underwear, and stretched out on his right side on a cot and began reading his *Stimmen der Zeit*.

After the terrible flash—which, Father Kleinsorge later realized, reminded him of something he had read as a boy about a large meteor colliding with the earth—he had time (since he was 1,400 yards from the center) for one thought: A bomb has fallen directly on us. Then, for a few seconds or minutes, he went out of his mind.

Father Kleinsorge never knew how he got out of the house. The next things he was conscious of were that he was wandering around in the mission's vegetable garden in his underwear, bleeding slightly from small cuts along his left flank; that all the buildings roundabout had fallen down except the Jesuits' mission house, which had long before been braced and double-braced by a priest named Gropper, who was terrified of earthquakes; that the day had turned dark; and that Murata-*san*, the housekeeper, was nearby, crying over and over, "*Shu Jesusu, awaremi tamai!* Our Lord Jesus, have pity on us!"

On the train on the way into Hiroshima from the country, where he lived with his mother, Dr. Terufumi Sasaki, the Red Cross Hospital surgeon, thought over an unpleasant nightmare he had had the night before. His mother's home was in Mukaihara, thirty miles from the city, and it took him two hours by train and tram to reach the hospital. He had slept uneasily all night and had wakened an hour earlier than usual, and, feeling sluggish and slightly feverish, had debated whether to go to the hospital at all; his sense of duty finally forced him to go, and he had started out on an earlier train than he took most mornings. The dream had particularly frightened him because it was so closely associated, on the surface at least, with a disturbing actuality. He was only twenty-five years old and had just completed his training at the Eastern Medical University, in Tsingtao, China. He was something of an idealist and was much distressed by the inadequacy of medical facilities in the country town where his mother lived. Quite on his own, and without a permit, he had begun visiting a few sick people out there in the evenings, after his eight hours at the hospital and four hours' commuting. He had recently learned that the penalty for practicing without a permit was severe; a fellow-doctor whom he had asked about it had given him a serious scolding. Nevertheless, he had continued to practice. In his dream, he had been at the bedside of a country patient when the police and the doctor he had consulted burst into the room, seized him, dragged him outside, and beat him up cruelly. On the train, he just about decided to give up the work in Mukaihara, since he felt it would be impossible to get a permit, because the authorities would hold that it would conflict with his duties at the Red Cross Hospital.

At the terminus, he caught a streetcar at once. (He later calculated that if he had taken his customary train that morning, and if he had had to wait a few minutes for the streetcar, as often happened, he would have been close to the center at the time of the explosion and would surely have perished.) He arrived at the hospital at seven-forty and reported to the chief surgeon. A few minutes later, he went to a room on the first floor and drew blood from the arm of a man in order to perform a Wassermann test. The laboratory containing the incubators for the test was on the third floor. With the blood specimen in his left hand, walking in a kind of distraction he had felt all morning, probably because of the dream and his restless night, he started along the main corridor on his way toward the stairs. He was one step beyond an open window when the light of the bomb was reflected, like a gigantic photographic flash, in the corridor. He ducked down on one knee and said to himself, as only a Japanese would, "Sasaki, *gambare!* Be brave!" Just then (the building was 1,650 yards from the center), the blast ripped through the hospital. The glasses he was wearing flew off his face; the bottle of blood crashed against one wall; his Japanese slippers zipped out from under his feet—but otherwise, thanks to where he stood, he was untouched.

Dr. Sasaki shouted the name of the chief surgeon and rushed around to the man's office and found him terribly cut by glass. The hospital was in horrible confusion: heavy partitions and ceilings had fallen on patients, beds had overturned, windows had blown in and cut people, blood was spattered on the walls and floors, instruments were everywhere, many of the patients were running about screaming, many more lay dead. (A colleague working in the laboratory to which Dr. Sasaki had been walking was dead; Dr. Sasaki's patient, whom he had just left and who a few moments before had been dreadfully afraid of syphilis, was also dead.) Dr. Sasaki found himself the only doctor in the hospital who was unhurt.

Dr. Sasaki, who believed that the enemy had hit only the building he was in, got bandages and began to bind the wounds of those inside the hospital; while outside, all over Hiroshima, maimed and dying citizens turned their unsteady steps toward the Red Cross Hospital to begin an invasion that was to make Dr. Sasaki forget his private nightmare for a long, long time.

Miss Toshiko Sasaki, the East Asia Tin Works clerk, who is not related to Dr. Sasaki, got up at three o'clock in the morning on the day the bomb fell. There was extra housework to do. Her eleven-month-old brother, Akio, had come down the day before with a serious stomach upset; her mother had taken him to the Tamura Pediatric Hospital and was staying there with him. Miss Sasaki, who was about twenty, had to cook breakfast for her father, a brother, a sister, and herself, and— since the hospital, because of the war, was unable to provide food—to prepare a whole day's meals for her mother and the baby, in time for her father, who worked in a factory making rubber earplugs for artillery crews, to take the food by on his way to the plant. When she had finished and had cleaned and put away the cooking things, it was nearly seven. The family lived in Koi, and she had a forty-five-minute trip to the tin works, in the section of town called Kannonmachi. She was in charge of the personnel records in the factory. She left Koi at seven, and as soon as she reached the plant, she went with some of the other girls from the personnel department to the factory auditorium. A prominent local Navy man, a former employee, had committed suicide the day before by throwing himself under a train—a death considered honorable enough to warrant a memorial service, which was to be held at the tin works at ten o'clock that morning. In the large hall, Miss Sasaki and the others made suitable preparations for the meeting. This work took about twenty minutes.

Miss Sasaki went back to her office and sat down at her desk. She was quite far from the windows, which were off to her left, and behind her were a couple of tall bookcases containing all the books of the factory library, which the personnel department had organized. She settled herself at her desk, put some things in a drawer, and shifted papers. She thought that before she began to make entries in her lists of new employees, discharges, and departures for the Army, she would chat for a moment with the girl at her right. Just as she turned her head away from the windows, the room was filled with a blinding light. She was paralyzed by fear, fixed still in her chair for a long moment (the plant was 1,600 yards from the center).

Everything fell, and Miss Sasaki lost consciousness. The ceiling dropped suddenly and the wooden floor above collapsed in splinters and the people up there came down and the roof above them gave way; but principally and first of all, the bookcases right behind her swooped forward and the contents threw her down, with her left leg horribly twisted and breaking underneath her. There, in the tin factory, in the first moment of the atomic age, a human being was crushed by books.

II · The Fire

IMMEDIATELY after the explosion, the Reverend Mr. Kiyoshi Tanimoto, having run wildly out of the Matsui estate and having looked in wonderment at the bloody soldiers at the mouth of the dugout they had been digging, attached himself sympathetically to an old lady who was walking along in a daze, holding her head with her left hand, supporting a small boy of three or four on her back with her right, and crying, "I'm hurt! I'm hurt! I'm hurt!" Mr. Tanimoto transferred the child to his own back and led the woman by the hand down the street, which was darkened by what seemed to be a local column of dust. He took the woman to a grammar school not far away that had previously been designated for use as a temporary hospital in case of emergency. By this solicitous behavior, Mr. Tanimoto at once got rid of his terror. At the school, he was much surprised to see glass all over the floor and fifty or sixty injured people already waiting to be treated. He reflected that, although the all-clear had sounded and he had heard no planes, several bombs must have been dropped. He thought of a hillock in the rayon man's garden from which he could get a view of the whole of Koi—of the whole of Hiroshima, for that matter —and he ran back up to the estate.

From the mound, Mr. Tanimoto saw an astonishing panorama. Not just a patch of Koi, as he had expected, but as much of Hiroshima as he could see through the clouded air was giving off a thick, dreadful miasma. Clumps of smoke, near and far, had begun to push up through the general dust. He wondered how such extensive damage could have been dealt out of a silent sky; even a few planes, far up, would have been audible. Houses nearby were burning, and when huge drops of water the size of marbles began to fall, he half thought that they must be coming from the hoses of firemen fighting the blazes. (They were actually drops of condensed moisture falling from the turbulent tower of dust, heat, and fission fragments that had already risen miles into the sky above Hiroshima.)

Mr. Tanimoto turned away from the sight when he heard Mr. Matsuo call out to ask whether he was all right. Mr. Matsuo had been safely cushioned within the falling house by the bedding stored in the front hall and had worked his way out. Mr. Tanimoto scarcely answered. He had thought of his wife and baby, his church, his home, his parishioners, all of them down in that awful murk. Once more he began to run in fear— toward the city.

Mrs. Hatsuyo Nakamura, the tailor's widow, having struggled up from under the ruins of her house after the explosion, and seeing Myeko, the youngest of her three children, buried breast-deep and unable to move, crawled across the debris, hauled at timbers, and flung tiles aside, in a hurried effort to free the child. Then, from what seemed to be caverns far below, she heard two small voices crying, "*Tasukete! Tasukete!* Help! Help!"

She called the names of her ten-year-old son and eight-year-old daughter: "Toshio! Yaeko!"

The voices from below answered.

Mrs. Nakamura abandoned Myeko, who at least could breathe, and in a frenzy made the wreckage fly above the crying voices. The children had been sleeping nearly ten feet apart, but now their voices seemed to come from the same place. Toshio, the boy, apparently had some freedom to move, because she could feel him undermining the pile of wood and tiles as she worked from above. At last she saw his head, and she hastily pulled him out by it. A mosquito net was wound intricately, as if it had been carefully wrapped, around his feet. He said he had been blown right across the room and had been on top of his sister Yaeko under the wreckage. She now said, from underneath, that she could not move, because there was something on her legs. With a bit more digging, Mrs. Nakamura cleared a hole above the child and began to pull her arm. "*Itai!* It hurts!" Yaeko cried. Mrs. Nakamura shouted, "There's no time now to say whether it hurts or not," and yanked her whimpering daughter up. Then she freed Myeko. The children were filthy and bruised, but none of them had a single cut or scratch.

Mrs. Nakamura took the children out into the street. They had nothing on but underpants, and although the day was very hot, she worried rather confusedly about their being cold, so she went back into the wreckage and burrowed underneath and found a bundle of clothes she had packed for an emergency, and she dressed them in pants, blouses, shoes, padded-cotton air-raid helmets called *bokuzuki*, and even, irrationally, overcoats. The children were silent, except for the five-year-old, Myeko, who kept asking questions: "Why is it night already? Why did our house fall down? What happened?" Mrs. Nakamura, who did not know what had happened (had not the all-clear sounded?), looked around and saw through the darkness that all the houses in her neighborhood had collapsed. The house next door, which its owner had been tearing down to make way for a fire lane, was now very thoroughly, if crudely, torn down; its owner, who had been sacrificing his home for the community's safety, lay dead. Mrs. Nakamoto, wife of the head of the local air-raid-defense Neighborhood Association, came across the street with her head all bloody, and said that

263

her baby was badly cut; did Mrs. Nakamura have any bandage?
Mrs. Nakamura did not, but she crawled into the remains of
her house again and pulled out some white cloth that she had
been using in her work as a seamstress, ripped it into strips,
and gave it to Mrs. Nakamoto. While fetching the cloth, she
noticed her sewing machine; she went back in for it and dragged
it out. Obviously, she could not carry it with her, so she un-
thinkingly plunged her symbol of livelihood into the receptacle
which for weeks had been her symbol of safety—the cement
tank of water in front of her house, of the type every household
had been ordered to construct against a possible fire raid.

A nervous neighbor, Mrs. Hataya, called to Mrs. Nakamura to
run away with her to the woods in Asano Park—an estate, by
the Kyo River not far off, belonging to the wealthy Asano
family, who once owned the Toyo Kisen Kaisha steamship line.
The park had been designated as an evacuation area for their
neighborhood. Seeing fire breaking out in a nearby ruin (except
at the very center, where the bomb itself ignited some fires,
most of Hiroshima's citywide conflagration was caused by in-
flammable wreckage falling on cookstoves and live wires), Mrs.
Nakamura suggested going over to fight it. Mrs. Hataya said,
"Don't be foolish. What if planes come and drop more bombs?"
So Mrs. Nakamura started out for Asano Park with her children and Mrs. Hataya, and she carried her rucksack of emergency clothing, a blanket, an umbrella, and a suitcase of things
she had cached in her air-raid shelter. Under many ruins, as
they hurried along, they heard muffled screams for help. The
only building they saw standing on their way to Asano Park
was the Jesuit mission house, alongside the Catholic kindergarten to which Mrs. Nakamura had sent Myeko for a time. As
they passed it, she saw Father Kleinsorge, in bloody underwear,
running out of the house with a small suitcase in his hand.

Right after the explosion, while Father Wilhelm Kleinsorge, S.J., was wandering around in his underwear in the vegetable garden, Father Superior LaSalle came around the corner of the building in the darkness. His body, especially his back, was bloody; the flash had made him twist away from his window, and tiny pieces of glass had flown at him. Father Kleinsorge, still bewildered, managed to ask, "Where are the rest?" Just then, the two other priests living in the mission house appeared —Father Cieslik, unhurt, supporting Father Schiffer, who was covered with blood that spurted from a cut above his left ear and who was very pale. Father Cieslik was rather pleased with himself, for after the flash he had dived into a doorway, which he had previously reckoned to be the safest place inside the building, and when the blast came, he was not injured. Father LaSalle told Father Cieslik to take Father Schiffer to a doctor before he bled to death, and suggested either Dr. Kanda, who lived on the next corner, or Dr. Fujii, about six blocks away. The two men went out of the compound and up the street.

The daughter of Mr. Hoshijima, the mission catechist, ran up to Father Kleinsorge and said that her mother and sister were buried under the ruins of their house, which was at the back of the Jesuit compound, and at the same time the priests noticed that the house of the Catholic-kindergarten teacher at the front of the compound had collapsed on her. While Father LaSalle and Mrs. Murata, the mission housekeeper, dug the teacher out, Father Kleinsorge went to the catechist's fallen house and began lifting things off the top of the pile. There was not a sound underneath; he was sure the Hoshijima women had been killed. At last, under what had been a corner of the kitchen, he saw Mrs. Hoshijima's head. Believing her dead, he began to haul her out by the hair, but suddenly she screamed, "Itai! Itai! It hurts! It hurts!" He dug some more and lifted her out. He managed, too, to find her daughter in the rubble and free her. Neither was badly hurt.

A public bath next door to the mission house had caught fire, but since there the wind was southerly, the priests thought their house would be spared. Nevertheless, as a precaution, Father Kleinsorge went inside to fetch some things he wanted to save. He found his room in a state of weird and illogical confusion. A first-aid kit was hanging undisturbed on a hook on the wall, but his clothes, which had been on other hooks nearby, were nowhere to be seen. His desk was in splinters all over the room, but a mere papier-mâché suitcase, which he had hidden under the desk, stood handle-side up, without a scratch on it, in the doorway of the room, where he could not miss it. Father Kleinsorge later came to regard this as a bit of Providential interference, inasmuch as the suitcase contained his breviary, the account books for the whole diocese, and a considerable amount of paper money belonging to the mission, for which he was responsible. He ran out of the house and deposited the suitcase in the mission air-raid shelter.

At about this time, Father Cieslik and Father Schiffer, who was still spurting blood, came back and said that Dr. Kanda's house was ruined and that fire blocked them from getting out of what they supposed to be the local circle of destruction to Dr. Fujii's private hospital, on the bank of the Kyo River.

Dr. Masakazu Fujii's hospital was no longer on the bank of the Kyo River; it was in the river. After the overturn, Dr. Fujii was so stupefied and so tightly squeezed by the beams gripping his chest that he was unable to move at first, and he hung there about twenty minutes in the darkened morning. Then a thought which came to him—that soon the tide would be running in through the estuaries and his head would be submerged

—inspired him to fearful activity; he wriggled and turned and exerted what strength he could (though his left arm, because of the pain in his shoulder, was useless), and before long he had freed himself from the vise. After a few moments' rest, he climbed onto the pile of timbers and, finding a long one that slanted up to the river-bank, he painfully shinnied up it.

Dr. Fujii, who was in his underwear, was now soaking and dirty. His undershirt was torn, and blood ran down it from bad cuts on his chin and back. In this disarray, he walked out onto Kyo Bridge, beside which his hospital had stood. The bridge had not collapsed. He could see only fuzzily without his glasses, but he could see enough to be amazed at the number of houses that were down all around. On the bridge, he encountered a friend, a doctor named Machii, and asked in bewilderment, "What do you think it was?"

Dr. Machii said, "It must have been a *Molotoffano hanakago*" —a Molotov flower basket, the delicate Japanese name for the "bread basket," or self-scattering cluster of bombs.

At first, Dr. Fujii could see only two fires, one across the river from his hospital site and one quite far to the south. But at the same time, he and his friend observed something that puzzled them, and which, as doctors, they discussed: although there were as yet very few fires, wounded people were hurrying across the bridge in an endless parade of misery, and many of them exhibited terrible burns on their faces and arms. "Why do you suppose it is?" Dr. Fujii asked. Even a theory was comforting that day, and Dr. Machii stuck to his. "Perhaps because it was a Molotov flower basket," he said.

There had been no breeze earlier in the morning when Dr. Fujii had walked to the railway station to see his friend off, but now brisk winds were blowing every which way; here on the bridge the wind was easterly. New fires were leaping up, and they spread quickly, and in a very short time terrible blasts of hot air and showers of cinders made it impossible to stand on the bridge any more. Dr. Machii ran to the far side of the river and along a still unkindled street. Dr. Fujii went down into the water under the bridge, where a score of people had already taken refuge, among them his servants, who had extricated themselves from the wreckage. From there, Dr. Fujii saw a nurse hanging in the timbers of his hospital by her legs, and then another painfully pinned across the breast. He enlisted the help of some of the others under the bridge and freed both of them. He thought he heard the voice of his niece for a moment, but he could not find her; he never saw her again. Four of his nurses and the two patients in the hospital died, too. Dr. Fujii went back into the water of the river and waited for the fire to subside.

The lot of Drs. Fujii, Kanda, and Machii right after the explosion—and, as these three were typical, that of the majority of the physicians and surgeons of Hiroshima—with their offices and hospitals destroyed, their equipment scattered, their own bodies incapacitated in varying degrees, explained why so many citizens who were hurt went untended and why so many who might have lived died. Of a hundred and fifty doctors in the city, sixty-five were already dead and most of the rest were wounded. Of 1,780 nurses, 1,654 were dead or too badly hurt to work. In the biggest hospital, that of the Red Cross, only six doctors out of thirty were able to function, and only ten nurses out of more than two hundred. The sole uninjured doctor on the Red Cross Hospital staff was Dr. Sasaki. After the explosion, he hurried to a storeroom to fetch bandages. This room, like everything he had seen as he ran through the hospital, was chaotic—bottles of medicines thrown off shelves and broken, salves spattered on the walls, instruments strewn everywhere. He grabbed up some bandages and an unbroken bottle of mercurochrome, hurried back to the chief surgeon, and bandaged his cuts. Then he went out into the corridor and began patching up the wounded patients and the doctors and nurses there. He blundered so without his glasses that he took a pair off the face of a wounded nurse, and although they only approximately compensated for the errors of his vision, they were better than nothing. (He was to depend on them for more than a month.)

Dr. Sasaki worked without method, taking those who were nearest him first, and he noticed soon that the corridor seemed to be getting more and more crowded. Mixed in with the abrasions and lacerations which most people in the hospital had suffered, he began to find dreadful burns. He realized that casualties were pouring in from outdoors. There were so many that he began to pass up the lightly wounded; he decided that all he could hope to do was to stop people from bleeding to death. Before long, patients lay and crouched on the floors of the wards and the laboratories and all the other rooms, and in the corridors, and on the stairs, and in the front hall, and under the porte-cochère, and on the stone front steps, and in the driveway and courtyard, and for blocks each way in the streets outside. Wounded people supported maimed people; disfigured families leaned together. Many people were vomiting. A tremendous number of schoolgirls—some of those who had been taken from their classrooms to work outdoors, clearing fire lanes —crept into the hospital. In a city of two hundred and forty-five thousand, nearly a hundred thousand people had been killed or doomed at one blow; a hundred thousand more were hurt. At least ten thousand of the wounded make their way to the best hospital in town, which was altogether unequal to such a trampling, since it had only six hundred beds, and they had all been occupied. The people in the suffocating crowd inside the hospital wept and cried, for Dr. Sasaki to hear, "Sensei! Doctor!," and the less seriously wounded came and pulled at his sleeve and begged him to go to the aid of the worse wounded. Tugged here and there in his stockinged feet, bewildered by the numbers, staggered by so much raw flesh, Dr. Sasaki lost all sense of profession and stopped working as a skillful surgeon and a sympathetic man; he became an automaton, mechanically wiping, daubing, winding, wiping, daubing, winding.

Some of the wounded in Hiroshima were unable to enjoy the questionable luxury of hospitalization. In what had been the personnel office of the East Asia Tin Works, Miss Sasaki lay doubled over, unconscious, under the tremendous pile of books and plaster and wood and corrugated iron. She was wholly unconscious (she later estimated) for about three hours. Her first sensation was of dreadful pain in her left leg. It was so black under the books and debris that the borderline between awareness and unconsciousness was fine; she apparently crossed it several times, for the pain seemed to come and go. At the moments when it was sharpest, she felt that her leg had been cut off somewhere below the knee. Later, she heard someone walking on top of the wreckage above her, and anguished voices spoke up, evidently from within the mess around her: "Please help! Get us out!"

Father Kleinsorge stemmed Father Schiffer's spurting cut as well as he could with some bandage that Dr. Fujii had given the priests a few days before. When he finished, he ran into the mission house again and found the jacket of his military uniform and an old pair of gray trousers. He put them on and went outside. A woman from next door ran up to him and shouted that her husband was buried under her house and the house was on fire; Father Kleinsorge must come and save him.

Father Kleinsorge, already growing apathetic and dazed in the presence of the cumulative distress, said, "We haven't much time." Houses all around were burning, and the wind was now blowing hard. "Do you know exactly which part of the house he is under?" he asked.

"Yes, yes," she said. "Come quickly."

They went around to the house, the remains of which blazed violently, but when they got there, it turned out that the woman had no idea where her husband was. Father Kleinsorge shouted several times, "Is anyone there?" There was no answer. Father Kleinsorge said to the woman, "We must get away or we will all die." He went back to the Catholic compound and told the Father Superior that the fire was coming closer on the wind, which had swung around and was now from the north; it was time for everybody to go.

Just then, the kindergarten teacher pointed out to the priests Mr. Fukai, the secretary of the diocese, who was standing in his window on the second floor of the mission house, facing in the direction of the explosion, weeping. Father Cieslik, because he thought the stairs unusable, ran around to the back of the mission house to look for a ladder. There he heard people crying for help under a nearby fallen roof. He called to passers-by running away in the street to help him lift it, but nobody paid any attention, and he had to leave the buried ones to die. Father Kleinsorge ran inside the mission house and scrambled up the stairs, which were awry and piled with plaster and lathing, and called to Mr. Fukai from the doorway of his room.

Mr. Fukai, a very short man of about fifty, turned around slowly, with a queer look, and said, "Leave me here."

Father Kleinsorge went into the room and took Mr. Fukai by the collar of his coat and said, "Come with me or you'll die."

Mr. Fukai said, "Leave me here to die."

Father Kleinsorge began to shove and haul Mr. Fukai out of

271

the room. Then the theological student came up and grabbed Mr. Fukai's feet, and Father Kleinsorge took his shoulders, and together they carried him downstairs and outdoors. "I can't walk!" Mr. Fukai cried. "Leave me here!" Father Kleinsorge got his paper suitcase with the money in it and took Mr. Fukai up pickaback, and the party started for the East Parade Ground, their district's "safe area." As they went out of the gate, Mr. Fukai, quite childlike now, beat on Father Kleinsorge's shoulders and said, "I won't leave. I won't leave." Irrelevantly, Father Kleinsorge turned to Father LaSalle and said, "We have lost all our possessions but not our sense of humor."

The street was cluttered with parts of houses that had slid into it, and with fallen telephone poles and wires. From every second or third house came the voices of people buried and abandoned, who invariably screamed, with formal politeness, *"Tasukete kure!* Help, if you please!" The priests recognized several ruins from which these cries came as the homes of friends, but because of the fire it was too late to help. All the way, Mr. Fukai whimpered, "Let me stay." The party turned right when they came to a block of fallen houses that was one flame. At Sakai Bridge, which would take them across to the East Parade Ground, they saw that the whole community on the opposite side of the river was a sheet of fire; they dared not cross and decided to take refuge in Asano Park, off to their left. Father Kleinsorge, who had been weakened for a couple of days by his bad case of diarrhea, began to stagger under his protesting burden, and as he tried to climb up over the wreckage of several houses that blocked their way to the park, he stumbled, dropped Mr. Fukai, and plunged down, head over heels, to the edge of the river. When he picked himself up, he saw Mr. Fukai running away. Father Kleinsorge shouted to a dozen soldiers, who were standing by the bridge, to stop him. As Father Kleinsorge started back to get Mr. Fukai, Father La-Salle called out, "Hurry! Don't waste time!" So Father Kleinsorge just requested the soldiers to take care of Mr. Fukai. They said they would, but the little, broken man got away from them, and the last the priests could see of him, he was running back toward the fire.

M r. Tanimoto, fearful for his family and church, at first ran toward them by the shortest route, along Koi Highway. He was the only person making his way into the city; he met hundreds and hundreds who were fleeing, and every one of them seemed to be hurt in some way. The eyebrows of some were burned off and skin hung from their faces and hands. Others, because of pain, held their arms up as if carrying something in both hands. Some were vomiting as they walked. Many were naked or in shreds of clothing. On some undressed bodies, the burns had made patterns—of undershirt straps and suspenders and, on the skin of some women (since white repelled the heat from the bomb and dark clothes absorbed it and conducted it to the skin), the shapes of flowers they had had on their kimonos. Many, although injured themselves, supported relatives who were worse off. Almost all had their heads bowed, looked straight ahead, were silent, and showed no expression whatever.

After crossing Koi Bridge and Kannon Bridge, having run the whole way, Mr. Tanimoto saw, as he approached the center, that all the houses had been crushed and many were afire. Here the trees were bare and their trunks were charred. He tried at several points to penetrate the ruins, but the flames always stopped him. Under many houses, people screamed for help, but no one helped; in general, survivors that day assisted only their relatives or immediate neighbors, for they could not comprehend or tolerate a wider circle of misery. The wounded limped past the screams, and Mr. Tanimoto ran past them. As a Christian he was filled with compassion for those who were trapped, and as a Japanese he was overwhelmed by the shame of being unhurt, and he prayed as he ran, "God help them and take them out of the fire."

He thought he would skirt the fire, to the left. He ran back to Kannon Bridge and followed for a distance one of the rivers. He tried several cross streets, but all were blocked, so he turned far left and ran out to Yokogawa, a station on a railroad line that detoured the city in a wide semicircle, and he followed the rails until he came to a burning train. So impressed was he by this time by the extent of the damage that he ran north two miles to Gion, a suburb in the foothills. All the way, he overtook dreadfully burned and lacerated people, and in his guilt he turned to right and left as he hurried and said to some of them, "Excuse me for having no burden like yours." Near Gion, he began to meet country people going toward the city to help, and when they saw him, several exclaimed, "Look! There is one who is not wounded." At Gion, he bore toward the right bank of the main river, the Ota, and ran down it until he reached fire again. There was no fire on the other side of the river, so he threw off his shirt and shoes and plunged into it. In midstream, where the current was fairly strong, exhaustion and fear finally caught up with him—he had run nearly seven miles—and he became limp and drifted in the water. He prayed, "Please, God, help me to cross. It would be nonsense for me to be drowned when I am the only uninjured one." He managed a few more strokes and fetched up on a spit downstream.

Mr. Tanimoto climbed up the bank and ran along it until, near a large Shinto shrine, he came to more fire, and as he turned left to get around it, he met, by incredible luck, his wife. She was carrying their infant son. Mr. Tanimoto was now so emotionally worn out that nothing could surprise him. He did not embrace his wife; he simply said, "Oh, you are safe." She told him that she had got home from her night in Ushida just in time for the explosion; she had been buried under the parsonage with the baby in her arms. She told how the wreckage had pressed down on her, how the baby had cried. She saw a chink of light, and by reaching up with a hand, she worked the hole bigger, bit by bit. After about half an hour, she heard the crackling noise of wood burning. At last the opening was big enough for her to push the baby out, and afterward she crawled out herself. She said she was now going out to Ushida again. Mr. Tanimoto said he wanted to see his church and take care of the people of his Neighborhood Association. They parted as casually—as bewildered—as they had met.

Mr. Tanimoto's way around the fire took him across the East Parade Ground, which, being an evacuation area, was now the scene of a gruesome review: rank on rank of the burned and bleeding. Those who were burned moaned, *"Mizu, mizu!* Water, water!" Mr. Tanimoto found a basin in a nearby street and located a water tap that still worked in the crushed shell of a house, and he began carrying water to the suffering strangers. When he had given drink to about thirty of them, he realized he was taking too much time. "Excuse me," he said loudly to those nearby who were reaching out their hands to him and crying their thirst. "I have many people to take care of." Then he ran away. He went to the river again, the basin in his hand, and jumped down onto a sandspit. There he saw hundreds of people so badly wounded that they could not get up to go farther from the burning city. When they saw a man erect and unhurt, the chant began again: *"Mizu, mizu, mizu."* Mr. Tanimoto could not resist them; he carried them water from the river—a mistake, since it was tidal and brackish. Two or three small boats were ferrying hurt people across the river from Asano Park, and when one touched the spit, Mr. Tanimoto again made his loud, apologetic speech and jumped into the boat. It took him across to the park. There, in the underbrush, he found some of his charges of the Neighborhood Association, who had come there by his previous instructions, and saw many acquaintances, among them Father Kleinsorge and the other Catholics. But he missed Fukai, who had been a close friend. "Where is Fukai-*san?*" he asked.

"He didn't want to come with us," Father Kleinsorge said. "He ran back."

When Miss Sasaki heard the voices of the people caught along with her in the dilapidation at the tin factory, she began speaking to them. Her nearest neighbor, she discovered, was a high-school girl who had been drafted for factory work, and who said her back was broken. Miss Sasaki replied, "I am lying here and I can't move. My left leg is cut off."

Some time later, she again heard somebody walk overhead and then move off to one side, and whoever it was began burrowing. The digger released several people, and when he had uncovered the high-school girl, she found that her back was not broken, after all, and she crawled out. Miss Sasaki spoke to the rescuer, and he worked toward her. He pulled away a great number of books, until he had made a tunnel to her. She could see his perspiring face as he said, "Come out, Miss." She tried. "I can't move," she said. The man excavated some more and told her to try with all her strength to get out. But books were heavy on her hips, and the man finally saw that a bookcase was leaning on the books and that a heavy beam pressed down on the bookcase. "Wait," he said. "I'll get a crowbar."

The man was gone a long time, and when he came back, he was ill-tempered, as if her plight were all her fault. "We have no men to help you!" he shouted in through the tunnel. "You'll have to get out by yourself."

"That's impossible," she said. "My left leg . . ." The man went away.

Much later, several men came and dragged Miss Sasaki out. Her left leg was not severed, but it was badly broken and cut and it hung askew below the knee. They took her out into a courtyard. It was raining. She sat on the ground in the rain. When the downpour increased, someone directed all the wounded people to take cover in the factory's air-raid shelters. "Come along," a torn-up woman said to her. "You can hop." But Miss Sasaki could not move, and she just waited in the rain. Then a man propped up a large sheet of corrugated iron as a kind of lean-to, and took her in his arms and carried her to it. She was grateful until he brought two horribly wounded people—a woman with a whole breast sheared off and a man whose face was all raw from a burn—to share the simple shed with her. No one came back. The rain cleared and the cloudy afternoon was hot; before nightfall the three grotesques under the slanting piece of twisted iron began to smell quite bad.

The former head of the Nobori-cho Neighborhood Association to which the Catholic priests belonged was an energetic man named Yoshida. He had boasted, when he was in charge of the district air-raid defenses, that fire might eat away all of Hiroshima but it would never come to Nobori-cho. The bomb blew down his house, and a joist pinned him by the legs, in full view of the Jesuit mission house across the way and of the people hurrying along the street. In their confusion as they hurried past, Mrs. Nakamura, with her children, and Father Kleinsorge, with Mr. Fukai on his back, hardly saw him; he was just part of the general blur of misery through which they moved. His cries for help brought no response from them; there were so many people shouting for help that they could not hear him separately. They and all the others went along. Nobori-cho became absolutely deserted, and the fire swept through it. Mr.

Yoshida saw the wooden mission house—the only erect building in the area—go up in a lick of flame, and the heat was
terrific on his face. Then flames came along his side of the
street and entered his house. In a paroxysm of terrified strength,
he freed himself and ran down the alleys of Nobori-cho,
hemmed in by the fire he had said would never come. He began at once to behave like an old man; two months later his
hair was white.

As Dr. Fujii stood in the river up to his neck to avoid the
heat of the fire, the wind blew stronger and stronger, and soon,
even though the expanse of water was small, the waves grew so
high that the people under the bridge could no longer keep
their footing. Dr. Fujii went close to the shore, crouched down,
and embraced a large stone with his usable arm. Later it became possible to wade along the very edge of the river, and
Dr. Fujii and his two surviving nurses moved about two hundred yards upstream, to a sandspit near Asano Park. Many
wounded were lying on the sand. Dr. Machii was there with
his family; his daughter, who had been outdoors when the
bomb burst, was badly burned on her hands and legs but fortunately not on her face. Although Dr. Fujii's shoulder was by
now terribly painful, he examined the girl's burns curiously.
Then he lay down. In spite of the misery all around, he was
ashamed of his appearance, and he remarked to Dr. Machii that
he looked like a beggar, dressed as he was in nothing but torn
and bloody underwear. Later in the afternoon, when the fire
began to subside, he decided to go to his parental house, in
the suburb of Nagatsuka. He asked Dr. Machii to join him, but
the Doctor answered that he and his family were going to spend
the night on the spit, because of his daughter's injuries. Dr.
Fujii, together with his nurses, walked first to Ushida, where, in

the partially damaged house of some relatives, he found first-aid materials he had stored there. The two nurses bandaged him and he them. They went on. Now not many people walked in the streets, but a great number sat and lay on the pavement, vomited, waited for death, and died. The number of corpses on the way to Nagatsuka was more and more puzzling. The Doctor wondered: Could a Molotov flower basket have done all this?

Dr. Fujii reached his family's house in the evening. It was five miles from the center of town, but its roof had fallen in and the windows were all broken.

All day, people poured into Asano Park. This private estate was far enough away from the explosion so that its bamboos, pines, laurel, and maples were still alive, and the green place invited refugees—partly because they believed that if the Americans came back, they would bomb only buildings; partly because the foliage seemed a center of coolness and life, and the estate's exquisitely precise rock gardens, with their quiet pools and arching bridges, were very Japanese, normal, secure; and also partly (according to some who were there) because of an irresistible, atavistic urge to hide under leaves. Mrs. Nakamura and her children were among the first to arrive, and they settled in the bamboo grove near the river. They all felt terribly thirsty, and they drank from the river. At once they were nauseated and began vomiting, and they retched the whole day. Others were also nauseated; they all thought (probably because of the strong odor of ionization, an "electric smell" given off by the bomb's fission) that they were sick from a gas the Americans had dropped. When Father Kleinsorge and the other priests came into the park, nodding to their friends as they passed, the Nakamuras were all sick and prostrate. A woman named Iwasaki, who lived in the neighborhood of the mission and who was sitting near the Nakamuras, got up and asked the priests if she should stay where she was or go with them. Father Kleinsorge said, "I hardly know where the safest place is." She stayed there, and later in the day, though she had no visible wounds or burns, she died. The priests went farther along the river and settled down in some underbrush. Father LaSalle lay down and went right to sleep. The theological student, who was wearing slippers, had carried with him a bundle of clothes, in which he had packed two pairs of leather shoes. When he sat down with the others, he found that the bundle had broken open and a couple of shoes had fallen out and now he had only two lefts. He retraced his steps and found one right. When he rejoined the priests, he said, "It's funny, but things don't matter any more. Yesterday, my shoes were my most important possessions. Today, I don't care. One pair is enough."

Father Cieslik said, "I know. I started to bring my books along, and then I thought, 'This is no time for books.' "

When Mr. Tanimoto, with his basin still in his hand, reached the park, it was very crowded, and to distinguish the living from the dead was not easy, for most of the people lay still, with their eyes open. To Father Kleinsorge, an Occidental, the silence in the grove by the river, where hundreds of gruesomely wounded suffered together, was one of the most dreadful and awesome phenomena of his whole experience. The hurt ones were quiet; no one wept, much less screamed in pain; no one complained; none of the many who died did so noisily; not even the children cried; very few people even spoke. And when Father Kleinsorge gave water to some whose faces had been almost blotted out by flash burns, they took their share and then raised themselves a little and bowed to him, in thanks.

Mr. Tanimoto greeted the priests and then looked around for other friends. He saw Mrs. Matsumoto, wife of the director of the Methodist School, and asked her if she was thirsty. She was, so he went to one of the pools in the Asanos' rock gardens and got water for her in his basin. Then he decided to try to get back to his church. He went into Nobori-cho by the way the priests had taken as they escaped, but he did not get far; the fire along the streets was so fierce that he had to turn back. He walked to the riverbank and began to look for a boat in which he might carry some of the most severely injured across the river from Asano Park and away from the spreading fire. Soon he found a good-sized pleasure punt drawn up on the bank, but in and around it was an awful tableau—five dead men, nearly naked, badly burned, who must have expired more or less all at once, for they were in attitudes which suggested that they had been working together to push the boat down into the river. Mr. Tanimoto lifted them away from the boat, and as he did so, he experienced such horror at disturbing the dead—preventing them, he momentarily felt, from launching their craft and going on their ghostly way—that he said out loud, "Please forgive me for taking this boat. I must use it for others, who are alive." The punt was heavy, but he managed to slide it into the water. There were no oars, and all he could find for propulsion was a thick bamboo pole. He worked the boat upstream to the most crowded part of the park and began to ferry the wounded. He could pack ten or twelve into the boat for each crossing, but as the river was too deep in the center to pole his way across, he had to paddle with the bamboo, and consequently each trip took a very long time. He worked several hours that way.

Early in the afternoon, the fire swept into the woods of Asano Park. The first Mr. Tanimoto knew of it was when, returning in his boat, he saw that a great number of people had moved toward the riverside. On touching the bank, he went up to investigate, and when he saw the fire, he shouted, "All the young men who are not badly hurt come with me!" Father Kleinsorge moved Father Schiffer and Father LaSalle close to the edge of the river and asked people there to get them across if the fire came too near, and then joined Tanimoto's volunteers. Mr. Tanimoto sent some to look for buckets and basins and told others to beat the burning underbrush with their clothes; when utensils were at hand, he formed a bucket chain from one of the pools in the rock gardens. The team fought the fire for more than two hours, and gradually defeated the flames. As Mr. Tanimoto's men worked, the frightened people in the park pressed closer and closer to the river, and finally the mob began to force some of the unfortunates who were on the very bank into the water. Among those driven into the river and drowned were Mrs. Matsumoto, of the Methodist School, and her daughter.

When Father Kleinsorge got back after fighting the fire, he found Father Schiffer still bleeding and terribly pale. Some Japanese stood around and stared at him, and Father Schiffer whispered, with a weak smile, "It is as if I were already dead." "Not yet," Father Kleinsorge said. He had brought Dr. Fujii's first-aid kit with him, and he had noticed Dr. Kanda in the crowd, so he sought him out and asked him if he would dress Father Schiffer's bad cuts. Dr. Kanda had seen his wife and daughter dead in the ruins of his hospital; he sat now with his head in his hands. "I can't do anything," he said. Father Kleinsorge bound more bandage around Father Schiffer's head, moved him to a steep place, and settled him so that his head was high, and soon the bleeding diminished.

The roar of approaching planes was heard about this time. Someone in the crowd near the Nakamura family shouted, "It's some Grummans coming to strafe us!" A baker named Nakashima stood up and commanded, "Everyone who is wearing anything white, take it off." Mrs. Nakamura took the blouses off her children, and opened her umbrella and made them get under it. A great number of people, even badly burned ones, crawled into bushes and stayed there until the hum, evidently of a reconnaissance or weather run, died away.

It began to rain. Mrs. Nakamura kept her children under the umbrella. The drops grew abnormally large, and someone shouted, "The Americans are dropping gasoline. They're going to set fire to us!" (This alarm stemmed from one of the theories being passed through the park as to why so much of Hiroshima had burned: it was that a single plane had sprayed gasoline on the city and then somehow set fire to it in one flashing moment.) But the drops were palpably water, and as they fell, the wind grew stronger and stronger, and suddenly—probably because of the tremendous convection set up by the blazing city—a whirlwind ripped through the park. Huge trees crashed down; small ones were uprooted and flew into the air. Higher, a wild array of flat things revolved in the twisting funnel— pieces of iron roofing, papers, doors, strips of matting. Father Kleinsorge put a piece of cloth over Father Schiffer's eyes, so that the feeble man would not think he was going crazy. The gale blew Mrs. Murata, the mission housekeeper, who was sitting close by the river, down the embankment at a shallow rocky place, and she came out with her bare feet bloody. The vortex moved out onto the river, where it sucked up a waterspout and eventually spent itself.

After the storm, Mr. Tanimoto began ferrying people again, and Father Kleinsorge asked the theological student to go across and make his way out to the Jesuit Novitiate at Nagatsuka, about three miles from the center of town, and to request the priests there to come with help for Fathers Schiffer and LaSalle. The student got into Mr. Tanimoto's boat and went off with him. Father Kleinsorge asked Mrs. Nakamura if she would like to go out to Nagatsuka with the priests when they came. She said she had some luggage and her children were sick—they were still vomiting from time to time, and so, for that matter, was she—and therefore she feared she could not. He said he thought the fathers from the Novitiate could come back the next day with a pushcart to get her.

Late in the afternoon, when he went ashore for a while, Mr. Tanimoto, upon whose energy and initiative many had come to depend, heard people begging for food. He consulted Father Kleinsorge, and they decided to go back into town to get some rice from Mr. Tanimoto's Neighborhood Association shelter and from the mission shelter. Father Cieslik and two or three others went with them. At first, when they got among the rows of prostrate houses, they did not know where they were; the change was too sudden, from a busy city of two hundred and forty-five thousand that morning to a mere pattern of residue in the afternoon. The asphalt of the streets was still so soft and hot from the fires that walking was uncomfortable. They encountered only one person, a woman, who said to them as they passed, "My husband is in those ashes." At the mission, where Mr. Tanimoto left the party, Father Kleinsorge was dismayed to see the building razed. In the garden, on the way to the shelter, he noticed a pumpkin roasted on the vine. He and Father Cieslik tasted it and it was good. They were surprised at their hunger, and they ate quite a bit. They got out several bags of rice and gathered up several other cooked pumpkins and dug up some potatoes that were nicely baked under the ground, and started back. Mr. Tanimoto rejoined them on the way. One of the people with him had some cooking utensils. In the park, Mr. Tanimoto organized the lightly wounded women of his neighborhood to cook. Father Kleinsorge offered the Nakamura family some pumpkin, and they tried it, but they could not keep it on their stomachs. Altogether, the rice was enough to feed nearly a hundred people.

Just before dark, Mr. Tanimoto came across a twenty-year-old girl, Mrs. Kamai, the Tanimoto's next-door neighbor. She was crouching on the ground with the body of her infant daughter in her arms. The baby had evidently been dead all day. Mrs. Kamai jumped up when she saw Mr. Tanimoto and said, "Would you please try to locate my husband?"

Mr. Tanimoto knew that her husband had been inducted into the Army just the day before; he and Mrs. Tanimoto had entertained Mrs. Kamai in the afternoon, to make her forget. Kamai had reported to the Chugoku Regional Army Headquarters—near the ancient castle in the middle of town—where some four thousand troops were stationed. Judging by the many maimed soldiers Mr. Tanimoto had seen during the day, he surmised that the barracks had been badly damaged by whatever it was that had hit Hiroshima. He knew he hadn't a chance of finding Mrs. Kamai's husband, even if he searched, but he wanted to humor her. "I'll try," he said.

"You've got to find him," she said. "He loved our baby so much. I want him to see her once more."

III · Details Are Being Investigated

Early in the evening of the day the bomb exploded, a Japanese naval launch moved slowly up and down the seven rivers of Hiroshima. It stopped here and there to make an announcement—alongside the crowded sandspits, on which hundreds of wounded lay; at the bridges, on which others were crowded; and eventually, as twilight fell, opposite Asano Park. A young officer stood up in the launch and shouted through a megaphone, "Be patient! A naval hospital ship is coming to take care of you!" The sight of the shipshape launch against the background of the havoc across the river; the unruffled young man in his neat uniform; above all, the promise of medical help—the first word of possible succor anyone had heard in nearly twelve awful hours—cheered the people in the park tremendously. Mrs. Nakamura settled her family for the night with the assurance that a doctor would come and stop their retching. Mr. Tanimoto resumed ferrying the wounded across the river. Father Kleinsorge lay down and said the Lord's Prayer and a Hail Mary to himself, and fell right asleep; but no sooner had he dropped off than Mrs. Murata, the conscientious mission housekeeper, shook him and said, "Father Kleinsorge! Did you remember to repeat your evening prayers?" He answered rather grumpily, "Of course," and he tried to go back to sleep but could not. This, apparently, was just what Mrs. Murata wanted. She began to chat with the exhausted priest. One of the questions she raised was when he thought the priests from the Novitiate, for whom he had sent a messenger in midafternoon, would arrive to evacuate Father Superior LaSalle and Father Schiffer.

The messenger Father Kleinsorge had sent—the theological student who had been living at the mission house—had arrived at the Novitiate, in the hills about three miles out, at half past four. The sixteen priests there had been doing rescue work in the outskirts; they had worried about their colleagues in the city but had not known how or where to look for them. Now they hastily made two litters out of poles and boards, and the student led half a dozen of them back into the devastated area. They worked their way along the Ota above the city; twice the heat of the fire forced them into the river. At Misasa Bridge, they encountered a long line of soldiers making a bizarre forced march away from the Chugoku Regional Army Headquarters in the center of the town. All were grotesquely burned, and they supported themselves with staves or leaned on one another. Sick, burned horses, hanging their heads, stood on the bridge. When the rescue party reached the park, it was after dark, and progress was made extremely difficult by the tangle of fallen trees of all sizes that had been knocked down by the whirlwind that afternoon. At last—not long after Mrs. Murata asked her question—they reached their friends, and gave them wine and strong tea.

The priests discussed how to get Father Schiffer and Father LaSalle out to the Novitiate. They were afraid that blundering through the park with them would jar them too much on the

287

wooden litters, and that the wounded men would lose too much blood. Father Kleinsorge thought of Mr. Tanimoto and his boat, and called out to him on the river. When Mr. Tanimoto reached the bank, he said he would be glad to take the injured priests and their bearers upstream to where they could find a clear roadway. The rescuers put Father Schiffer onto one of the stretchers and lowered it into the boat, and two of them went aboard with it. Mr. Tanimoto, who still had no oars, poled the punt upstream.

About half an hour later, Mr. Tanimoto came back and excitedly asked the remaining priests to help him rescue two children he had seen standing up to their shoulders in the river. A group went out and picked them up—two young girls who had lost their family and were both badly burned. The priests stretched them on the ground next to Father Kleinsorge and then embarked Father LaSalle. Father Cieslik thought he could make it out to the Novitiate on foot, so he went aboard with the others. Father Kleinsorge was too feeble; he decided to wait in the park until the next day. He asked the men to come back with a handcart, so that they could take Mrs. Nakamura and her sick children to the Novitiate.

Mr. Tanimoto shoved off again. As the boatload of priests moved slowly upstream, they heard weak cries for help. A woman's voice stood out especially: "There are people here about to be drowned! Help us! The water is rising!" The sounds came from one of the sandspits, and those in the punt could see, in the reflected light of the still-burning fires, a number of wounded people lying at the edge of the river, already partly covered by the flooding tide. Mr. Tanimoto wanted to help them, but the priests were afraid that Father Schiffer would die if they didn't hurry, and they urged their ferryman along. He dropped them where he had put Father Schiffer down and then started back alone toward the sandspit.

The night was hot, and it seemed even hotter because of the fires against the sky, but the younger of the two girls Mr. Tanimoto and the priests had rescued complained to Father Kleinsorge that she was cold. He covered her with his jacket. She and her older sister had been in the salt water of the river for a couple of hours before being rescued. The younger one had huge, raw flash burns on her body; the salt water must have been excruciatingly painful to her. She began to shiver heavily, and again said it was cold. Father Kleinsorge borrowed a blanket from someone nearby and wrapped her up, but she shook more and more, and said again, "I am so cold," and then she suddenly stopped shivering and was dead.

Mr. Tanimoto found about twenty men and women on the sandspit. He drove the boat onto the bank and urged them to get aboard. They did not move and he realized that they were too weak to lift themselves. He reached down and took a woman by the hands, but her skin slipped off in huge, glove-like pieces. He was so sickened by this that he had to sit down for a moment. Then he got out into the water and, though a small man, lifted several of the men and women, who were naked, into his boat. Their backs and breasts were clammy, and he remembered uneasily what the great burns he had seen during the day had been like: yellow at first, then red and swollen, with the skin sloughed off, and finally, in the evening, suppurated and smelly. With the tide risen, his bamboo pole was now too short and he had to paddle most of the way across with it. On the other side, at a higher spit, he lifted the slimy living bodies out and carried them up the slope away from the tide. He had to keep consciously repeating to himself, "These are human beings." It took him three trips to get them all across the river. When he had finished, he decided he had to have a rest, and he went back to the park.

As Mr. Tanimoto stepped up the dark bank, he tripped over someone, and someone else said angrily, "Look out! That's my hand." Mr. Tanimoto, ashamed of hurting wounded people, embarrassed at being able to walk upright, suddenly thought of the naval hospital ship, which had not come (it never did), and he had for a moment a feeling of blind, murderous rage at the crew of the ship, and then at all doctors. Why didn't they come to help these people?

D̲r. Fujii lay in dreadful pain throughout the night on the floor of his family's roofless house on the edge of the city. By the light of a lantern, he had examined himself and found: left clavicle fractured; multiple abrasions and lacerations of face and body, including deep cuts on the chin, back, and legs; extensive contusions on chest and trunk; a couple of ribs possibly fractured. Had he not been so badly hurt, he might have been at Asano Park, assisting the wounded.

B̲y nightfall, ten thousand victims of the explosion had invaded the Red Cross Hospital, and Dr. Sasaki, worn out, was moving aimlessly and dully up and down the stinking corridors with wads of bandage and bottles of mercurochrome, still wearing the glasses he had taken from the wounded nurse, binding up the worst cuts as he came to them. Other doctors were putting compresses of saline solution on the worst burns. That was all they could do. After dark, they worked by the light of the city's fires and by candles the ten remaining nurses held for them. Dr. Sasaki had not looked outside the hospital all day; the scene inside was so terrible and so compelling that it had not occurred to him to ask any questions about what had happened beyond the windows and doors. Ceilings and partitions had fallen; plaster, dust, blood, and vomit were everywhere. Patients were dying by the hundreds, but there was nobody to carry away the corpses. Some of the hospital staff distributed biscuits and rice balls, but the charnel-house smell was so strong that few were hungry. By three o'clock the next morning, after nineteen straight hours of his gruesome work, Dr. Sasaki was incapable of dressing another wound. He and some other survivors of the hospital staff got straw mats and went outdoors— thousands of patients and hundreds of dead were in the yard and on the driveway—and hurried around behind the hospital and lay down in hiding to snatch some sleep. But within an hour wounded people had found them; a complaining circle formed around them: "Doctors! Help us! How can you sleep?" Dr. Sasaki got up again and went back to work. Early in the day, he thought for the first time of his mother, at their country home in Mukaihara, thirty miles from town. He usually went home every night. He was afraid she would think he was dead.

Near the spot upriver to which Mr. Tanimoto had transported the priests, there sat a large case of rice cakes which a rescue party had evidently brought for the wounded lying thereabouts but hadn't distributed. Before evacuating the wounded priests, the others passed the cakes around and helped themselves. A few minutes later, a band of soldiers came up, and an officer, hearing the priests speaking a foreign language, drew his sword and hysterically asked who they were. One of the priests calmed him down and explained that they were Germans—allies. The officer apologized and said that there were reports going around that American parachutists had landed.

The priests decided that they should take Father Schiffer

first. As they prepared to leave, Father Superior LaSalle said he felt awfully cold. One of the Jesuits gave up his coat, another his shirt; they were glad to wear less in the muggy night. The stretcher bearers started out. The theological student led the way and tried to warn the others of obstacles, but one of the priests got a foot tangled in some telephone wire and tripped and dropped his corner of the litter. Father Schiffer rolled off, lost consciousness, came to, and then vomited. The bearers picked him up and went on with him to the edge of the city, where they had arranged to meet a relay of other priests, left him with them, and turned back and got the Father Superior.

The wooden litter must have been terribly painful for Father LaSalle, in whose back scores of tiny particles of window glass were embedded. Near the edge of town, the group had to walk around an automobile burned and squatting on the narrow road, and the bearers on one side, unable to see their way in the darkness, fell into a deep ditch. Father LaSalle was thrown onto the ground and the litter broke in two. One priest went ahead to get a handcart from the Novitiate, but he soon found one beside an empty house and wheeled it back. The priests lifted Father LaSalle into the cart and pushed him over the bumpy road the rest of the way. The rector of the Novitiate, who had been a doctor before he entered the religious order, cleaned the wounds of the two priests and put them to bed between clean sheets, and they thanked God for the care they had received.

Thousands of people had nobody to help them. Miss Sasaki was one of them. Abandoned and helpless, under the crude lean-to in the courtyard of the tin factory, beside the woman who had lost a breast and the man whose burned face was scarcely a face any more, she suffered awfully that night from the pain in her broken leg. She did not sleep at all; neither did she converse with her sleepless companions.

In the park, Mrs. Murata kept Father Kleinsorge awake all night by talking to him. None of the Nakamura family were able to sleep, either; the children, in spite of being very sick, were interested in everything that happened. They were delighted when one of the city's gas-storage tanks went up in a tremendous burst of flame. Toshio, the boy, shouted to the others to look at the reflection in the river. Mr. Tanimoto, after his long run and his many hours of rescue work, dozed uneasily. When he awoke, in the first light of dawn, he looked across the river and saw that he had not carried the festered, limp bodies high enough on the sandspit the night before. The tide had risen above where he had put them; they had not had the strength to move; they must have drowned. He saw a number of bodies floating in the river.

Early that day, August 7th, the Japanese radio broadcast for the first time a succinct announcement that very few, if any, of the people most concerned with its content, the survivors in Hiroshima, happened to hear: "Hiroshima suffered considerable damage as the result of an attack by a few B-29s. It is believed that a new type of bomb was used. The details are being investigated." Nor is it probable that any of the survivors happened to be tuned in on a short-wave rebroadcast of an extraordinary announcement by the President of the United States, which identified the new bomb as atomic: "That bomb had more power than twenty thousand tons of TNT. It had more than two thousand times the blast power of the British

Grand Slam, which is the largest bomb ever yet used in the history of warfare." Those victims who were able to worry at all about what had happened thought of it and discussed it in more primitive, childish terms—gasoline sprinkled from an airplane, maybe, or some combustible gas, or a big cluster of incendiaries, or the work of parachutists; but, even if they had known the truth, most of them were too busy or too weary or too badly hurt to care that they were the objects of the first great experiment in the use of atomic power, which (as the voices on the short wave shouted) no country except the United States, with its industrial know-how, its willingness to throw two billion gold dollars into an important wartime gamble, could possibly have developed.

Mr. Tanimoto was still angry at doctors. He decided that he would personally bring one to Asano Park—by the scruff of the neck, if necessary. He crossed the river, went past the Shinto shrine where he had met his wife for a brief moment the day before, and walked to the East Parade Ground. Since this had long before been designated as an evacuation area, he thought he would find an aid station there. He did find one, operated by an Army medical unit, but he also saw that its doctors were hopelessly overburdened, with thousands of patients sprawled among corpses across the field in front of it. Nevertheless, he went up to one of the Army doctors and said, as reproachfully as he could, "Why have you not come to Asano Park? You are badly needed there."

Without even looking up from his work, the doctor said in a tired voice, "This is my station."

"But there are many dying on the riverbank over there."

"The first duty," the doctor said, "is to take care of the slightly wounded."

"Why—when there are many who are heavily wounded on the riverbank?"

The doctor moved to another patient. "In an emergency like this," he said, as if he were reciting from a manual, "the first task is to help as many as possible—to save as many lives as possible. There is no hope for the heavily wounded. They will die. We can't bother with them."

"That may be right from a medical standpoint—" Mr. Tanimoto began, but then he looked out across the field, where the many dead lay close and intimate with those who were still living, and he turned away without finishing his sentence, angry now with himself. He didn't know what to do; he had promised some of the dying people in the park that he would bring them medical aid. They might die feeling cheated. He saw a ration stand at one side of the field, and he went to it and begged some rice cakes and biscuits, and he took them back, in lieu of doctors, to the people in the park.

The morning, again, was hot. Father Kleinsorge went to fetch water for the wounded in a bottle and a teapot he had borrowed. He had heard that it was possible to get fresh tap water outside Asano Park. Going through the rock gardens, he had to climb over and crawl under the trunks of fallen pine trees; he found he was weak. There were many dead in the gardens. At a beautiful moon bridge, he passed a naked, living woman who seemed to have been burned from head to toe and was red all over. Near the entrance to the park, an Army doctor was working, but the only medicine he had was iodine, which he painted over cuts, bruises, slimy burns, everything—and by now everything that he painted had pus on it. Outside the gate of the park, Father Kleinsorge found a faucet that still worked —part of the plumbing of a vanished house—and he filled his vessels and returned. When he had given the wounded the water, he made a second trip. This time, the woman by the bridge was dead. On his way back with the water, he got lost on a detour around a fallen tree, and as he looked for his way through the woods, he heard a voice ask from the underbrush, "Have you anything to drink?" He saw a uniform. Thinking there was just one soldier, he approached with the water. When he had penetrated the bushes, he saw there were about twenty men, and they were all in exactly the same nightmarish state: their faces were wholly burned, their eyesockets were hollow, the fluid from their melted eyes had run down their cheeks. (They must have had their faces upturned when the bomb went off; perhaps they were anti-aircraft personnel.) Their mouths were mere swollen, pus-covered wounds, which they could not bear to stretch enough to admit the spout of the teapot. So Father Kleinsorge got a large piece of grass and drew out the stem so as to make a straw, and gave them all water to drink that way. One of them said, "I can't see anything." Father Kleinsorge answered, as cheerfully as he could, "There's a doctor at the entrance to the park. He's busy now, but he'll come soon and fix your eyes, I hope."

Since that day, Father Kleinsorge has thought back to how queasy he had once been at the sight of pain, how someone else's cut finger used to make him turn faint. Yet there in the park he was so benumbed that immediately after leaving this horrible sight he stopped on a path by one of the pools and discussed with a lightly wounded man whether it would be safe to eat the fat, two-foot carp that floated dead on the surface of the water. They decided, after some consideration, that it would be unwise.

Father Kleinsorge filled the containers a third time and went back to the riverbank. There, amid the dead and dying, he saw a young woman with a needle and thread mending her kimono, which had been slightly torn. Father Kleinsorge joshed her. "My, but you're a dandy!" he said. She laughed.

He felt tired and lay down. He began to talk with two engaging children whose acquaintance he had made the afternoon before. He learned that their name was Kataoka; the girl was thirteen, the boy five. The girl had been just about to set out for a barbershop when the bomb fell. As the family started for Asano Park, their mother decided to turn back for some food and extra clothing; they became separated from her in the crowd of fleeing people, and they had not seen her since. Occasionally they stopped suddenly in their perfectly cheerful playing and began to cry for their mother.

It was difficult for all the children in the park to sustain the sense of tragedy. Toshio Nakamura got quite excited when he saw his friend Seichi Sato riding up the river in a boat with his family, and he ran to the bank and waved and shouted, "Sato! Sato!"

The boy turned his head and shouted, "Who's that?"

"Nakamura."

"Hello, Toshio!"

"Are you all safe?"

"Yes. What about you?"

"Yes, we're all right. My sisters are vomiting, but I'm fine."

Father Kleinsorge began to be thirsty in the dreadful heat, and he did not feel strong enough to go for water again. A little before noon, he saw a Japanese woman handing something out. Soon she came to him and said in a kindly voice, "These are tea leaves. Chew them, young man, and you won't feel thirsty." The woman's gentleness made Father Kleinsorge suddenly want to cry. For weeks, he had been feeling oppressed by the hatred of foreigners that the Japanese seemed increasingly to show, and he had been uneasy even with his Japanese friends. This stranger's gesture made him a little hysterical.

Around noon, the priests arrived from the Novitiate with the handcart. They had been to the site of the mission house in the city and had retrieved some suitcases that had been stored in the air-raid shelter and had also picked up the remains of melted holy vessels in the ashes of the chapel. They now packed Father Kleinsorge's papier-mâché suitcase and the things belonging to Mrs. Murata and the Nakamuras into the cart, put the two Nakamura girls aboard, and prepared to start out. Then one of the Jesuits who had a practical turn of mind remembered that they had been notified some time before that if they suffered property damage at the hands of the enemy, they could enter a claim for compensation with the prefectural police. The holy men discussed this matter there in the park, with the wounded as silent as the dead around them, and decided that Father Kleinsorge, as a former resident of the destroyed mission, was the one to enter the claim. So, as the others went off with the handcart, Father Kleinsorge said goodbye to the Kataoka children and trudged to a police station. Fresh, clean-uniformed policemen from another town were in charge, and a crowd of dirty and disarrayed citizens crowded around them, mostly asking after lost relatives. Father Kleinsorge filled out a claim form and started walking through the center of the town on his way to Nagatsuka. It was then that he first realized the extent of the damage; he passed block after block of ruins, and even after all he had seen in the park, his breath was taken away. By the time he reached the Novitiate, he was sick with exhaustion. The last thing he did as he fell into bed was request that someone go back for the motherless Kataoka children.

Altogether, Miss Sasaki was left two days and two nights under the piece of propped-up roofing with her crushed leg and her two unpleasant comrades. Her only diversion was when men came to the factory air-raid shelters, which she could see from under one corner of her shelter, and hauled corpses up out of them with ropes. Her leg became discolored, swollen, and putrid. All that time, she went without food and water.

On the third day, August 8th, some friends who supposed she was dead came to look for her body and found her. They told her that her mother, father, and baby brother, who at the time of the explosion were in the Tamura Pediatric Hospital, where the baby was a patient, had all been given up as certainly dead, since the hospital was totally destroyed. Her friends then left her to think that piece of news over. Later, some men picked her up by the arms and legs and carried her quite a distance to a truck. For about an hour, the truck moved over a bumpy road, and Miss Sasaki, who had become convinced that she was dulled to pain, discovered that she was not. The men lifted her out at a relief station in the section of Inokuchi, where two Army doctors looked at her. The moment one of them touched her wound, she fainted. She came to in time to hear them discuss whether or not to cut off her leg; one said there was gas gangrene in the lips of the wound and predicted she would die unless they amputated, and the other said that was too bad, because they had no equipment with which to do the job. She fainted again. When she recovered consciousness, she was being carried somewhere on a stretcher. She was put aboard a launch, which went to the nearby island of Ninoshima, and she was taken to a military hospital there. Another doctor examined her and said that she did not have gas gangrene, though she did have a fairly ugly compound fracture. He said quite coldly that he was sorry, but this was a hospital for operative surgical cases only, and because she had no gangrene, she would have to return to Hiroshima that night. But then the doctor took her temperature, and what he saw on the thermometer made him decide to let her stay.

That day, August 8th, Father Cieslik went into the city to look for Mr. Fukai, the Japanese secretary of the diocese, who had ridden unwillingly out of the flaming city on Father Kleinsorge's back and then had run back crazily into it. Father Cieslik started hunting in the neighborhood of Sakai Bridge, where the Jesuits had last seen Mr. Fukai; he went to the East Parade Ground, the evacuation area to which the secretary might have gone, and looked for him among the wounded and dead there; he went to the prefectural police and made inquiries. He could not find any trace of the man. Back at the Novitiate that evening, the theological student, who had been rooming with Mr. Fukai at the mission house, told the priests that the secretary had remarked to him, during an air-raid alarm one day not long before the bombing, "Japan is dying. If there is a real air raid here in Hiroshima, I want to die with our country." The priests concluded that Mr. Fukai had run back to immolate himself in the flames. They never saw him again.

At the Red Cross Hospital, Dr. Sasaki worked for three straight days with only one hour's sleep. On the second day, he began to sew up the worst cuts, and right through the following night and all the next day he stitched. Many of the wounds were festered. Fortunately, someone had found intact a supply of *narucopon*, a Japanese sedative, and he gave it to many who were in pain. Word went around among the staff that there must have been something peculiar about the great bomb, because on the second day the vice-chief of the hospital went down in the basement to the vault where the X-ray plates were stored and found the whole stock exposed as they lay. That day, a fresh doctor and ten nurses came in from the city of Yamaguchi with extra bandages and antiseptics, and the third day another physician and a dozen more nurses arrived from Matsue— yet there were still only eight doctors for ten thousand patients. In the afternoon of the third day, exhausted from his foul tailoring, Dr. Sasaki became obsessed with the idea that his mother thought he was dead. He got permission to go to Mukaihara. He walked out to the first suburbs, beyond which the electric train service was still functioning, and reached home late in the evening. His mother said she had known he was all right all along; a wounded nurse had stopped by to tell her. He went to bed and slept for seventeen hours.

Before dawn on August 8th, someone entered the room at the Novitiate where Father Kleinsorge was in bed, reached up to the hanging light bulb, and switched it on. The sudden flood of light, pouring in on Father Kleinsorge's half sleep, brought him leaping out of bed, braced for a new concussion. When he realized what had happened, he laughed confusedly and went back to bed. He stayed there all day.

On August 9th, Father Kleinsorge was still tired. The rector looked at his cuts and said they were not even worth dressing, and if Father Kleinsorge kept them clean, they would heal in three or four days. Father Kleinsorge felt uneasy; he could not yet comprehend what he had been through; as if he were guilty of something awful, he felt he had to go back to the scene of the violence he had experienced. He got up out of bed and walked into the city. He scratched for a while in the ruins of the mission house, but he found nothing. He went to the sites of a couple of schools and asked after people he knew. He looked for some of the city's Japanese Catholics, but he found only fallen houses. He walked back to the Novitiate, stupefied and without any new understanding.

At two minutes after eleven o'clock on the morning of August 9th, the second atomic bomb was dropped, on Nagasaki. It was several days before the survivors of Hiroshima knew they had company, because the Japanese radio and newspapers were being extremely cautious on the subject of the strange weapon.

On August 9th, Mr. Tanimoto was still working in the park. He went to the suburb of Ushida, where his wife was staying with friends, and got a tent which he had stored there before the bombing. He now took it to the park and set it up as a shelter for some of the wounded who could not move or be moved. Whatever he did in the park, he felt he was being watched by the twenty-year-old girl, Mrs. Kamai, his former neighbor, whom he had seen on the day the bomb exploded, with her dead baby daughter in her arms. She kept the small corpse in her arms for four days, even though it began smelling bad on the second day. Once, Mr. Tanimoto sat with her for a while, and she told him that the bomb had buried her under their house with the baby strapped to her back, and that when she had dug herself free, she had discovered that the baby was choking, its mouth full of dirt. With her little finger, she had carefully cleaned out the infant's mouth, and for a time the child had breathed normally and seemed all right; then suddenly it had died. Mrs. Kamai also talked about what a fine man her husband was, and again urged Mr. Tanimoto to search for him. Since Mr. Tanimoto had been all through the city the first day and had seen terribly burned soldiers from Kamai's post, the Chugoku Regional Army Headquarters, everywhere, he knew it would be impossible to find Kamai, even if he were living, but of course he didn't tell her that. Every time she saw Mr. Tanimoto, she asked whether he had found her husband. Once, he tried to suggest that perhaps it was time to cremate the baby, but Mrs. Kamai only held it tighter. He began to keep away from her, but whenever he looked at her, she was staring at him and her eyes asked the same question. He tried to escape her glance by keeping his back turned to her as much as possible.

The Jesuits took about fifty refugees into the exquisite chapel of the Novitiate. The rector gave them what medical care he could—mostly just the cleaning away of pus. Each of the Naka-muras was provided with a blanket and a mosquito net. Mrs. Nakamura and her younger daughter had no appetite and ate nothing; her son and other daughter ate, and lost, each meal they were offered. On August 10th, a friend, Mrs. Osaki, came to see them and told them that her son Hideo had been burned alive in the factory where he worked. This Hideo had been a kind of hero to Toshio, who had often gone to the plant to watch him run his machine. That night, Toshio woke up screaming. He had dreamed that he had seen Mrs. Osaki com-ing out of an opening in the ground with her family, and then he saw Hideo at his machine, a big one with a revolving belt, and he himself was standing beside Hideo, and for some reason this was terrifying.

On August 10th, Father Kleinsorge, having heard from some-one that Dr. Fujii had been injured and that he had eventually gone to the summer house of a friend of his named Okuma, in the village of Fukawa, asked Father Cieslik if he would go and see how Dr. Fujii was. Father Cieslik went to Misasa station, outside Hiroshima, rode for twenty minutes on an electric train, and then walked for an hour and a half in a terribly hot sun to Mr. Okuma's house, which was beside the Ota River at the foot of a mountain. He found Dr. Fujii sitting in a chair in a kimono, applying compresses to his broken collarbone. The

Doctor told Father Cieslik about having lost his glasses and said that his eyes bothered him. He showed the priest huge blue and green stripes where beams had bruised him. He offered the Jesuit first a cigarette and then whiskey, though it was only eleven in the morning. Father Cieslik thought it would please Dr. Fujii if he took a little, so he said yes. A servant brought some Suntory whiskey, and the Jesuit, the Doctor, and the host had a very pleasant chat. Mr. Okuma had lived in Hawaii, and he told some things about Americans. Dr. Fujii talked a bit about the disaster. He said that Mr. Okuma and a nurse had gone into the ruins of his hospital and brought back a small safe which he had moved into his air-raid shelter. This contained some surgical instruments, and Dr. Fujii gave Father Cieslik a few pairs of scissors and tweezers for the rector at the Novitiate. Father Cieslik was bursting with some inside dope he had, but he waited until the conversation turned naturally to the mystery of the bomb. Then he said he knew what kind of bomb it was; he had the secret on the best authority—that of a Japanese newspaperman who had dropped in at the Novitiate. The bomb was not a bomb at all; it was a kind of fine magnesium powder sprayed over the whole city by a single plane, and it exploded when it came into contact with the live wires of the city power system. "That means," said Dr. Fujii, perfectly satisfied, since after all the information came from a newspaperman, "that it can only be dropped on big cities and only in the daytime, when the tram lines and so forth are in operation."

After five days of ministering to the wounded in the park, Mr. Tanimoto returned, on August 11th, to his parsonage and dug around in the ruins. He retrieved some diaries and church records that had been kept in books and were only charred around the edges, as well as some cooking utensils and pottery.

While he was at work, a Miss Tanaka came and said that her father had been asking for him. Mr. Tanimoto had reason to hate her father, the retired shipping-company official who, though he made a great show of his charity, was notoriously selfish and cruel, and who, just a few days before the bombing, had said openly to several people that Mr. Tanimoto was a spy for the Americans. Several times he had derided Christianity and called it un-Japanese. At the moment of the bombing, Mr. Tanaka had been walking in the street in front of the city's radio station. He received serious flash burns, but he was able to walk home. He took refuge in his Neighborhood Association shelter and from there tried hard to get medical aid. He expected all the doctors of Hiroshima to come to him, because he was so rich and so famous for giving his money away. When none of them came, he angrily set out to look for them; leaning on his daughter's arm, he walked from private hospital to private hospital, but all were in ruins, and he went back and lay down in the shelter again. Now he was very weak and knew he was going to die. He was willing to be comforted by any religion.

Mr. Tanimoto went to help him. He descended into the tomblike shelter and, when his eyes were adjusted to the darkness, saw Mr. Tanaka, his face and arms puffed up and covered with pus and blood, and his eyes swollen shut. The old man smelled very bad, and he moaned constantly. He seemed to recognize Mr. Tanimoto's voice. Standing at the shelter stairway to get light, Mr. Tanimoto read loudly from a Japanese-language pocket Bible: "For a thousand years in Thy sight are but as yesterday when it is past, and as a watch in the night. Thou carriest the children of men away as with a flood; they are as a sleep; in the morning they are like grass which groweth up. In the morning it flourisheth and groweth up; in the evening it is cut down, and withereth. For we are consumed by Thine anger and by Thy wrath are we troubled. Thou hast set our iniquities before Thee, our secret sins in the light of Thy

305

countenance. For all our days are passed away in Thy wrath: we spend our years as a tale that is told. . . ."

Mr. Tanaka died as Mr. Tanimoto read the psalm.

O n August 11th, word came to the Ninoshima Military Hospital that a large number of military casualties from the Chugoku Regional Army Headquarters were to arrive on the island that day, and it was deemed necessary to evacuate all civilian patients. Miss Sasaki, still running an alarmingly high fever, was put on a large ship. She lay out on deck, with a pillow under her leg. There were awnings over the deck, but the vessel's course put her in the sunlight. She felt as if she were under a magnifying glass in the sun. Pus oozed out of her wound, and soon the whole pillow was covered with it. She was taken ashore at Hatsukaichi, a town several miles to the southwest of Hiroshima, and put in the Goddess of Mercy Primary School, which had been turned into a hospital. She lay there for several days before a specialist on fractures came from Kobe. By then her leg was red and swollen up to her hip. The doctor decided he could not set the breaks. He made an incision and put in a rubber pipe to drain off the putrescence.

A t the Novitiate, the motherless Kataoka children were inconsolable. Father Cieslik worked hard to keep them distracted. He put riddles to them. He asked, "What is the cleverest animal in the world?," and after the thirteen-year-old girl had guessed the ape, the elephant, the horse, he said, "No, it must be the hippopotamus," because in Japanese that animal is *kaba*, the reverse of *baka*, stupid. He told Bible stories, beginning, in the order of things, with the Creation. He showed them a scrapbook of snapshots taken in Europe. Nevertheless, they cried most of the time for their mother.

Several days later, Father Cieslik started hunting for the children's family. First, he learned through the police that an uncle had been to the authorities in Kure, a city not far away, to inquire for the children. After that, he heard that an older brother had been trying to trace them through the post office in Ujina, a suburb of Hiroshima. Still later, he heard that the mother was alive and was on Goto Island, off Nagasaki. And at last, by keeping a check on the Ujina post office, he got in touch with the brother and returned the children to their mother.

About a week after the bomb dropped, a vague, incomprehensible rumor reached Hiroshima—that the city had been destroyed by the energy released when atoms were somehow split in two. The weapon was referred to in this word-of-mouth report as *genshi bakudan*—the root characters of which can be translated as "original child bomb." No one understood the idea or put any more credence in it than in the powdered magnesium and such things. Newspapers were being brought in from other cities, but they were still confining themselves to extremely general statements, such as Domei's assertion on August 12th: "There is nothing to do but admit the tremendous power of this inhuman bomb." Already, Japanese physicists had entered the city with Lauritsen electroscopes and Neher electrometers; they understood the idea all too well.

On August 12th, the Nakamuras, all of them still rather sick, went to the nearby town of Kabe and moved in with Mrs. Nakamura's sister-in-law. The next day, Mrs. Nakamura, although she was too ill to walk much, returned to Hiroshima alone, by electric car to the outskirts, by foot from there. All week, at the Novitiate, she had worried about her mother, brother, and older sister, who had lived in the part of town called Fukuro, and besides, she felt drawn by some fascination, just as Father Kleinsorge had been. She discovered that her family were all dead. She went back to Kabe so amazed and depressed by what she had seen and learned in the city that she could not speak that evening.

A comparative orderliness, at least, began to be established at the Red Cross Hospital. Dr. Sasaki, back from his rest, undertook to classify his patients (who were still scattered everywhere, even on the stairways). The staff gradually swept up the debris. Best of all, the nurses and attendants started to remove the corpses. Disposal of the dead, by decent cremation and enshrinement, is a greater moral responsibility to the Japanese than adequate care of the living. Relatives identified most of the first day's dead in and around the hospital. Beginning on the second day, whenever a patient appeared to be moribund, a piece of paper with his name on it was fastened to his clothing. The corpse detail carried the bodies to a clearing outside, placed them on pyres of wood from ruined houses, burned them, put some of the ashes in envelopes intended for exposed X-ray plates, marked the envelopes with the names of the deceased, and piled them, neatly and respectfully, in stacks in the main office. In a few days, the envelopes filled one whole side of the impromptu shrine.

In Kabe, on the morning of August 15th, ten-year-old Toshio Nakamura heard an airplane overhead. He ran outdoors and identified it with a professional eye as a B-29. "There goes Mr. B!" he shouted.

One of his relatives called out to him, "Haven't you had enough of Mr. B?"

The question had a kind of symbolism. At almost that very moment, the dull, dispirited voice of Hirohito, the Emperor Tenno, was speaking for the first time in history over the radio: "After pondering deeply the general trends of the world and the actual conditions obtaining in Our Empire today, We have decided to effect a settlement of the present situation by resorting to an extraordinary measure. . . ."

Mrs. Nakamura had gone to the city again, to dig up some rice she had buried in her Neighborhood Association air-raid shelter. She got it and started back for Kabe. On the electric car, quite by chance, she ran into her younger sister, who had not been in Hiroshima the day of the bombing. "Have you heard the news?" her sister asked.

"What news?"

"The war is over."

"Don't say such a foolish thing, sister."

"But I heard it over the radio myself." And then, in a whisper, "It was the Emperor's voice."

"Oh," Mrs. Nakamura said (she needed nothing more to make her give up thinking, in spite of the atomic bomb, that Japan still had a chance to win the war), "in that case . . ."

Some time later, in a letter to an American, Mr. Tanimoto described the events of that morning. "At the time of the Post-War, the marvelous thing in our history happened. Our Emperor broadcasted his own voice through radio directly to us, common people of Japan. Aug. 15th we were told that some news of great importance could be heard & all of us should hear

it. So I went to Hiroshima railway station. There set a loud-
speaker in the ruins of the station. Many civilians, all of them
were in boundage, some being helped by shoulder of their
daughters, some sustaining their injured feet by sticks, they
listened to the broadcast and when they came to realize the fact
that it was the Emperor, they cried with full tears in their eyes,
'What a wonderful blessing it is that Tenno himself call on us
and we can hear his own voice in person. We are thoroughly
satisfied in such a great sacrifice.' When they came to know the
war was ended—that is, Japan was defeated, they, of course,
were deeply disappointed, but followed after their Emperor's
commandment in calm spirit, making whole-hearted sacrifice
for the everlasting peace of the world—and Japan started her
new way."

IV · Panic Grass and Feverfew

ON AUGUST 18TH, twelve days after the bomb burst, Father Kleinsorge set out on foot for Hiroshima from the Novitiate with his papier-mâché suitcase in his hand. He had begun to think that this bag, in which he kept his valuables, had a talismanic quality, because of the way he had found it after the explosion, standing handle-side up in the doorway of his room, while the desk under which he had previously hidden it was in splinters all over the floor. Now he was using it to carry the yen belonging to the Society of Jesus to the Hiroshima branch of the Yokohama Specie Bank, already reopened in its half-ruined building. On the whole, he felt quite well that morning. It is true that the minor cuts he had received had not healed in three or four days, as the rector of the Novitiate, who had examined them, had positively promised they would, but Father Kleinsorge had rested well for a week and considered that he was again ready for hard work. By now he was accustomed to the terrible scene through which he walked on his way into the city: the large rice field near the Novitiate, streaked with brown; the houses on the outskirts of the city, standing but decrepit, with broken windows and dishevelled tiles; and then, quite suddenly, the beginning of the four square miles of reddish-brown scar, where nearly everything had been buffeted down and burned; range on range of collapsed city blocks, with here and there a crude sign erected on a pile of ashes and tiles ("Sister, where are you?" or "All safe and we live at Toyosaka"); naked trees and canted telephone poles; the few standing, gutted buildings only accentuating the horizontality of everything else (the Museum of Science and Industry, with its dome stripped to its steel frame, as if for an autopsy; the modern Chamber of Commerce Building, its tower as cold, rigid, and unassailable after the blow as before; the huge, low-lying, camouflaged city hall; the row of dowdy banks, caricaturing a shaken economic system); and in the streets a macabre traffic—hundreds of crumpled bicycles, shells of streetcars and automobiles, all halted in mid-motion. The whole way, Father Kleinsorge was oppressed by the thought that all the damage he saw had been done in one instant by one bomb. By the time he reached the center of town, the day had become very hot. He walked to the Yokohama Bank, which was doing business in a temporary wooden stall on the ground floor of its building, deposited the money, went by the mission compound just to have another look at the wreckage, and then started back to the Novitiate. About halfway there, he began to have peculiar sensations. The more or less magical suitcase, now empty, suddenly seemed terribly heavy. His knees grew weak. He felt excruciatingly tired. With a considerable expenditure of spirit, he managed to reach the Novitiate. He did not think his weakness was worth mentioning to the other Jesuits. But a couple of days later, while attempting to say Mass, he had an onset of faintness and even after three attempts was unable to go through with the service, and the next morning the rector, who had examined Father Kleinsorge's apparently negligible but unhealed cuts daily, asked in surprise, "What have you done to your wounds?" They had suddenly opened wider and were swollen and inflamed.

As she dressed on the morning of August 20th, in the home

of her sister-in-law in Kabe, not far from Nagatsuka, Mrs. Nakamura, who had suffered no cuts or burns at all, though she had been rather nauseated all through the week she and her children had spent as guests of Father Kleinsorge and the other Catholics at the Novitiate, began fixing her hair and noticed, after one stroke, that her comb carried with it a whole handful of hair; the second time, the same thing happened, so she stopped combing at once. But in the next three or four days, her hair kept falling out of its own accord, until she was quite bald. She began living indoors, practically in hiding. On August 26th, both she and her younger daughter, Myeko, woke up feeling extremely weak and tired, and they stayed on their bedrolls. Her son and other daughter, who had shared every experience with her during and after the bombing, felt fine.

At about the same time—he lost track of the days, so hard was he working to set up a temporary place of worship in a private house he had rented in the outskirts—Mr. Tanimoto fell suddenly ill with a general malaise, weariness, and feverishness, and he, too, took to his bedroll on the floor of the half-wrecked house of a friend in the suburb of Ushida.

These four did not realize it, but they were coming down with the strange, capricious disease which came later to be known as radiation sickness.

Miss Sasaki lay in steady pain in the Goddess of Mercy Primary School, at Hatsukaichi, the fourth station to the southwest of Hiroshima on the electric train. An internal infection still prevented the proper setting of the compound fracture of her lower left leg. A young man who was in the same hospital and who seemed to have grown fond of her in spite of her unremitting preoccupation with her suffering, or else just pitied her because of it, lent her a Japanese translation of de Maupassant, and she

313

tried to read the stories, but she could concentrate for only four or five minutes at a time.

The hospitals and aid stations around Hiroshima were so crowded in the first weeks after the bombing, and their staffs were so variable, depending on their health and on the unpredictable arrival of outside help, that patients had to be constantly shifted from place to place. Miss Sasaki, who had already been moved three times, twice by ship, was taken at the end of August to an engineering school, also at Hatsukaichi. Because her leg did not improve but swelled more and more, the doctors at the school bound it with crude splints and took her by car, on September 9th, to the Red Cross Hospital in Hiroshima. This was the first chance she had had to look at the ruins of Hiroshima; the last time she had been carried through the city's streets, she had been hovering on the edge of unconsciousness. Even though the wreckage had been described to her, and though she was still in pain, the sight horrified and amazed her, and there was something she noticed about it that particularly gave her the creeps. Over everything—up through the wreckage of the city, in gutters, along the riverbanks, tangled among tiles and tin roofing, climbing on charred tree trunks—was a blanket of fresh, vivid, lush, optimistic green; the verdancy rose even from the foundations of ruined houses. Weeds already hid the ashes, and wild flowers were in bloom among the city's bones. The bomb had not only left the underground organs of plants intact; it had stimulated them. Everywhere were bluets and Spanish bayonets, goosefoot, morning glories and day lilies, the hairy-fruited bean, purslane and clotbur and sesame and panic grass and feverfew. Especially in a circle at the center, sickle senna grew in extraordinary regeneration, not only standing among the charred remnants of the same plant but pushing up in new places, among bricks and through cracks in the asphalt. It actually seemed as if a load of sickle-senna seed had been dropped along with the bomb.

At the Red Cross Hospital, Miss Sasaki was put under the care of Dr. Sasaki. Now, a month after the explosion, something like order had been reëstablished in the hospital; which is to say that the patients who still lay in the corridors at least had mats to sleep on and that the supply of medicines, which had given out in the first few days, had been replaced, though inadequately, by contributions from other cities. Dr. Sasaki, who had had one seventeen-hour sleep at his home on the third night, had ever since then rested only about six hours a night, on a mat at the hospital; he had lost twenty pounds from his very small body; he still wore the borrowed glasses.

Since Miss Sasaki was a woman and was so sick (and perhaps, he afterward admitted, just a little bit because she was named Sasaki), Dr. Sasaki put her on a mat in a semi-private room, which at that time had only eight people in it. He questioned her and put down on her record card, in the correct, scrunched-up German in which he wrote all his records: "*Mittelgrosse Patientin in gutem Ernährungszustand. Fraktur am linken Unterschenkelknochen mit Wunde; Anschwellung in der linken Unterschenkelgegend. Haut und sichtbare Schleimhäute mässig durchblutet und kein Oedema*," noting that she was a medium-sized female patient in good general health; that she had a compound fracture of the left tibia, with swelling of the left lower leg; that her skin and visible mucous membranes were heavily spotted with *petechiae*, which are hemorrhages about the size of grains of rice, or even as big as soybeans; and, in addition, that her head, eyes, throat, lungs, and heart were apparently normal; and that she had a fever. He wanted to set her fracture and put her leg in a cast, but he had run out of plaster of Paris long since, so he just stretched her out on a mat and prescribed aspirin for her fever, and glucose intravenously and diastase orally for her undernourishment (which he had not entered on her record because everyone suffered from it). She exhibited only one of the queer symptoms so many of his patients were just then beginning to show—the spot hemorrhages.

D r. Fujii was still pursued by bad luck, which still was connected with rivers. Now he was living in the summer house of Mr. Okuma, in Fukawa. This house clung to the steep banks of the Ota River. Here his injuries seemed to make good progress, and he even began to treat refugees who came to him from the neighborhood, using medical supplies he had retrieved from a cache in the suburbs. He noticed in some of his patients a curious syndrome of symptoms that cropped out in the third and fourth weeks, but he was not able to do much more than swathe cuts and burns. Early in September, it began to rain, steadily and heavily. The river rose. On September 17th, there came a cloudburst and then a typhoon, and the water crept higher and higher up the bank. Mr. Okuma and Dr. Fujii became alarmed and scrambled up the mountain to a peasant's house. (Down in Hiroshima, the flood took up where the bomb had left off—swept away bridges that had survived the blast, washed out streets, undermined foundations of buildings that still stood—and ten miles to the west, the Ono Army Hospital, where a team of experts from Kyoto Imperial University was studying the delayed affliction of the patients, suddenly slid down a beautiful, pine-dark mountainside into the Inland Sea and drowned most of the investigators and their mysteriously diseased patients alike.) After the storm, Dr. Fujii and Mr. Okuma went down to the river and found that the Okuma house had been washed altogether away.

B ecause so many people were suddenly feeling sick nearly a month after the atomic bomb was dropped, an unpleasant rumor began to move around, and eventually it made its way to the house in Kabe where Mrs. Nakamura lay bald and ill. It was that the atomic bomb had deposited some sort of poison on Hiroshima which would give off deadly emanations for seven years; nobody could go there all that time. This especially upset Mrs. Nakamura, who remembered that in a moment of confusion on the morning of the explosion she had literally sunk her entire means of livelihood, her Sankoku sewing machine, in the small cement water tank in front of what was left of her house; now no one would be able to go and fish it out. Up to this time, Mrs. Nakamura and her relatives had been quite resigned and passive about the moral issue of the atomic bomb, but this rumor suddenly aroused them to more hatred and resentment of America than they had felt all through the war.

Japanese physicists, who knew a great deal about atomic fission (one of them owned a cyclotron), worried about lingering radiation at Hiroshima, and in mid-August, not many days after President Truman's disclosure of the type of bomb that had been dropped, they entered the city to make investigations. The first thing they did was roughly to determine a center by observing the side on which telephone poles all around the heart of the town were scorched; they settled on the torii gateway of the Gokoku Shrine, right next to the parade ground of the Chugoku Regional Army Headquarters. From there, they worked north and south with Lauritsen electroscopes, which are sensitive to both beta particles and gamma rays. These indicated that the highest intensity of radioactivity, near the torii, was 4.2 times the average natural "leak" of ultra-short waves for the earth of that area. The scientists noticed that the flash of the bomb had discolored concrete to a light reddish tint, had scaled off the surface of granite, and had scorched certain other types of building material, and that consequently the bomb had, in some places, left prints of the shadows that had been cast by its light. The experts found, for instance, a permanent shadow thrown on the roof of the Chamber of Commerce Building

(220 yards from the rough center) by the structure's rectangular tower; several others in the lookout post on top of the Hypothec Bank (2,050 yards); another in the tower of the Chugoku Electric Supply Building (800 yards); another projected by the handle of a gas pump (2,630 yards); and several on granite tombstones in the Gokoku Shrine (385 yards). By triangulating these and other such shadows with the objects that formed them, the scientists determined that the exact center was a spot a hundred and fifty yards south of the torii and a few yards southeast of the pile of ruins that had once been the Shima Hospital. (A few vague human silhouettes were found, and these gave rise to stories that eventually included fancy and precise details. One story told how a painter on a ladder was monumentalized in a kind of bas-relief on the stone façade of a bank building on which he was at work, in the act of dipping his brush into his paint can; another, how a man and his cart on the bridge near the Museum of Science and Industry, almost under the center of the explosion, were cast down in an embossed shadow which made it clear that the man was about to whip his horse.) Starting east and west from the actual center, the scientists, in early September, made new measurements, and the highest radiation they found this time was 3.9 times the natural "leak." Since radiation of at least a thousand times the natural "leak" would be required to cause serious effects on the human body, the scientists announced that people could enter Hiroshima without any peril at all.

As soon as this reassurance reached the household in which Mrs. Nakamura was concealing herself—or, at any rate, within a short time, after her hair had started growing back again—her whole family relaxed their extreme hatred of America, and Mrs. Nakamura sent her brother-in-law to look for the sewing machine. It was still submerged in the water tank, and when he brought it home, she saw, to her dismay, that it was all rusted and useless.

By the end of the first week in September, Father Kleinsorge was in bed at the Novitiate with a fever of 102.2, and since he seemed to be getting worse, his colleagues decided to send him to the Catholic International Hospital in Tokyo. Father Cieslik and the rector took him as far as Kobe and a Jesuit from that city took him the rest of the way, with a message from a Kobe doctor to the Mother Superior of the International Hospital: "Think twice before you give this man blood transfusions, because with atomic-bomb patients we aren't at all sure that if you stick needles in them, they'll stop bleeding."

When Father Kleinsorge arrived at the hospital, he was terribly pale and very shaky. He complained that the bomb had upset his digestion and given him abdominal pains. His white blood count was three thousand (five to seven thousand is normal), he was seriously anemic, and his temperature was 104. A doctor who did not know much about these strange manifestations—Father Kleinsorge was one of a handful of atomic patients who had reached Tokyo—came to see him, and to the patient's face he was most encouraging. "You'll be out of here in two weeks," he said. But when the doctor got out in the corridor, he said to the Mother Superior, "He'll die. All these bomb people die—you'll see. They go along for a couple of weeks and then they die."

The doctor prescribed suralimentation for Father Kleinsorge. Every three hours, they forced some eggs or beef juice into him, and they fed him all the sugar he could stand. They gave him vitamins, and iron pills and arsenic (in Fowler's solution) for his anemia. He confounded both the doctor's predictions; he neither died nor got up in a fortnight. Despite the fact that the message from the Kobe doctor deprived him of transfusions, which would have been the most useful therapy of all, his fever and his digestive troubles cleared up fairly quickly. His white count went up for a while, but early in October it dropped again, to 3,600; then, in ten days, it suddenly climbed above normal, to 8,800; and it finally settled at 5,800. His ridiculous scratches puzzled everyone. For a few days, they would mend, and then, when he moved around, they would open up again. As soon as he began to feel well, he enjoyed himself tremendously. In Hiroshima he had been one of thousands of sufferers; in Tokyo he was a curiosity. American Army doctors came by the dozen to observe him. Japanese experts questioned him. A newspaper interviewed him. And once, the confused doctor came and shook his head and said, "Baffling cases, these atomic-bomb people."

Mrs. Nakamura lay indoors with Myeko. They both continued sick, and though Mrs. Nakamura vaguely sensed that their trouble was caused by the bomb, she was too poor to see a doctor and so never knew exactly what the matter was. Without any treatment at all, but merely resting, they began gradually to feel better. Some of Myeko's hair fell out, and she had a tiny burn on her arm which took months to heal. The boy, Toshio, and the older girl, Yaeko, seemed well enough, though they, too, lost some hair and occasionally had bad headaches. Toshio was still having nightmares, always about the nineteen-year-old mechanic, Hideo Osaki, his hero, who had been killed by the bomb.

On his back with a fevor of 104, Mr. Tanimoto worried about all the funerals he ought to be conducting for the deceased of his church. He thought he was just overtired from the hard work he had done since the bombing, but after the fever had persisted for a few days, he sent for a doctor. The doctor was too busy to visit him in Ushida, but he dispatched a nurse, who recognized his symptoms as those of mild radiation disease and came back from time to time to give him injections of Vitamin B_1. A Buddhist priest with whom Mr. Tanimoto was acquainted called on him and suggested that moxibustion might give him relief; the priest showed the pastor how to give himself the ancient Japanese treatment, by setting fire to a twist of the stimulant herb moxa placed on the wrist pulse. Mr. Tanimoto found that each moxa treatment temporarily reduced his fever one degree. The nurse had told him to eat as much as possible, and every few days his mother-in-law brought him vegetables and fish from Tsuzu, twenty miles away, where she lived. He spent a month in bed, and then went ten hours by train to his father's home in Shikoku. There he rested another month.

D r. Sasaki and his colleagues at the Red Cross Hospital watched the unprecedented disease unfold and at last evolved a theory about its nature. It had, they decided, three stages. The first stage had been all over before the doctors even knew they were dealing with a new sickness; it was the direct reaction to the bombardment of the body, at the moment when the bomb went off, by neutrons, beta particles, and gamma rays. The apparently uninjured people who had died so mysteriously in the first few hours or days had succumbed in this first stage. It killed ninety-five per cent of the people within a half mile of the center, and many thousands who were farther away. The doctors realized in retrospect that even though most of these dead had also suffered from burns and blast effects, they had absorbed enough radiation to kill them. The rays simply destroyed body cells—caused their nuclei to degenerate and broke their walls. Many people who did not die right away came down with nausea, headache, diarrhea, malaise, and fever, which lasted several days. Doctors could not be certain whether some of these symptoms were the result of radiation or nervous shock. The second stage set in ten or fifteen days after the bombing. Its first symptom was falling hair. Diarrhea and fever, which in some cases went as high as 106, came next. Twenty-five to thirty days after the explosion, blood disorders appeared: gums bled, the white-blood-cell count dropped sharply, and *petechiae* appeared on the skin and mucous membranes. The drop in the number of white blood corpuscles reduced the patient's capacity to resist infection, so open wounds were unusually slow in healing and many of the sick developed sore throats and mouths. The two key symptoms, on which the doctors came to base their prognosis, were fever and the lowered white-corpuscle count. If fever remained steady and high, the patient's chances for survival were poor. The white count almost always dropped below four thousand; a patient whose count fell below one thousand had little hope of living. Toward the end of the second stage, if the patient survived, anemia, or a drop in the red blood count, also set in. The third stage was the reaction that came when the body struggled to compensate for its ills —when, for instance, the white count not only returned to normal but increased to much higher than normal levels. In this stage, many patients died of complications, such as infections in the chest cavity. Most burns healed with deep layers of pink, rubbery scar tissue, known as keloid tumors. The duration of the disease varied, depending on the patient's constitution and the amount of radiation he had received. Some victims recovered in a week; with others the disease dragged on for months.

As the symptoms revealed themselves, it became clear that many of them resembled the effects of overdoses of X-ray, and the doctors based their therapy on that likeness. They gave victims liver extract, blood transfusions, and vitamins, especially B_1. The shortage of supplies and instruments hampered them. Allied doctors who came in after the surrender found plasma and penicillin very effective. Since the blood disorders were, in the long run, the predominant factor in the disease, some of the Japanese doctors evolved a theory as to the seat of the delayed sickness. They thought that perhaps gamma rays, entering the body at the time of the explosion, made the phosphorus in the victims' bones radioactive, and that they in turn emitted beta particles, which, though they could not penetrate far through flesh, could enter the bone marrow, where blood is manufactured, and gradually tear it down. Whatever its source, the disease had some baffling quirks. Not all the patients exhibited all the main symptoms. People who suffered flash burns were protected, to a considerable extent, from radiation sickness. Those who had lain quietly for days or even hours after the bombing were much less liable to get sick than those who had been active. Gray hair seldom fell out. And, as if nature were protecting man against his own ingenuity, the reproductive processes were affected for a time; men became sterile, women had miscarriages, menstruation stopped.

For ten days after the flood, Dr. Fujii lived in the peasant's house on the mountain above the Ota. Then he heard about a vacant private clinic in Kaitaichi, a suburb to the east of Hiroshima. He bought it at once, moved there, and hung out a sign inscribed in English, in honor of the conquerors:

M. FUJII, M.D.

MEDICAL & VENEREAL

Quite recovered from his wounds, he soon built up a strong practice, and he was delighted, in the evenings, to receive members of the occupying forces, on whom he lavished whiskey and practiced English.

Giving Miss Sasaki a local anaesthetic of procaine, Dr. Sasaki made an incision in her leg on October 23rd, to drain the infection, which still lingered on eleven weeks after the injury. In the following days, so much pus formed that he had to dress the opening each morning and evening. A week later, she complained of great pain, so he made another incision; he cut still a third, on November 9th, and enlarged it on the twenty-sixth. All this time, Miss Sasaki grew weaker and weaker, and her spirits fell low. One day, the young man who had lent her his translation of de Maupassant at Hatsukaichi came to visit her; he told her that he was going to Kyushu but that when he came back, he would like to see her again. She didn't care. Her leg had been so swollen and painful all along that the doctor had not even tried to set the fractures, and though an X-ray taken in November showed that the bones were mending, she could see under the sheet that her left leg was nearly three inches shorter than her right and that her left foot was turning inward. She thought often of the man to whom she had been engaged. Someone told her he was back from overseas. She wondered what he had heard about her injuries that made him stay away.

Father Kleinsorge was discharged from the hospital in Tokyo on December 19th and took a train home. On the way, two days later, at Yokogawa, a stop just before Hiroshima, Dr. Fujii boarded the train. It was the first time the two men had met since before the bombing. They sat together. Dr. Fujii said he was going to the annual gathering of his family, on the anniversary of his father's death. When they started talking about their experiences, the Doctor was quite entertaining as he told how his places of residence kept falling into rivers. Then he asked Father Kleinsorge how he was, and the Jesuit talked about his stay in the hospital. "The doctors told me to be cautious," he said. "They ordered me to have a two-hour nap every afternoon."

Dr. Fujii said, "It's hard to be cautious in Hiroshima these days. Everyone seems to be so busy."

A new municipal government, set up under Allied Military Government direction, had gone to work at last in the city hall. Citizens who had recovered from various degrees of radiation sickness were coming back by the thousand—by November 1st, the population, mostly crowded into the outskirts, was already 137,000, more than a third of the wartime peak—and the government set in motion all kinds of projects to put them to work rebuilding the city. It hired men to clear the streets, and others to gather scrap iron, which they sorted and piled in mountains opposite the city hall. Some returning residents were putting up their own shanties and huts, and planting small squares of winter wheat beside them, but the city also authorized and built four hundred one-family "barracks." Utilities were repaired—electric lights shone again, trams started running, and employees of the waterworks fixed seventy thousand leaks in mains and plumbing. A Planning Conference, with an enthusiastic young Military Government officer, Lieutenant John D. Montgomery, of Kalamazoo, as its adviser, began to consider what sort of city the new Hiroshima should be. The ruined city had flourished—and had been an inviting target—mainly because it had been one of the most important military-command and communications centers in Japan, and would have become the Imperial headquarters had the islands been invaded and Tokyo been captured. Now there would be no huge military establishments to help revive the city. The Planning Conference, at a loss as to just what importance Hiroshima could have, fell back on rather vague cultural and paving projects. It drew maps with avenues a hundred yards wide and thought seriously of erecting a group of buildings as a monument to the disaster, and naming them the Institute of International Amity. Statistical workers gathered what figures they could on the effects of the bomb. They reported that 78,150 people had been killed, 13,983 were missing, and 37,425 had been injured. No one in the city government pretended that these figures were accurate—though the Americans accepted them as official—and as the months went by and more and more hundreds of corpses were dug up from the ruins, and as the number of unclaimed urns of ashes at the Zempoji Temple in Koi rose into the thousands, the statisticians began to say that at least a hundred thousand people had lost their lives in the bombing. Since many people died of a combination of causes, it was impossible to figure exactly how many were killed by each cause, but the statisticians calculated that about twenty-five per cent had died of direct burns from the bomb, about fifty per cent from other injuries, and about twenty per cent as a result of radiation effects. The statisticians' figures on property damage were more reliable: sixty-two thousand out of ninety thousand buildings destroyed, and six thousand more damaged beyond repair. In the heart of the city, they found only five modern buildings that could be used again without major repairs. This small number was by no means the fault of flimsy Japanese construction. In fact, since the 1923 earthquake, Japanese building regulations had required that the roof of each large building be able to bear a minimum load of seventy pounds per square foot, whereas American regulations do not normally specify more than forty pounds per square foot.

Scientists swarmed into the city. Some of them measured the force that had been necessary to shift marble gravestones in the cemeteries, to knock over twenty-two of the forty-seven railroad cars in the yards at Hiroshima station, to lift and move the con-

crete roadway on one of the bridges, and to perform other note-
worthy acts of strength, and concluded that the pressure exerted by the explosion varied from 5.3 to 8.0 tons per square
yard. Others found that mica, of which the melting point is
900° C., had fused on granite gravestones three hundred and
eighty yards from the center; that telephone poles of *Crypto-
meria japonica*, whose carbonization temperature is 240° C., had
been charred at forty-four hundred yards from the center; and
that the surface of gray clay tiles of the type used in Hiroshima,
whose melting point is 1,300° C., had dissolved at six hundred
yards; and, after examining other significant ashes and melted
bits, they concluded that the bomb's heat on the ground at the
center must have been 6,000° C. And from further measurements of radiation, which involved, among other things, the
scraping up of fission fragments from roof troughs and drain-
pipes as far away as the suburb of Takasu, thirty-three hundred
yards from the center, they learned some far more important
facts about the nature of the bomb. General MacArthur's headquarters systematically censored all mention of the bomb in
Japanese scientific publications, but soon the fruit of the scientists' calculations became common knowledge among Japanese
physicists, doctors, chemists, journalists, professors, and, no
doubt, those statesmen and military men who were still in circu-
lation. Long before the American public had been told, most
of the scientists and lots of non-scientists in Japan knew—from
the calculations of Japanese nuclear physicists—that a uranium
bomb had exploded at Hiroshima and a more powerful one, of
plutonium, at Nagasaki. They also knew that theoretically one
ten times as powerful—or twenty—could be developed. The
Japanese scientists thought they knew the exact height at
which the bomb at Hiroshima was exploded and the approxi-
mate weight of the uranium used. They estimated that, even
with the primitive bomb used at Hiroshima, it would require a
shelter of concrete fifty inches thick to protect a human being

entirely from radiation sickness. The scientists had these and
other details which remained subject to security in the United
States printed and mimeographed and bound into little books.
The Americans knew of the existence of these, but tracing them
and seeing that they did not fall into the wrong hands would
have obliged the occupying authorities to set up, for this one
purpose alone, an enormous police system in Japan. Altogether,
the Japanese scientists were somewhat amused at the efforts of
their conquerors to keep security on atomic fission.

Late in February, 1946, a friend of Miss Sasaki's called on
Father Kleinsorge and asked him to visit her in the hospital. She
had been growing more and more depressed and morbid; she
seemed little interested in living. Father Kleinsorge went to see
her several times. On his first visit, he kept the conversation
general, formal, and yet vaguely sympathetic, and did not mention religion. Miss Sasaki herself brought it up the second time
he dropped in on her. Evidently she had had some talks with a
Catholic. She asked bluntly, "If your God is so good and kind,
how can he let people suffer like this?" She made a gesture
which took in her shrunken leg, the other patients in her room,
and Hiroshima as a whole.

"My child," Father Kleinsorge said, "man is not now in the
condition God intended. He has fallen from grace through sin."
And he went on to explain all the reasons for everything.

It came to Mrs. Nakamura's attention that a carpenter from
Kabe was building a number of wooden shanties in Hiroshima
which he rented for fifty yen a month—$3.33, at the fixed rate

of exchange. Mrs. Nakamura had lost the certificates for her bonds and other wartime savings, but fortunately she had copied off all the numbers just a few days before the bombing and had taken the list to Kabe, and so, when her hair had grown in enough for her to be presentable, she went to her bank in Hiroshima, and a clerk there told her that after checking her numbers against the records the bank would give her her money. As soon as she got it, she rented one of the carpenter's shacks. It was in Nobori-cho, near the site of her former house, and though its floor was dirt and it was dark inside, it was at least a home in Hiroshima, and she was no longer dependent on the charity of her in-laws. During the spring, she cleared away some nearby wreckage and planted a vegetable garden. She cooked with utensils and ate off plates she scavenged from the debris. She sent Myeko to the kindergarten which the Jesuits reopened, and the two old children attended Nobori-cho Primary School, which, for want of buildings, held classes out of doors. Toshio wanted to study to be a mechanic, like his hero, Hideo Osaki. Prices were high; by midsummer Mrs. Nakamura's savings were gone. She sold some of her clothes to get food. She had once had several expensive kimonos, but during the war one had been stolen, she had given one to a sister who had been bombed out in Tokuyama, she had lost a couple in the Hiroshima bombing, and now she sold her last one. It brought only a hundred yen, which did not last long. In June, she went to Father Kleinsorge for advice about how to get along, and in early August, she was still considering the two alternatives he suggested—taking work as a domestic for some of the Allied occupation forces, or borrowing from her relatives enough money, about five hundred yen, or a bit more than thirty dollars, to repair her rusty sewing machine and resume the work of a seamstress.

329

When Mr. Tanimoto returned from Shikoku, he draped a
tent he owned over the roof of the badly damaged house he had
rented in Ushida. The roof still leaked, but he conducted services in the damp living room. He began thinking about raising
money to restore his church in the city. He became quite
friendly with Father Kleinsorge and saw the Jesuits often. He
envied them their Church's wealth; they seemed to be able to
do anything they wanted. He had nothing to work with except
his own energy, and that was not what it had been.

The Society of Jesus had been the first institution to build a
relatively permanent shanty in the ruins of Hiroshima. That
had been while Father Kleinsorge was in the hospital. As soon
as he got back, he began living in the shack, and he and another priest, Father Laderman, who had joined him in the mission, arranged for the purchase of three of the standardized
"barracks," which the city was selling at seven thousand yen
apiece. They put two together, end to end, and made a pretty
chapel of them; they ate in the third. When materials were
available, they commissioned a contractor to build a three-story
mission house exactly like the one that had been destroyed in
the fire. In the compound, carpenters cut timbers, gouged
mortises, shaped tenons, whittled scores of wooden pegs and
bored holes for them, until all the parts for the house were in a
neat pile; then, in three days, they put the whole thing together,
like an Oriental puzzle, without any nails at all. Father Kleinsorge was finding it hard, as Dr. Fujii had suggested he would,
to be cautious and to take his naps. He went out every day on
foot to call on Japanese Catholics and prospective converts. As
the months went by, he grew more and more tired. In June, he

read an article in the Hiroshima *Chugoku* warning survivors against working too hard—but what could he do? By July, he was worn out, and early in August, almost exactly on the anniversary of the bombing, he went back to the Catholic International Hospital, in Tokyo, for a month's rest.

Whether or not Father Kleinsorge's answers to Miss Sasaki's questions about life were final and absolute truths, she seemed quickly to draw physical strength from them. Dr. Sasaki noticed it and congratulated Father Kleinsorge. By April 15th, her temperature and white count were normal and the infection in the wound was beginning to clear up. On the twentieth, there was almost no pus, and for the first time she jerked along a corridor on crutches. Five days later, the wound had begun to heal, and on the last day of the month she was discharged.

During the early summer, she prepared herself for conversion to Catholicism. In that period she had ups and downs. Her depressions were deep. She knew she would always be a cripple. Her fiancé never came to see her. There was nothing for her to do except read and look out, from her house on a hillside in Koi, across the ruins of the city where her parents and brother died. She was nervous, and any sudden noise made her put her hands quickly to her throat. Her leg still hurt; she rubbed it often and patted it, as if to console it.

It took six months for the Red Cross Hospital, and even longer for Dr. Sasaki, to get back to normal. Until the city restored electric power, the hospital had to limp along with the aid of a Japanese Army generator in its back yard. Operating tables, X-ray machines, dentist chairs, everything complicated and essential came in a trickle of charity from other cities. In Japan, face is important even to institutions, and long before the Red Cross Hospital was back to par on basic medical equipment, its directors put up a new yellow brick veneer façade, so the hospital became the handsomest building in Hiroshima—from the street. For the first four months, Dr. Sasaki was the only surgeon on the staff and he almost never left the building; then, gradually, he began to take an interest in his own life again. He got married in March. He gained back some of the weight he lost, but his appetite remained only fair; before the bombing, he used to eat four rice balls at every meal, but a year after it he could manage only two. He felt tired all the time. "But I have to realize," he said, "that the whole community is tired."

A year after the bomb was dropped, Miss Sasaki was a cripple; Mrs. Nakamura was destitute; Father Kleinsorge was back in the hospital; Dr. Sasaki was not capable of the work he once could do; Dr. Fujii had lost the thirty-room hospital it took him many years to acquire, and had no prospects of rebuilding it; Mr. Tanimoto's church had been ruined and he no longer had his exceptional vitality. The lives of these six people, who were among the luckiest in Hiroshima, would never be the same. What they thought of their experiences and of the use of the atomic bomb was, of course, not unanimous. One feeling they did seem to share, however, was a curious kind of elated community spirit, something like that of the Londoners after their blitz—a pride in the way they and their fellow-survivors had stood up to a dreadful ordeal. Just before the anniversary, Mr. Tanimoto wrote in a letter to an American some words which expressed this feeling: "What a heartbreaking scene this was the first night! About midnight I landed on the riverbank. So many

injured people lied on the ground that I made my way by strid-
ing over them. Repeating 'Excuse me,' I forwarded and carried
a tub of water with me and gave a cup of water to each one of
them. They raised their upper bodies slowly and accepted a cup
of water with a bow and drunk quietly and, spilling any rem-
nant, gave back a cup with hearty expression of their thankful-
ness, and said, 'I couldn't help my sister, who was buried under
the house, because I had to take care of my mother who got a
deep wound on her eye and our house soon set fire and we
hardly escaped. Look, I lost my home, my family, and at last
my-self bitterly injured. But now I have gotted my mind to dedi-
cate what I have and to complete the war for our country's
sake.' Thus they pledged to me, even women and children did
the same. Being entirely tired I lied down on the ground
among them, but couldn't sleep at all. Next morning I found
many men and women dead, whom I gave water last night. But,
to my great surprise, I never heard any one cried in disorder,
even though they suffered in great agony. They died in silence,
with no grudge, setting their teeth to bear it. All for the country!

"Dr. Y. Hiraiwa, professor of Hiroshima University of Literature and Science, and one of my church members, was buried
by the bomb under the two storied house with his son, a student
of Tokyo University. Both of them could not move an inch
under tremendously heavy pressure. And the house already
caught fire. His son said, 'Father, we can do nothing except
make our mind up to consecrate our lives for the country. Let
us give *Banzai* to our Emperor.' Then the father followed after
his son, '*Tenno-heika, Banzai, Banzai, Banzai!*' In the result,
Dr. Hiraiwa said, 'Strange to say, I felt calm and bright and
peaceful spirit in my heart, when I chanted *Banzai* to Tenno.'
Afterward his son got out and digged down and pulled out his
father and thus they were saved. In thinking of their experience
of that time Dr. Hiraiwa repeated, 'What a fortunate that we

333

are Japanese! It was my first time I ever tasted such a beautiful spirit when I decided to die for our Emperor.'

"Miss Kayoko Nobutoki, a student of girl's high school, Hiroshima Jazabuin, and a daughter of my church member, was taking rest with her friends beside the heavy fence of the Buddhist Temple. At the moment the atomic bomb was dropped, the fence fell upon them. They could not move a bit under such a heavy fence and then smoke entered into even a crack and choked their breath. One of the girls begun to sing *Kimi ga yo*, national anthem, and others followed in chorus and died. Meanwhile one of them found a crack and struggled hard to get out. When she was taken in the Red Cross Hospital she told how her friends died, tracing back in her memory to singing in chorus our national anthem. They were just 13 years old.

"Yes, people of Hiroshima died manly in the atomic bombing, believing that it was for Emperor's sake."

A surprising number of the people of Hiroshima remained more or less indifferent about the ethics of using the bomb. Possibly they were too terrified by it to want to think about it at all. Not many of them even bothered to find out much about what it was like. Mrs. Nakamura's conception of it—and awe of it—was typical. "The atom bomb," she would say when asked about it, "is the size of a matchbox. The heat of it is six thousand times that of the sun. It exploded in the air. There is some radium in it. I don't know just how it works, but when the radium is put together, it explodes." As for the use of the bomb, she would say, "It was war and we had to expect it." And then she would add, "*Shikata ga nai*," a Japanese expression as common as, and corresponding to, the Russian word "*nichevo*": "It can't be helped. Oh, well. Too bad." Dr. Fujii said approximately the same thing about the use of the bomb to Father Kleinsorge one evening, in German: "*Da ist nichts zu machen.* There's nothing to be done about it."

Many citizens of Hiroshima, however, continued to feel a hatred for Americans which nothing could possibly erase. "I see," Dr. Sasaki once said, "that they are holding a trial for war criminals in Tokyo just now. I think they ought to try the men who decided to use the bomb and they should hang them all."

Father Kleinsorge and the other German Jesuit priests, who, as foreigners, could be expected to take a relatively detached view, often discussed the ethics of using the bomb. One of them, Father Siemes, who was out at Nagatsuka at the time of the attack, wrote in a report to the Holy See in Rome: "Some of us consider the bomb in the same category as poison gas and were against its use on a civilian population. Others were of the opinion that in total war, as carried on in Japan, there was no difference between civilians and soldiers, and that the bomb itself was an effective force tending to end the bloodshed, warning Japan to surrender and thus to avoid total destruction. It seems logical that he who supports total war in principal cannot complain of a war against civilians. The crux of the matter is whether total war in its present form is justifiable, even when it serves a just purpose. Does it not have material and spiritual evil as its consequences which far exceed whatever good might result? When will our moralists give us a clear answer to this question?"

It would be impossible to say what horrors were embedded in the minds of the children who lived through the day of the bombing in Hiroshima. On the surface, their recollections, months after the disaster, were of an exhilarating adventure. Toshio Nakamura, who was ten at the time of the bombing, was soon able to talk freely, even gaily, about the experience, and a few weeks before the anniversary he wrote the following matter-of-fact essay for his teacher at Nobori-cho Primary School: "The day before the bomb, I went for a swim. In the morning, I was eating peanuts. I saw a light. I was knocked to little sister's sleeping place. When we were saved, I could only see as far as the tram. My mother and I started to pack our things. The neighbors were walking around burned and bleeding. Hataya-*san* told me to run away with her. I said I wanted to wait for my mother. We went to the park. A whirlwind came. At night a gas tank burned and I saw the reflection in the river. We stayed in the park one night. Next day I went to Taiko Bridge and met my girl friends Kikuki and Murakami. They were looking for their mothers. But Kikuki's mother was wounded and Murakami's mother, alas, was dead."